Jesus and Buddha

Jesus and Buddha

Friends in Conversation

PAUL KNITTER
ROGER HAIGHT

ORBIS BOOKS

Maryknoll, New York 10545

ORBIS BOOKS
Maryknoll, New York 10545

Founded in 1970, Orbis Books endeavors to publish works that enlighten the mind, nourish the spirit, and challenge the conscience. The publishing arm of the Maryknoll Fathers and Brothers, Orbis seeks to explore the global dimensions of the Christian faith and mission, to invite dialogue with diverse cultures and religious traditions, and to serve the cause of reconciliation and peace. The books published reflect the views of their authors and do not represent the official position of the Maryknoll Society. To learn more about Maryknoll and Orbis Books, please visit our website at www.maryknollsociety.org.

Library of Congress Cataloging-in-Publication Data

Knitter, Paul F.
    Jesus and Buddha : friends in conversation / Paul Knitter, Roger Haight.
        pages cm
    Includes bibliographical references and index.
        ISBN 978–1–62698–151–5 (pbk.)
        1. Christianity and other religions—Buddhism. 2. Buddhism—Relations—Christianity. I. Title.
BR128.B8K55 2015
261.2'43—dc23

                                                                    2015018005

Contents

Introduction

In the spring semester of 2012 Paul Knitter offered a course at Union Theological Seminary that bore the title "Jesus and Buddha in Dialogue: An Exploratory Seminar." Roger Haight served as a resource person for the discussions on Christian spirituality. The course was dedicated to exploring whether followers of Buddha and Jesus can communicate in a way that influences each other's spirituality, that is, whether they can meet on another, deeper level beyond mutual cognitive understanding and disagreement.

The exploration set out along the following path: First, we looked at the stories of Jesus and of Buddha, not in any exhaustive detail, but enough to lift up their basic teaching within their historical and social context. Then, we took some time to look alternatively at how the story of Jesus might be presented in an objective way to Buddhists, and reciprocally, how various authors have presented Buddha to outsiders such as Christians. This involved reading essays that introduced Buddha and Jesus and that kept the analysis close to the teachings of these historical figures as distinct from later speculative interpretations of the two developed religions: Buddhism and Christianity. We then moved into another phase that considered authors who represented ways in which Jesus has been received by Buddhists and Buddha has been appropriated by Christians. These multiple criss-crossing but complementary views of the two figures fostered a relatively deep appreciation of differences and, across them, some analogous ways of seeing things.

At the beginning of this course we shared a conviction that spirituality offered a unique entry into these two faith traditions, an approach that comparison of doctrines ordinarily does not enjoy. We noticed, too, that the term *spirituality* itself is ambiguous;

it needs definition in order to be useful. Yet no single conception will be acceptable to everyone because spirituality is too rich a reality to be so contained. Thus it remains a somewhat open concept that will be further developed in the text according to this shared guideline: spirituality is essentially a form of practice that has multiple layers that include sets of beliefs and teachings but is still distinguishable from them. We were led by the conviction that spirituality represented a level of commitment that is more widely shared within a tradition than any particular appropriation of the more intellectually generated beliefs and teachings. We agreed that spirituality possesses a certain existential priority to doctrines and that the spiritual life practiced in the two spiritual traditions is more readily accessible than the belief structures that accompany and shape spirituality. These impressions grew as the course unfolded.

But before describing further how this course stimulated a joint effort at a comparative spirituality, here are brief introductions of us as authors. It will help to situate the work.

Paul Knitter finished his graduate studies in theology at the Pontifical Gregorian University in Rome in 1966 and earned a doctorate in theology from the University of Marburg, Germany, in 1972. A member of the Society of the Divine Word for some twenty years, he left the ministerial priesthood in 1975 and began teaching at Xavier University in Cincinnati, Ohio. Retired from Xavier in 2002, he subsequently accepted the position of Paul Tillich Professor of World Religions and Culture at Union Theological Seminary in 2007. Retired again in 2013, he now lives with his wife, Cathy Cornell, in Madison, Wisconsin.

Roger Haight is an American Jesuit who did his graduate studies in theology at the Divinity School of the University of Chicago. He began teaching theology at Loyola School of Theology at the Ateneo de Manila University. He subsequently moved to Jesuit faculties of theology in Chicago, Toronto, and Cambridge, Massachusetts. In 2004 he became a Scholar in Residence at Union Theological Seminary in New York, where he is currently the director of the PhD program.

One can get the drift of what interests theologians from the trail of their writings. Haight has reflected upon Christian teachings that may be called fundamental issues of the Christian life. He has produced works on the saving relationship between God and human beings that is called grace, the multifaceted liberating power of Christian faith, the basic grammar of Christian theology, and the application of theological method to a technical understanding of Jesus as the Christ. He has also worked on the theology of the church and most recently has explored the meaning of spirituality and how it grounds the theological enterprise. So this project fits into the pattern of exploring how and where as human beings Buddhists and Christians share some fundamental experiences of ultimate reality that might bind them together.

Since his doctoral dissertation, which dealt with Protestant theologies of religious pluralism, Knitter's teaching and writing have dealt primarily with the challenges that religious diversity poses for Christian belief and practice. Since the mid 1980s, influenced by his work with an ecumenical group called Christians for Peace in El Salvador and experiencing the realities of injustice and the struggles of liberation communities and theologians, he has sought to further a liberative theology and dialogue of religions. Recently, as exemplified in this book, he has been trying to develop a liberative, comparative theology in dialogue with Buddhism.

We have known each other since the mid 1970s and have followed each other's writings. Thus it seemed right that, when we found ourselves together at Union Theological Seminary, we do something together. Paul initiated and taught the course described earlier, and Roger attended as an informant relative to Christian spirituality. The book, while different from the course, bears features of the earlier collaboration upon which we agree. For example, we share a broad agreement on a method of correlation. This entails placing in conjunction the tradition of a given faith with an understanding of the present situation in which the inquirer exists. The question that is always being asked is how the tradition makes sense for life in a given context and, vice versa, how life illumines the tradition. Such a method strives to generate an understanding that will be faithful to the given faith tradition and relevant in the present and thereby provide a stimulus to liberating, life-enhancing action.

We also share a large structural understanding of comparative theology. This consists in placing side by side two faith traditions on a particular point, noting their historical contexts, entering into the other tradition as best one can, not without the help of current interpreters, and then bringing back to one's own tradition an expanded view of the subject matter. This easy formula harbors countless nuances and difficulties in its execution, but the goal is clear: to learn positive new things that will influence the understanding and practice of one's own tradition.

It is true that the method of correlation, which has its own problems, is further complicated by a comparative method, that is, by the fact that we are not only interpreting two traditions but then laying them side by side as if they were commensurable. This complication, however, is no greater than what is experienced every day in real life. In many respects the largest portion of this volume is given over to descriptive writing, to representing what a great number of people ask about when they encounter people from another faith or allow another tradition to raise questions for their own faith.

In keeping with that presupposition, the audience of this book can best be described as broad and general. It is not intended for academics, but it may be used by academics in teaching undergraduates—perhaps graduates as well. It aims mainly at Christians who are aware of the religious pluralism that constitutes the atmosphere in which we now live and who are asking questions of its bearing upon their own Christian faith. The book is intended for Christians rather than Buddhists because it measures most pointedly the influence that Buddhism might have on Christian spirituality. Our book is a conversation between a Christian and a Buddhist Christian. Knitter is not a formally trained Buddhist scholar but a Christian who has done his best to understand the variety of Buddhist traditions. He remains close to the audience for which we write. He has incorporated Buddhism into his own Christian spirituality and speaks in particular out of his study and practice of Tibetan Buddhism. He is a "double belonger." And while Haight is a single belonger, for the last three decades he has written about Christian matters from an ecumenical perspective enjoined by Vatican II with an awareness of the fact that there are other religions and that they are listening. But he too is a particular interpreter and does not pretend to speak for the whole Christian tradition.

Many implicit goals motivate this work. In the first place we want to discuss in an open and accessible way—a way that is sometimes more and sometimes less formal, but disciplined and structured—issues that currently occupy the consciousness of not only Christians but also members of other religions. The desire for mutual understanding and accord, if not actual sharing of experiences, still demands a rationale, and our conversation seeks to supply that. We are also striving for mutual enrichment.

But our situation at this moment also has an urgent side; the new closeness of other religions, actual interaction with people of other faiths, can cause a degree of confusion. In reaction to various degrees of puzzlement this book aims at overcoming fear of religious pluralism. It invites people to see our new pluralistic religious situation as a positive phenomenon and to recognize that Christian faith and spirituality have all the resources necessary to engage it constructively and be enriched by it. Especially in the area of spiritual enrichment the Buddhist-Christian dialogue has had a tremendous influence on Christian spirituality.

The other situation that adds urgency to this conversation has been addressed by liberation theologies: the question of massive social and environmental suffering to which our history bears witness. The faith traditions cannot move forward in a way that is inattentive to massive human and planetary degradation. The comparison of these two sources of spirituality cannot be reduced to the area of prayer and meditation but has to attend to the demands for social activism. We are searching for a spirituality that is both mystical *and* prophetic. Both of us have had some experience in such a search. Paul has been engaged with Buddhism for over thirty years and has participated in social movements. Roger has written a book and numerous articles about liberation theology.

An overview of our conversations. We have noted that our conversations here do not follow the structure of the course in which we worked together at Union Theological Seminary. The engagement of students requires its own particular logic. Here our dialogue lies open to a larger audience, and it required some formulation of the premises and concepts entailed in the interchange.

In the first chapter, for example, we talk about what we mean when we use the word *spirituality.* This is a work in comparative spirituality. But what people imagine when they hear the word varies so radically that we felt we had to begin by sharing with each other how we—that is, each of us, with slightly different nuances—use the term. From there we easily slide, in Chapter 2, into a dialogue about interreligious dialogue and how each of us thinks it works and what we feel it might accomplish. We have to say something about this up front.

This work is trying to make connections and to open a conversation between these two traditions. This is a complex endeavor that requires care in the choice of language. Frequently we are looking for "bridge concepts" and "functional analogies" that can relate to and be appreciated by both traditions. A good example is found in the terms that are commonly used to point to ultimate reality: such terms as *the really Real, Emptiness, Interbeing, the pure act of Being, the ground of being, Transcendence, absolute Mystery, God.* Some of these terms might function for both Christians and Buddhists as fingers pointing to the moon. Others, such as *Transcendence,* inevitably suggest an idea that projects *God* outside and above the finite order rather than immanent to it as its ground of being. One of the reasons for adopting a conversational method is to draw people in rather than push them away with close scholastic analysis.

Chapters 3 and 4 go right into the subject matter of the conversation. We lay out for one another in Chapter 3 how each of us conceives in a condensed way what Buddha and what Jesus taught. That this is done in one short chapter shows that this is not a scholarly work. It takes some courage to synopsize the teachings of these two figures in such a short space. But the sketches are drawn from a larger fund of resources, and they should be received as they are intended, as interpretive portraits. The chapter aims not at a precise, detailed account but at painting a picture with a wide brush in order to contrast these historical figures. Chapter 4 asks who these figures were and how they were understood, and this ambiguous question yields a rich exchange because its answer always depends on interpretation. Both Buddha and Jesus were interpreted in many different ways by their immediate followers, and that interpreting is still going on. This chapter does not come to a definitive conclusion that will be accepted by all.

The next two chapters may be looked upon as companions. Both of them stray into the teachings of Buddhism and Christianity, the extended communities that contain the large imaginative frameworks within which Buddha and Jesus are lodged. So, in Chapter 5 we talk about the background of non-theism, where ultimate reality is not "a person," in contrast with the theism of Jesus. Here the merging of person, teaching, and worldview on each side of the dialogue is brought to the surface, and we talk about possible connections across the chasms of difference. Can we think of non-theism as promoting a pervasive presence of ultimate reality that is a dimension of finite history? And how does this relate to the creating power of being whose source is the creator God? Here comparison becomes interesting and difficult, and so we have to keep reminding ourselves of what we are after. It cannot amount to reductions of one to another in either direction. It has to involve trying to imagine what the other is saying by some analogy with one's own experience, because this is the only way one can understand another. And one has to try to understand others in order to learn from them.

Chapter 6 turns to the world as the counterpart of ultimate reality. In Buddhism nirvana encompasses *samara*, the continuum of everyday world and history. In Christianity, God is "Creator of heaven and earth." We briefly lay these things out and exchange views on these macro doctrines that come to bear on the concrete spiritualities of the followers of Buddha and Jesus.

In Chapters 7 and 8 we talk about human nature, the teachings of Buddhists and Christians on basic anthropology. In the first of the two chapters we ask about the problem of human nature, the distress in which we find ourselves, and the resolution or "salvation" that is offered through the sources of these traditions. The next chapter follows up with a discussion of the vision of human potential as these two traditions see it. These are delicate comparisons because so much is going on: Buddha, his teachings, the traditions that arose around him, and current schools of Buddhist teaching all interact with the same layers in Christian self-understanding.

The next three chapters, 9, 10, and 11, return to more concrete issues of the spiritual life. These include the tensions among silence and speech and action as expressions of the encounter with the really Real. We discuss styles of spirituality as they are exhibited in the followers of Buddha and Jesus, or in various tendencies that are mediated in these two traditions and communities.

Of special concern here is social engagement as an antidote to the supposed introversion of religious spirituality or any type of escape from the human project.

In the final chapter we raise the question of double religious belonging. What does this mean for each spiritual tradition? In the academy there is much debate on whether dual belonging is possible; on the spiritual level dual belongers speak of the richness of their ability to live in both worlds.

Each chapter follows a similar pattern. Both of us make an opening statement, followed by a response, each to the other. Each chapter ends with an "It Seems to Us" statement that tries to articulate where we agree and where there are differences that either have to be further explored or simply accepted. These statements are the fruit of almost a week of day-long discussions at America House in New York City after we had finished all our opening statements and responses. They are truly the result of two companions of Jesus and Buddha in conversation.

Such is the conversation upon which we have embarked, with our different background, voices, and styles. These will be noticeable; we have not tried to sing with one voice. We have tried to sing together and hope that the duet is harmonious.

We have many people to thank for their support in this project.

- The students at Union Theological Seminary who joined us for "Jesus and Buddha in Dialogue: An Exploratory Seminar" in the Spring 2012 semester added their voices and enthusiasm to our initial conversations.
- The perspectives of some experienced Buddhist-Christian practitioners were also part of those seminar conversations: Mr. (now Dr.) Kyeongil Jung, our teaching fellow; Catholic priest and Zen sensei Michael Holleran; and Roshis Paul Genki Kahn and Ann Ankai Wagner, both of the Zen Garland community in Airmont, New York.
- Paul's men's group in Madison, Wisconsin (The Wise Guys) discussed and offered helpful suggestions for an early draft of the manuscript. We are grateful to John Buscemi, Ed Emmenegger, George Nestler, Dick Russo, Bob Smith, Tom Zanzig, and Steve Zwettler.

- We are most grateful to retired lawyer Patrick Amer for his keen editing of the final draft of the book. His close reading ferreted out many unclear passages and proffered alternative wording.
- Very special thanks to Robert Ellsberg, wise and skilled editor in chief at Orbis Books, who encouraged this work from the beginning and helped draw it out of us.
- Finally, Paul expresses a warm thank you to the Jesuit Community of America House in Manhattan who offered him and his wife, Cathy Cornell, typical Jesuit hospitality for the week of conversations in which Roger and Paul formulated the "It Seems to Us" sections of each chapter.

1.

What Is Spirituality?

This chapter explores our differing, but complementary, views of the basic theme of our conversations: spirituality. Understanding spirituality as both a way of living and as a particular practice, we recognize what Buddhist and Christian spiritualities seem to have in common: an encounter with Mystery and a grounding in morality.

A Buddhist Perspective: Paul

From my study and practice as a Buddhist Christian, I can offer a starkly simple answer to the question that occupies this chapter—an answer that, I believe, fits the teachings and the example of both Jesus and Buddha: *spirituality is what one does to stay connected.*

For both Buddha and Jesus, if we are not connected, if we are not in some way extended beyond our self-awareness, we're going to have a hard time putting our lives together. Staying connected enables us to know, or feel, what life is all about. Moving beyond our own limited, individual sense of self—in both our awareness and in our actions—was for both Buddha and Jesus essential to the process of what Buddha called waking up and what Jesus termed conversion.

If I may put it in more general and contemporary terms: both of them offered us means by which we can come to the living, stirring realization that we are part of a "Bigger Picture."

Being part of this Bigger Picture is what provides us with two ingredients that are essential for living a satisfying human life: *meaning* and *energy*. The meaning or purpose of living our lives comes from the awareness that we are part of something larger than ourselves, something that connects us with others and with the world around us, and in so connecting us, provides us with a sense of "this is what it's all about." But living out these connections with others—a process of giving to and receiving from them—sure isn't easy. We need energy to do so. We need some form of empowerment, an empowerment, however, that comes from outside of us but at the same time can be realized only within and through us.

Such meaning-linked-with-energy arises out of—or is given in the very nature of—what contemporary Buddhists call interconnectedness, or *Interbeing*. Jesus and his followers use the term *Spirit*—the loving, or interconnecting, Spirit. (We'll be exploring these symbols in coming chapters.) Both of them are pointing to the Bigger Picture that we are already part of, but that we have to open ourselves to and learn to be aware of.

Spirituality is what we do in order to be so aware and so open. The word Buddhists use for spirituality is *practice*. Spirituality, therefore, is a matter of *doing*, but for Buddha it's a doing that aims to move beyond all doing. It's a doing that ultimately ends up in the realization that we don't have to do anything at all. All that we need is already given to us. As we shall see more clearly in the following pages, our spiritual practice leads us to that realization. We do, we practice, in order not to have to do or to practice anything at all. We are already held in Interbeing and in the Love of the Spirit. But what a difference it makes when we wake up to what we already are.

A paradigm shift in self-awareness. So for Buddhists—and I think we have empirical grounds to say for all (or most) religions—when spiritual practice begins to work, it brings about a fundamental shift in the way a person feels about both self and world. To adopt current jargon, spirituality triggers a *paradigm shift*. It's a shift from *self-centeredness to other-centeredness*. Or, from the little picture to the Big Picture. There is a growing sense of being *rooted* and of being *responsible*—rooted, or grounded, in something that is much larger than what we as individuals are and what we do. My Buddhist teachers use the words *held by*, even *cradled by*, an interconnecting energy.

This sense of being rooted or held has a dynamic or directionality. In grounding us inwardly, it propels us outwardly. At the same time that we feel held by this energy, we also feel part of, and therefore *responsible* for, other sentient beings. Simply stated: we find ourselves caring about other people. That doesn't exclude caring about ourselves, or about bugs and bears. But as spiritual praxis deepens, it's just all one big caring. We care about others just as much as we care about ourselves. And we do that not because we are told to, but because we simply have to. Being rooted in the Big Picture, we naturally care about every piece of it.

The rootedness and responsibility that result from the shift from self-centeredness to other-centeredness are what Buddhists are getting at in the teaching, found in all forms of Buddhism, that the two characteristics or results of spiritual practice are Wisdom and Compassion. Wisdom contains what we know and what we feel when we start waking up to our rootedness in the big interconnecting picture; such Wisdom conveys a deep peace that enables us to deal with whatever happens. But as we grow in Wisdom, we inevitably grow in Compassion. Rooted in the peace of Wisdom, we naturally reach out to others (and to ourselves!) in an all-embracing caring.

Spirituality and morality. The centrality of Compassion, which is an expression of the shift from self-centeredness to other-centeredness, enables us to appreciate the vital link for Buddhists between spirituality and morality. This is very clear in one of the pivotal pieces in Buddha's first sermons: the Eightfold Path. These eight neatly defined steps are like the handy "directions on the box" of all Buddhist spiritual practice. If the first two steps (right view and intention) invite us to trust and take the Buddha's message seriously, and if the last three directives (right effort, mindfulness, and concentration) call us to the practice of meditation, the three middle steps clear the way and provide the gas for everything else to move along. And these three enablers— right deeds, right words, and right job—are ethical to their core. Their message for anyone who wants to follow Buddha is clear: if you are harming others in any way—by the way you treat them, talk about them, or affect them in the profession you have—then no matter how deeply you study and comprehend Buddha's teachings, no matter how long and earnestly you sit in meditation, nothing is going to work! How you treat other living and sentient beings will determine what happens to you when you sit in silence or perform your rituals.

So for Buddhism—and I think also for Christianity—there is a vital link between ethics and spirituality. Really, they blur into each other to the extent that there is really no essential difference between them. For Buddhists, ethics—or the way you treat other sentient beings—is both the *condition for* and the *expression of* what spirituality is all about: waking up to the interconnecting Big Picture. If you are hurting others and using them for your own benefit, you are constructing an egotistical encasement around yourself that no amount of meditation or prayer can penetrate. Nothing is going to happen, no spiritual lights can go on, unless you first start making the effort to care about others. That's the *ethical condition* for the possibility of spiritual awakening. Ethics removes the obstacles and sets the stage for spiritual praxis.

But ethics does more. The very act of caring for another sentient being, the effort to contribute to or protect the well-being of another person or animal or tree, is *already* a spiritual practice. What moves you to such compassion, and what you feel in the act of extending compassion, is the reality and the happiness of Interbeing or of the interconnecting Spirit. In Buddhist language, Compassion *is* Wisdom. In Christian language, to love your neighbor *is* to love God. Initially this means that in loving God's creatures and friends one implicitly loves God their creator.

Non-dual and non-conceptual. This blending and blurring of morality and spirituality, of Compassion and Wisdom, of loving neighbor and loving God point to another defining character of Buddhist spirituality or praxis: *non-duality*. That's a philosophical term that Buddha and even most Buddhists don't use. A more mystical synonym would be *unity*. But *non-dual* brings out the depth of this unity that may not be immediately evident to Christians. For Buddhists, there is a *non-dual unity* between what we've called the Big Picture and the little pictures; or, in more philosophical or theological language, between the Infinite and the finite, between the Creator and the created. One of the most traditional Buddhist images of such non-dual unity is that between Emptiness and Form. "Emptiness is Form," the *Prajna-paramita Sutra* announces, and "Form is Emptiness." You can't have Emptiness without Form or Form without Emptiness.

So this, as we shall see in coming chapters, is the power and the beauty of what we discover in a non-dual spirituality: Emptiness and Form, the Big Picture and the Little Picture, God and the World are not two separable realities. But that doesn't mean they are simply one reality. They are both two and one. Distinguishable, yes. But not separable. Different from each other, they have their being in and through each other. Infinite Emptiness and finite Form *co-inhere*. They exist in each other. Without the other, neither is real.

And so if, as I suggested, spirituality for Buddhists is "what we do in order to stay connected," this is the kind of connection we're talking about—a non-dual, co-inhering unity between the Big Picture and my little picture. But such a realization of this non-dual unity is something that we can never comprehend or reach with our minds or our rational, thinking capacities. And here we come to another distinguishing aspect of Buddhist spirituality: it aims *to know by non-thinking*. It seeks to realize truth or reality by getting beyond thoughts, concepts, definitions. You might say it claims to know by not-knowing. Or as Christian mystics have put it, an authentic spirituality will lead us into a "cloud of unknowing." But it's a cloud in which we see, realize, understand in a different way—not an *irrational* way, but a *beyond rational* way. Maybe *intuitive* is an appropriate way of describing this way of knowing.

Buddhists therefore distinguish between what they term a *relative* way of knowing and an *ultimate* way of knowing. In our everyday lives of living and working with one another in this world, we have to operate through thinking and feeling, by using our head and being aware of our feelings. This is the relative level of knowing and deciding and acting. To call it relative doesn't mean, of course, that it is not real. But there is a deeper, fuller, truer way of grasping what's really going on. This is to wake up to, to sense, the interconnecting, always changing, creative Bigger Picture that is the ultimate reality of all the relative forms or expressions. Once we begin to wake up to this Bigger Picture, we don't abandon the little, always-changing, relative expressions of that picture. Indeed, we embrace them and live them with a newfound peace, vitality, and compassion.

But this distinction between the relative and the ultimate ways of knowing—between the conceptual and the mystical—doesn't mean that in Buddhist spiritual practice we simply check all our thoughts and feelings at the door of our meditation rooms. On the contrary, in most forms of Buddhist practice we make use of thoughts and images and feelings. But we use them as helpful, even necessary, ways of *getting beyond* them. For example, in some Zen practice we wrestle seriously and strenuously with try- ing to think our way through what are called *koans*—questions or puzzles that really have no logical answers (for instance, what is the sound of one hand clapping?). The object is to expend so much rational energy in trying to figure out an answer that you run out of energy and give up. In the Tibetan practice that I now follow, we carefully and elaborately imagine individuals who have totally embodied the Wisdom and Compassion that pervades all things—but then set aside the images as we realize that we are what they are. As the poets have put it, in such a spirituality, words and images are like music we listen to until we become the music and don't realize we are listening to it.

Silence and service. For me, as a disciple of Buddha and also a disciple of Jesus, I can summarize my Buddhist spiritual practice as a *spirituality of silence* that is also a *spirituality of service*. Silence is a necessary means of waking up to the Interbeing that pervades everything. But in hearing what this silence tells me, I also know that what I hear in silence I have already been *feel- ing* in the service of others and of the world. Silence that serves. Service that lives out of silence. I think that gets at the heart of Buddhist spirituality.

A Christian Response: Roger

I find your description of spirituality from a Buddhist-Christian perspective clear and persuasive. It goes directly to substance in contrast to my more formal and abstract reflections. You invite me to speak more specifically about aspects of Christian spiritual- ity that your description awakens by analogy. They revolve around the Big Picture found in the Christian conception of creation. This does not supplant a following of Jesus but provides a context for it.

The doctrine of creation rests on the experience that one does not possess within oneself the power that supports one's own being. Hedged in by nonexistence in the past and the future, we find ourselves existing by and within a power not our own that has brought us into existence. Creation means that God has formed our being out of nothing and continually sustains it. Our real, autonomous selves are not God but entirely held in being by the continual inner power of God symbolized as God's Spirit. This particular form of Christian non-duality, which is filled with tensions, was pictured by Augustine in an image of a sponge suffused and supported in existence by the ocean of God's power of being (*Confessions* 7.5). Meditation on the vectors of meaning released by creation-out-of-nothing provides a context in which Buddhist language begins to resonate with Christian convictions.

Being a creature makes me part of a reality that is larger than myself, bigger than the universe. On the one hand, the scientific story of the universe is my story, and I am its objective product. On the other hand, God as the power of being encompasses everything, holds me in being, and relates to me personally. The idea of being connected has an intimate personalist meaning for a follower of Jesus.

The idea of the interconnectedness of all reality finds another deep analogy in Christian spirituality that is shaped by the idea of creation. When evolution is drawn into an awareness of the ongoing creating power of God, it yields the conviction that human consciousness emerged out of the stuff of the universe by means of the life that preceded it. Through evolution supported by God's creating love the human becomes the material world's consciousness of itself. Human beings are the cosmos opened up into conscious freedom, so that we become responsible not simply for our individual selves but for our extended biosphere and the planet of which we are part and they part of us.

The Buddhist ideal of the bodhisattva draws spirituality and a sense of moral responsibility for others and for the world together. This has a parallel in a Christian spirituality that can't separate love of God from love of the world and other human beings. This allows a mutually enriching conversation between the two. The groundwork of intentional human activity inseparably unites these spiritualities. But every way of life is not wholesome; some spiritualities lead to ruin. Buddhism and Christianity converge in a deep sense of human responsibility for the well-being of others and the world.

A Christian Perspective: Roger

The area for this conversation between Paul and myself is *spirituality*. Few words have such a wide recognition and so many different meanings or interpretations. Not only does spirituality assume countless different shapes among the billions of people in our world, but the different understandings of what the term refers to make any discussion of it quite difficult. So we have decided to begin this exchange with clear statements of what each of us means by *spirituality* so that we might then work with our different approaches in order to establish some common ground for communication that respects the differences.

I approach this question somewhat didactically by stating a definition that clearly designates what I mean by spirituality in abstract terms, but which needs commentary to explain its rationale and provide it with some vital reference. *Spirituality consists in the way persons or groups live their lives in the face of what they consider ultimately important or real.*

Without probing the history of the term, I associate the word *spirituality* with the human spirit. It shows itself as that clear space where human beings are self-conscious and aware of themselves as autonomous subjects in the very act of knowing the world about them. This is also where we experience freedom. *Spirit* thus marks the difference of human beings from other animals on our planet. One's spirit refers to the deepest center of each individual person, so deep that others and even each individual self cannot fully apprehend it. Spirituality, then, is a characteristic of spiritual beings.

About this ability to know ourselves: even before Freud reflective thinkers were aware that self-knowledge is an ideal to be striven for, that self-deception is not uncommon, that human beings are not fully transparent even to themselves. Self-reflection never penetrates to the depths of one's inner spirit or self. Spirituality runs deep. Because of the depth of the human person, the complexity of the interior life, and the many motives that direct it, one may not completely know whether what we say about ourselves, as individuals or as communities, matches our deepest commitments or allegiances. This consideration supports the idea that the phrase "the way persons or groups live their lives" is not only an indicator of where a person's heart lies but also that, over the course of time, behavior constitutes what a person becomes. Not only can this or that action manifest the character of a person, but also the record of what one does or how one conducts one's life becomes the clearest window through which to assess the inner person. I do not mean to reduce a person to his or her external conduct, because the depth of one's human freedom and spiritual presence to oneself does not allow it. But human beings construct themselves by their decisions and actions, so that one's story provides a good measure of the inner person.

The lifestyle, or external pattern of a person's active life on the surface, requires more depth in order to correspond with the dimension of the human person to which that spirituality points. What do people live for? What constitutes the central meaning of their lives? These questions require inserting into the definition of spirituality that which confers substance to personhood, that which a person considers to be ultimately important. I use the phrase "ultimate reality" to signal on a descriptive level the thing that commands a central and a centering function in a person's life—that which is transcendent and goes beyond all else in its authority or ability to attract or command loyalty.

Two comments on this centering object of commitment relative to spirituality show how important it is. First, notice how this consideration begins to insert some hint of normativity into the domain of spirituality. This can be illustrated negatively by considering a complete commitment of a person's life or talent to something that clearly does not merit such allegiance. We sense that there should be a certain correspondence between human investment or dedication and the intrinsic merits of that to which it is given. This is tricky business, because the criteria for that judgment are not standardized. Yet on a formal level we might accept that, just as responses to value should be commensurate with the object in question, so too that which centers a human life should be worthy. As Paul Tillich advised, ultimate concern should be directed toward something ultimate.[1]

Second, the term *spirituality* has built into it two distinct levels that need to be considered. The one is existential, referring to any given person's actual spiritual life. The other level represents the theory or analytical description of an actually lived spirituality. Spirituality is a common noun that also refers to the discipline or field of spirituality that studies lived spiritualities. Thus, for example, Christian spirituality may refer to the way a Christian actually leads his or her life, that is, his or her spirituality. Or it may refer to the theoretical consideration of how Christians ought or are expected to lead their lives. It is one thing to describe how individual Christians, Jews, or Hindus live or how particular groups behave; it is quite another thing to describe on the basis of historical sources how the typical Christian, Jew, or Hindu lives or should live a distinctive pattern of life.

This approach to spirituality as defined by human behavior leads to a broad, open, and inclusive conception of this sphere of life. That inclusiveness has a couple of different senses. On the one hand, all people have a spirituality unless they are so scattered that they completely lack an identity. Since people's spirituality is lodged within the logic of their lives, it approaches what in secular or psychological terms might be called character. This removes the idea of spirituality from an esoteric corner of human life, a matter of special practices, and makes it the possession of everyone. On the other hand, inclusiveness also refers to the many factors that come together to make a person what he or she is. Spirituality includes virtually every facet of a person's intentional or deliberate life, because it draws up into itself all the things that contribute to his or her being. Spirituality includes the dynamic process by which persons make themselves the kind of persons they become. In short, spirituality applies to all people and folds into itself all the dimensions of personal life.

The relation of spirituality to religion raises a host of questions that elicit different views on the basis of the conception of spirituality one adopts and the approach one takes to analyze

---

[1] Paul Tillich, *Dynamics of Faith* (New York: Harper and Row, 158), 9.

it. Rather than enter into this complex discussion, I use a formula that is more functional than analytic or prescriptive but provides something with which we can work. Spirituality relates to religion the way individual persons relate to the communities to which they belong. In the secular analogue the communities referred to are not tangential but primary, those that give support to a person's life. Being a member of a community does not swallow individuality but supports and nourishes it. In so doing the community addresses basic needs relating to meaning, values, relationships, and an orienting context for life. So, too, although one should not reduce people's spirituality to the religion to which they belong, the spiritual relationship can be so strong that one's personal spirituality in large measure depends on the religious community. There is always a tension between individual persons and the communities to which they belong. In the end, spirituality is prior to religion because of the freedom of each person. Religion is ultimately constituted by the spiritualities of the members. Religion may be regarded as socially organized spirituality, and as such it bends back and has significant influence on individual members.

Turning to Christian spirituality, how does it relate to the Christian church? Ordinarily people live out their Christian spirituality as members of a Christian church. The communities or churches exist in order to support and to sustain Christian spirituality, and their members are precisely those who look for ministry that addresses their spirituality. But the ordinary situation does not apply in every case because many Christians today are not affiliated with any church. Also, the character of membership differs by degrees of participation. On the one hand, the relation of spirituality to the church is a variable; on the other hand, if there were no churches at all, Christian spirituality as such would gradually cease to exist. In this sense some connection with the church, distant or close, characterizes Christian spirituality.

One can explain the roots of the distinction between Christian spirituality and church membership by recalling how deeply spirituality pertains to the inner core of a person's freedom. Just as persons preserve an inner freedom relative to the communities to which they belong, so too Christians in their spirituality preserve a certain freedom in regard to their church. Each person is an individual and as such makes concrete a communitarian Christian spirituality in a particular way. This fact can be raised to the level of principle. All persons assume responsibility for their own spiritualities; one does not ultimately abdicate personal responsibility to any community.

The personal responsibility that characterizes Christian spirituality matches its defining characteristic of following Jesus. This attachment to Jesus as a follower constitutes the core of Christian spirituality. Following Jesus is prior to and lies beneath an acceptance of the common portrait of Jesus Christ represented by the churches.[2] According to the Gospels, beliefs about Jesus did not define following Jesus; following Jesus from the beginning provided the source for the beliefs about him. This shows that Christian spirituality understood as "following Jesus" designates the existential base from which many different forms of Christian spirituality developed.[3]

Before commenting on the many different forms of Christian spirituality, one should be aware of some common, essential, and unified traits. The "object" of Christian spirituality is God and God's rule as it was revealed in Jesus's ministry. Christian spirituality is frequently associated with the Spirit of God because God is experienced not only as the object of Jesus's teaching but also as an immanent power within the human spirit, not supplanting the human spirit but energizing it.

It would be hard to exaggerate the number of different forms that the spirituality of following Jesus has taken. Even the ways of measuring the variations are multiple. Following Jesus has

---

[2] In the tradition, "following Jesus" was often called "the imitation of Christ," which more frequently than not referred to Jesus of Nazareth since the distinction between Jesus the historical figure and the interpretations of him (Messiah or Christ) that developed after his ministry was not as pronounced as it is today. One way of showing this is to arrange the New Testament writings according to the estimated dates of their composition and examine how the interpretations of Jesus as the Christ developed over time. They developed out of the corporate spirituality of the Jesus movement.

[3] Within Christianity some authors deal with Christian spirituality as the limited area of specifically religious practices such as prayer, meditation, and patterns of worship and devotion. This contrasts with the expansive use of the term *Christian spirituality* employed here.

changed as Christianity has moved through different times, places, and cultures; it takes on contrary dominant styles; it differs according to different constituencies. These differences indicate that following Jesus cannot reduce Christian spirituality to a single defining characteristic.

In sum, defining spirituality as a form of behavior, and transporting that general definition into Christianity as following Jesus, has strategic importance in this work. It provides a ready access to Christianity through the following of Jesus of Nazareth. Jesus was a public figure and is so today through the gospel accounts.

A Buddhist Response: Paul

Roger, if there are any real differences that I as a disciple of Buddha have with your description of spirituality, they are much more a matter of emphasis than of substance. But emphasis can sometimes be just as important, or maybe more important, than substance.

In general, from my Buddhist perch, I found your working definition of spirituality—"spirituality consists in the way persons or groups live their lives in the face of what they consider ultimately important or real"—to be a bit too broad, too all-encompassing. So you start with how people live, and you then discern what their ultimate concern is by the logic of their lives. How they live and what they live for determines their character or spirituality. That makes sense. Beliefs are best seen in behavior.

Buddhists, I think, have a different starting point for their spirituality. They don't begin with one's understanding of ultimate reality in order to see how that influences one's actions. Rather, they begin with particular kinds of action that will clarify one's view of ultimate reality. More directly, spirituality for Buddhists begins with the suspicion that we really don't know what ultimate reality is. As we will hear again and again in these pages, for Buddhists, *ignorance* is our fundamental problem. Our understanding of ourselves and of ultimate reality (or what really matters) is out of sync with the way things really are. So the first thing we have to do is get things straight.

And to do that, Buddha offers us some very real, very practical things to do. That's what makes up spirituality. As I said in my initial statement, the Buddhist word for spirituality is *practice*. It's what you do in order to clear your mind and so get in touch with ultimate reality—often called your Buddha-nature. It's already there, already given to us, but for the most part we are ignorant of it. So practices such as meditation, mindfulness, and breath-awareness are meant to open our eyes and wake us up to what is already there. These practices are at the heart of spirituality.

This emphasis on practice points to how Buddhists might differ with your understanding of the relation between spirituality and religion. Yes, Buddha would agree that "spirituality is prior to religion" and that the religious community cannot replace the individual's responsibility. Buddha insisted that we must take refuge in ourselves; we have the primary responsibility. But he was also insistent that we must take refuge in the Dharma (the tradition) and the Sangha, or the community of fellow practitioners. It is the Sangha that will enable us to carry out the necessary practice without which we cannot clear up our ignorance. So, in a sense, I think Buddha is challenging contemporary notions by insisting that *we cannot be spiritual without being religious*. To be spiritual we have to practice. To practice we need a community that will guide us and sustain us.

Finally, Roger, your reminder that "following Jesus" is the "existential basis" for Christian spirituality resonates with the central place that Buddha holds in Buddhist practice. But instead of "following Buddha," my Buddhist teachers speak more of *being* Buddha. As I think Saint Paul understood it, in order to follow Christ we must realize—or wake up to the reality—that we are "in Christ."

Spirituality is what we do in order to wake up to what we really are.

It Seems to Us

We are not constructing these concluding observations systematically on the basis of pre-established first principles or foundations. They follow a conversation. This interchange between different persons provides a unique context. What follows both sums up and moves forward.

In our conversations about this chapter we agreed that *spirituality* describes the deepest conscious region of human existence. We want to show the depth at which one should enter into a conversation about spirituality. Spirituality has to do with the identity of a person and a community and the quality of their being. It has to be expansive enough to embrace the entire range of personal human development and cannot be shriveled up into occasional practices, even though certain specific activities may be central to who and what a person becomes. Our common reflections begin with spirituality itself and go on to note commonalities and differences that bear Buddhist and Christian nuances. We aim to open up areas where we agree and differ, and to offer our reflections for the consideration of others.

Imaginative frameworks. From our Buddhist and Christian viewpoints we see two quite different approaches to spirituality; but we end in basic agreement on the particulars that an authentic spirituality contains and produces. Roger, the Christian systematic theologian, describes *spirituality* as the "way persons or groups live their lives in the face of what they consider ultimately important and real." The imaginative framework completely encompasses the conscious life of human beings. Paul, with his Buddhist glasses, considers spirituality as the practical process of coming to an experience of what can be called ultimate reality or "the way things really are." This second imaginative framework focuses on practices that bring the many dimensions of life to an integrating self-possession.

Both conceptions of spirituality involve practice or action: either the full range of human behavior as it unites us to what is ultimately real, or spiritual practices that engender a consciousness that envelops and centers the whole of human life. In Roger's framework the ultimacy to which spirituality binds us arises out of "the experience that one does not possess within oneself the power that supports one's own being." Spirituality consists in a fundamental orientation and commitment to something beyond the self. In Paul's framework ultimate reality does not lie outside the self but fully encompasses the self; practice helps us mindfully to participate in it. It should be clear that we can build many bridges between these two frameworks. They provide a large space where a Christian and a Christian Buddhist can agree on a number of key characteristics of spirituality.

Activity and passivity. Spirituality is a dynamic clearinghouse of human response. The human person is both active and passive, a bundle of responsive freedom that also remains passive before the many limiting factors of life and the forces that impact it. The person is self-aware as a center of consciousness over against what is "other" than the self. Each one is an individual that is formed by the world around it. At the same time every person is biologically and socially constructed of the same stuff. To know is actively to interpret data that has been received. Within all this, human *spirit* refers to the inner dynamic core of freedom that constitutes the individual as an individual formed by the world around it.

In Paul's conception ultimate reality is given within the self; each one participates in a Buddha-nature that we become aware of through spiritual practice. Each one has within the self what it takes to become fully enlightened. Spiritual practices help us to tap into the inner resources of the ground of our own being. But a Buddhist also seeks refuge. A Buddhist takes the "Triple Refuge" in Buddha, the Dharma (the power of the teachings), and the Sangha (the community). The Triple Refuge gives concrete expression to Buddhist spirituality, a practice essential for finding and keeping in touch with what is of ultimate concern for followers of Buddha.

In Roger's conception, although ultimate reality is within the self, it is other than the self. That upon which we are ultimately dependent is non-self, even though it is the sustaining power of one's being. All persons, in degrees depending on their circumstances, have within them the power to act intentionally (freedom), and by their actions they define themselves in some measure. Yet all of us seek some kind of refuge that supports the self with meaning and value. Religious traditions are various ways of naming or pointing to that in which one seeks refuge. In terms of the activities and passivities of spirituality, Buddhists and Christians have a lot of analogous experience to talk about.

Absolute Mystery. "Taking refuge" presupposes that there *is* "something" in which we can take refuge. You've perhaps noticed that Roger the Christian likes the term *transcendent* or *ultimate reality*. The Buddhist side of Paul gravitates toward the even more amorphous *way things are, the really Real,* or *Emptiness*. We both agree that the source of refuge is not really a *some-thing*—that is, a reality that "is" or "exists" like everything else is and exists. One cannot simply call it "outside oneself" or "within oneself." Ultimate reality or the really Real may be imagined and symbolized in many ways but cannot be confined by any one form. Incomprehensible *Mystery,* that which is most real and utterly unfathomable, describes the source and object of spirituality with appropriate vagueness.

We agree that spiritualities can be good or bad, and more or less appropriate to humanity and to absolute Mystery. We recognize that spiritualities may relate authentically to absolute Mystery without giving it a name. Secular or humanistic spiritualities can be true and good. They may promote acting or living in ways that provide refuge and a path to human flourishing. Mindfulness-based Stress Reduction, Yoga, humanitarian projects—these stimulate spiritualities of commitment and refuge without any talk of God or Transcendence. Many argue that such loyalties imply something beyond themselves.

The moral dimension. An intrinsic element of spirituality lies in human intentionality, that ability to be aware of the self in its conscious relation to the non-self, the other, and the world. This is the sphere of morality, that is, the sphere of reflective awareness, of freedom, of responsibility for oneself and one's actions, and conceptions of right and wrong. Persons can reflect on their self-centeredness over against their concern for things outside the self. One can measure love of self and one's autonomous freedom over against concern for others or worry about the quality of one's impact on the world. We can be passive or aggressive, self-absorbed or thoughtful of others. We can contrast our grasping and clinging with our self-giving and letting go.

We agree, therefore, that spirituality engages human freedom and responsibility and cannot be reduced to innate character over which we have little or no control. But if our freedom truly suffuses the whole of our being, and we are to some degree responsible for ourselves, then we have a responsibility to develop a spirituality that is not just a given but in some measure a product of our freedom. Our spirituality is not our temperament, but rather what we do with it; it is not solely the imprint of our dependent origination but the path we have chosen to walk.

We agree, then, that for both Christians and Buddhists an authentic spirituality cannot be purely private. It has a personal and a social dimension; it embraces a concern for good and evil; it measures and critically judges; it is mystical and political, personal and prophetic. For Buddhists, the Wisdom of finding refuge is not authentic without compassion for others. For Christians, love of God and love of neighbor are inseparable. Spirituality may start with the individual. But if it stops there, it fails.

Spirituality and religion. The sphere of spirituality relates to religion, but religion and religious practice cannot limit the sphere of the spiritual. Spiritual practice so closely adheres to the essential inner core of a person that those who engage in no religious practices still possess a spirituality. This does not exclude spirituality from faith traditions, but spirituality transcends the sphere of organized religion.

While spirituality and religion are clearly distinct, we believe that spirituality tends toward community. *Religion*, for us, refers generically to the various socially organized ways of being spiritual in community. Spirituality is much like speaking: you need a socially given language in order to speak and a particular group or community of people with whom to speak. Religion provides the practice and the community in which to be spiritual.

But if we agree that community—whether religious or secular community—is necessary for spirituality, we believe that religion follows and should be measured by living spirituality. The Buddhist notion of *upaya* can help us get at this necessary though subordinate role of religion. *Upaya* means "skillful means"— whatever helps you to attain your goal. Religion is always a means to an end, not the end itself. So, as the Buddhists put it, use and practice your religion seriously and faithfully, but do not cling to it. Do not absolutize it. Use it to actualize your spirituality.

2.

How Does
Interreligious Dialogue Work?

Religions are trying to get along with each other through mutual respect, dialogue, and understanding. But what does the impulse for dialogue look like from the religious perspectives of Buddhism and Christianity? We are actually engaged in inter-spiritual dialogue. So we want to reflect on the premises, urgency, rules, and goals of our own conversation.

A Christian Perspective: Roger

Appreciation of interreligious dialogue increases with a recognition of the urgent need for it. Development of human life on our planet is dissolving many boundaries between human communities. As a result, an increasingly shared and interdependent life has enabled and forced sometimes intense exchanges between people of different religions. Religions that were known abstractly or at a distance have appeared close at hand. We know that different national cultures are marked by the predominance of other religions; now these religions participate in our culture. We read about different religions; now they are all in our cities and our children are marrying their members. Religious pluralism—different religions within a common sphere of interchange—may cause tensions, but it may also stimulate curiosity to learn about others' religious experiences. In both cases interreligious dialogue provides a way to engage our current reality and to move forward.

In this statement I try to express clearly and positively what interreligious dialogue might entail, describe its goals, reflect on its dynamics, and finally, enumerate some of its possible results.

The nature of interreligious dialogue. One can describe interreligious dialogue in a general abstract way in straightforward terms. It consists of reciprocal communication of religious beliefs and practices among people of different faith traditions; generally speaking, it should follow the rules of an authentic conversation. But these general terms become actual in many different ways. For example, a discussion group of women of many different faiths with no particular formal training in theology was formed to share spiritual aspects of their lives in the wake of 9/11.[1] Although the group did not dwell on religious beliefs, they were always there, and they came up, so that this group implicitly was an interreligious conversation. Its practice was nothing like the formal meetings of official representatives of different religions assembling to discuss an issue that directly pertained either to religious beliefs or to a religious response to a shared secular issue. In the first case the authenticity of the conversation would be measured primarily by the openness of the participants and the candidness of the exchanges. In the more formal conversation authenticity might be measured by the exactness with which the participants represented the essential or official beliefs of their religious organizations. Interreligious dialogue takes many different forms.

The goals of dialogue. Most conversations aim at successful communication and mutual understanding as their immediate goals. But different parties dealing with different subject matters may aim for different results. For example, people enter into dialogue to determine the terms of a contract, and each culture has its own informal rules for negotiating different kinds of agreements. The goal of business negotiation is a clear contract that satisfies all the parties concerned. The goals of those engaged in a dialogue will have significant bearing on its character. One can appreciate at least three obvious goals of an interreligious dialogue: objective dialogue understands another religion, in-

---

[1] Jeannine Hill Fletcher, *Motherhood as Metaphor: Engendering Interreligious Dialogue* (New York: Fordham University Press, 2013), 145–63.

terpersonal dialogue understands other religious persons, and spiritual dialogue seeks conversion of both parties, not away from anything, but to new depths.

The student is one who investigates or probes. If the emphasis in dialogue falls less on the persons involved and more on the objects of their belief, an interreligious conversation will have an objective character. This type of dialogue presupposes that the other religion has value and contains dimensions of truth about ultimate reality. The student wants to learn more about reality and to be expanded by a wider horizon of vision. This dialogue takes the partners as witnesses to beliefs with new and different content. Entering into such an interreligious dialogue does not presuppose any dissatisfaction with one's own religious beliefs, only recognition that no single religion can harness the infinite.

Another kind of interreligious dialogue is much more interpersonal. The goal is to learn more about the interlocutor in order to understand him or her better, even to the point of generating an affective relationship. Just as one's story up to the present opens up communication between two persons or groups, so too, receiving religious testimony about the religion of others can amount to intimate communication. Knowledge of another person does not in itself create friendship, but conversation about religious faith can elicit deep interpersonal sharing.

One might call persons who are looking for something they do not possess seekers. Seekers enter into interreligious dialogue in order to be spiritually enriched and possibly converted to what are for them fundamentally new religious attitudes toward reality. This level of dialogue is called spiritual, not to exclude the other motives, but to define the interchange as having a deep goal that may not be present or explicitly acknowledged in the other goals: a quest for a meaningful spiritual encounter.

The process of interreligious dialogue. Interreligious dialogue can designate so many different practices that speaking of "the" process can be misleading. Even the word *dialogue,* suggesting an interchange between two persons, too narrowly confines something that can take many forms. Dialogue does not require two people interacting. A standard description of the process of interreligious dialogue from the point of view of a given party would stipulate something like this: a person first enters into the system of language and values of the other religion, to some extent putting in parentheses one's own religious worldview, in order to learn about a different religious experience as manifested in beliefs and practices.[2] In a second move this new knowledge is appropriated and allowed, by comparison and contrast, to expand the self-understanding of the person. This should broaden the meaning of the person's own religious beliefs, values, and perhaps practices because these are now situated within a wider horizon. The whole process rests on the supposition that the other religion offers something of value to be learned.

The following account falls within this broad description. It draws from an actual protracted experience of entering into dialogue with Buddhist authors and entering into practices of Christian and Buddhist meditation. From that experience four notes are added to the template of exchange.

First, dialogue between different religions requires a common basis of communication; there has to be a medium across which understanding can pass. Social scientists tend to stress the differences among cultures because many antitheses lie on the surface of culture and at the same time penetrate deeply to the roots of human experience. Human beings can communicate, even though cross-cultural understanding is difficult. But it requires some shared basis in order for analogy between two different systems of thought and experience to operate. I postulate that a common basis for interreligious dialogue lies in the questions that human existence poses to itself: Whence, where, and whither am I? On the basis of that common question, for the three are aspects of one existential question of being, a person can have a first understanding of the logic of another religion's discourse; that is, it responds to ultimate questions. The answers to these questions provide a rationale for existence. To understand the self at this profound level is to understand the species. This maxim is enough to make another religion's response to the existential question of the human relevant to myself.

Second, I understand that all religious traditions have a beginning in history, that a specific historical mediation or mediator

---

[2] This straightforward statement could be implemented in countless different ways, from more formal and strictly controlled academic methods to more informal ways that highlight personal encounter.

stands at their source, however difficult it may be to isolate this figure or event. Usually in the course of a tradition's history, interpretation grows up around the core event or sacred place of a religion. One way of gaining access to a religion is to consider the most primitive and original core of its tradition. In the case of a Christian-Buddhist dialogue, the relationships of Christians to Jesus and Buddhists to Buddha provide a point of entry into the logic of each religion. If one imagines that these religions consist in some form of following Jesus and following the Buddha, the focus of attention on these relationships penetrates to something fundamental in the spirituality of each religion. Consideration of the relationship of Christians to Jesus and of Buddhists to the Buddha provides an appreciation of each religion on a level prior to the belief systems that developed on the basis of this core spirituality. The practical dialogue between the two spiritualities of following Jesus and following Buddha does not exclude considering each religion's set of beliefs and ethical values, but it relates them to something more basic, deeper, and yet more accessible, namely, the different ways in which Jesus and the Buddha influence Christian and Buddhist life respectively.

Third, the first two points combine to set up an abstract but common formal structure in which one can perceive analogies between these two religious figures and their spiritual followers. The common structure lies in the idea that Jesus the Christ and Gautama the Buddha are sources for responses to the existential questions of their followers. Seen from within that framework, interreligious dialogue will find analogies, both similarities and differences, between the spiritualities that each religion represents.

Fourth, the back and forth of religious dialogue will generate some degree of understandings of each other. Such an understanding has to respect differences, especially when it finds deep analogies between the two faiths. Ordinarily, people will begin to appreciate the other religious mediator in terms analogous to the way they relate to their own mediator. For example, Christians may be able to recognize that the Buddha functions like, and to that extent is, a "savior" figure. And Buddhists may be able to see that Jesus functions like, and to that extent is, an "enlightened" one. In the course of the dialogue it will become apparent that there is a tendency to show one's positive appreciation of the other precisely in the language of each one's own religion. Such is the logic of analogous perception and appreciation.[3] But this has to be accompanied by recognition of a wide cultural gap or difference. The process shows that the goal is not assimilation but appreciation of the other across a shared humanity.

The effects of interreligious dialogue. Effects differ from goals in their immediacy, concreteness, and practicality. They indicate what can happen to a person who engages another religious tradition. These effects depend on the seriousness with which a person enters into the dialogue. I use a personalist framework here, but what is said of a person can also happen to groups or societies.

One could develop a list of the potential benefits of interfaith dialogue. One gets to know another religion and, more important, the people of the other religious tradition. When this simple, obvious fact is contrasted with its opposite, which is reflected in the impatient question, Who are these people? one can immediately see how knowledge, especially personal knowledge, can overcome suspicion and mistrust. Dialogue allows a person or group to locate others within its own worldview. It expands personal horizons of knowledge, recognition of new values, and artistic sensibility.

But I wish to highlight what may be surprising effects of becoming familiar with another religious tradition. At a minimum, authentic dialogue with people of another religion will inevitably deepen one's understanding of one's own religion by means of contrast. This inescapably implied contrast heightens the distinctiveness of one's own beliefs and the rationale for them. Further, interreligious dialogue should enable or help one to learn more about transcendent reality than one's own religion by itself affords. The new perspectives on transcendent reality gradually combine with what one brings to the conversation

---

[3] David Tracy writes: "We understand one another, if at all, only through analogy. Who you are I know only by knowing what event, what focal meaning, you actually live by. And that I know only if I too have sensed some analogous guide in my own life." *The Analogical Imagination: Christian Theology and the Culture of Pluralism* (New York: Crossroad, 1981), 454–55.

to create wider categories that, in effect, can receive "more transcendence."

Still more deeply, entering into the world of another faith allows for the possibility of standing in solidarity with people of another faith before the absolute mystery of transcendence. This result appears most sharply in opposition to the suspicion that lack of knowledge about others often generates. One can transcend the dialogical situation, without completely leaving it behind, to a new plateau of human solidarity with other religious people before absolute mystery. At this level interreligious dialogue will expand one's spirituality beyond mutual understanding in unexpected ways.

A Buddhist Response: Paul

Let me comment on your input, Roger, by asking myself, What would Buddha say? After bowing in gratitude and appreciation, he might, I suspect, offer you three suggestions on the need to (1) prioritize the starting point for interreligious dialogue, (2) clarify what we must bring to the dialogue, and (3) intensify the necessity of dialogue.

To your observation that "the common basis" or the starting point for dialogue is to be found in the common "existential question of being"—that is, "whence, where, whither am I"?—Buddha might remind you of his famous parable of the man shot with a poisoned arrow (of which we will hear more in coming chapters). Briefly, the questions that the man asked of those who came to his assistance—"Who shot me? Where was he standing? What kind of arrow is it?"—really, as Buddha understatedly put it, "did not fit the case." The pressing questions were, "How do I get this arrow out? How do I counteract the poison?"

I surmise that Buddha would want to start religious dialogue not with "the one existential question of being" but with the "one existential question of suffering." That was the driving, unsettling concern that launched and then directed Buddha's spiritual search: how to stop the sufferings afflicting humanity and all sentient beings. These are the issues that, as I urge in this chapter, make interreligious dialogue so urgent. But they can also make the dialogue more productive. If religious people can first join in solidarity around shared commitments to reduce poverty and global warming, they will naturally form friendships that will enable them, more effectively perhaps, to share their wisdom about the "the existential question of being."

But when they do that, when Buddhists and Christians enter into what you describe as the "reciprocal communication of religious beliefs and practices," Buddha would remind them that they must state their beliefs *without clinging to those beliefs.* As Buddha's Second Noble Truth announces, the sufferings of the world, including the breakdown of relationships like dialogue, are generally caused by *tanha*—by greedily clinging to what we have or want, by refusing to let go and open ourselves to something new or different. So in the dialogue Buddha would call on all participants to be as clear and committed to their beliefs as they are ready and willing to modify or expand them. You put it nicely, Roger, in your statement: "no single religion can harness the infinite." There's always more to learn. Anyone who claims to have the only or the final truth spells the death of dialogue.

And that's why Buddha's third reminder is so important. No religion has the only or the final truth; religions have to keep talking to each other. What Buddha said about human beings is true of religions: we are *anattas*—non-individuals. We are relationships; we live out of connecting with each other. Abraham Heschel was echoing Buddhist teaching when he said that "no religion is an island." No religion can get along all by itself. If religions, like persons, are non-individuals, then dialogue is not an option. It is a necessity.

A Buddhist Perspective: Paul

Before we ask what interreligious dialogue is and how it works, we need to ponder a prior question: why is dialogue among religious believers important in the first place? My answer to that question is loud and clear: conversation and collaboration among religious communities, especially in today's world, is extremely important. Indeed, I would venture to say that it is *necessary.*

Interreligious dialogue is an ethical imperative. I say this not primarily because of religious or theological reasons, not because I am a Buddhist or a Christian. I say that because I am a human being who is trying to be aware of the world around me and to take some responsibility for it. The ethical imperative of interreligious dialogue arises out of the *state of our world*. To describe that world simply and starkly: it is a mess. And the religions, as more and more people are coming to realize, have a necessary contribution to make in trying to clean up that mess.

The kinds of problems that humanity faces today are *global* and they are *threatening*; they extend throughout this planet called earth, and they menace the well-being and often the very existence of the earth and its inhabitants. I'm talking especially about three categories of problems: (1) the horrible amount of suffering that results from the *unjust ways and structures* in which the goods of this earth are shared; (2) the *violence* that results from those who seek to impose or maintain unjust economic structures—and from the reactions of those who feel they are victims of those structures; and (3) the *environmental degradation and suffering* that results from the way humans are unjustly consuming the goods of this earth.

Such global, menacing problems, of course, call for the response of many different people and groups with differing expertise—politicians, political scientists, philosophers, grassroots activists, revolutionaries. But in this mix of responses we also need the contributions of the world's religions. Why? Mainly for two reasons.

First, the religions of the world, in their vast variety, offer the kind of values and visions that will counteract the selfishness and greed that are devastating both people and planet. What's more, religions also provide the *energy* or the *higher power* needed to live and be faithful to the values and vision needed for a different kind of world. Religions, we might say, offer an "impossible dream" and then the means and hope to make it possible.

The second reason why religions must contribute to "fixing the world" (as the Jewish tradition puts it) is paradoxical: They have been part of creating the mess in the first place. As religious history, especially recent history since 9/11, makes clear, religion has been used to justify or promote oppression, inequality, and violence. As Rabbi Jonathan Sachs has incisively observed: "If religion is not part of the solution, it will certainly be part of the problem."[4]

---

[4] Jonathan Sacks, *The Dignity of Difference: How to Avoid the Clash of Civilizations* (New York: Continuum, 2002), 9.

But for religions to make their contribution to relieving the sufferings of our world, they will have "to get their act together." They will have to act together, cooperatively, concertedly. Yes, each religious community will have its distinctive contribution to make, but it will be insufficient unless combined with other contributions. Going it alone will not only be ineffective, but it can also be dangerous. Any religion, like any nation, that thinks it has the only or the final solution to humanity's problems easily ends up a dictator rather than a liberator. Loners tend to think they are owners.

So Hans Küng's well-worn dictum is more accurate and urgent than ever: "There will be no peace among nations unless there is peace among religions. And there will be no peace among religions unless there is genuine dialogue among them."[5] The world is burning. Living beings are suffering. Religious people must set aside their bickering and their rivalry and act together, perhaps as never before, in order to help overcome this suffering. The ethical challenges facing the world make dialogue among religions an ethical imperative.

Buddha, I believe, would be in full agreement. What constitutes this "ethical imperative of interreligious dialogue" is what constituted and impelled Buddha's entire spiritual quest. It's what the First Noble Truth is all about: *The world is full of suffering.* And it was the need and the determination to alleviate this suffering that compelled Buddha to leave his palace in search of a religious practice and revelation that would enable human beings to deal with the sufferings that, according to the Second Noble Truth, were caused by greed. For Buddha, if religion does not remove suffering, it is false religion. It doesn't do the job that religion is supposed to take on, the job before all other jobs.

Therefore, for Buddha (and I suspect for Jesus too) the primary reason, and the primary starting point, for all interreligious dialogue is the ethical need for cooperation in order to remove suffering. If interreligious dialogue doesn't remove suffering, it would be, according to Buddha, a waste of time.

Interreligious dialogue as a spiritual imperative. But the need for dialogue is not only an ethical imperative. It is also a religious

---

[5] Hans Küng, *Global Responsibility: In Search of a New World Ethic* (New York: Crossroad, 1991), xv.

or spiritual imperative. It is based on a central teaching, or a pivotal recognition, that can be found in all religions; that is, all of them, in differing ways, confess that they really don't know what they are talking about! Let me explain how this sets up a spiritual demand for dialogue.

Of course, in every religious tradition we can hear a clear and proud announcement that it has been given, or has discovered, a truth or a revelation that is meaningful for everyone. But at the same time, paradoxically, all religions recognize, at least in their better moments, that the truth that they contain is a Truth that can never be grasped and contained fully and finally by any human being or any religion. In one way or another, all the religions know and teach that they are dealing with Mystery. The more they know of this Mystery, the more they realize that they really don't know it. Every discovery signals that there is so much more to discover.

This combination of the right to be proud with the necessity to be humble was captured inspiringly in the life and teachings of the Buddha. After his Enlightenment experience under the Bodhi tree, there was no doubt in his mind that he had discovered something that could revolutionize the lives of individuals and societies. He had to get up from his meditation perch and, as it is expressed in the early sutras, he had to "preach the Dharma until the last blade of grass was enlightened." But central to the message he preached was the warning to all his followers not to think that the words they were using captured the Truth they were preaching. Throughout his life he warned against *clinging* to our ideas, our beliefs, and our doctrines. As we will see in coming chapters, Buddha recognized the need for words, but he also recognized that when it comes to describing the experience of nirvana, no word could ever be the final word.

If this is so, if religion and religious experience deal with a Mystery that is as real as it is incomprehensible, if each religion knows something of the Truth but never the whole Truth, then in order to learn more of this Truth they all must learn more from one another. We might compare the reality of the Ultimate, or Truth, to the panoply of stars that expands before us on a clear night. To peer into it, we need telescopes. But each telescope, in its individual construction, does two things: it enables us to look into and understand the universe, but it also limits what we can see and understand. We see, but we see only a piece of the sky. The conclusion is evident: in order to see more of the universe than what I can see with my telescope, I need to borrow and look through yours.

Borrowing each other's religious telescopes in order to see more of the universe of Truth can serve as a metaphor for inter-religious dialogue. If, as one theologian has put it, "there is more religious truth in all religions together than in one particular religion," then interreligious dialogue is a spiritual imperative.[6]

What it takes to dialogue. So let me venture a description of interreligious dialogue: *an engagement and exchange between persons from differing religious traditions in the hope that thereby everyone can grow in the knowledge and the practice of what is true and real.*

If members of different religions can agree on this description of dialogue (and I trust they can), then they would also agree that effective dialogue requires both clear speaking and authentic listening, both witnessing and being witnessed to, both commitment to one's own tradition and openness to that of the other. Dialogue, therefore, is truly a two-way street. It's not just a matter of learning from someone else. It is also a matter of sharing with someone else. And sharing is a serious matter: it's not just like sharing a bite of my candy bar, which I think you would really enjoy but which you really don't need. Rather, it's like sharing a new kind of food that is not known in your culture and that can bring not just enjoyment but nutrients that perhaps are missing in your diet.

In dialogue we share truths that are of vital meaning for us— and that we think can make a real difference in our dialogue partner's life. We want not only to offer these truths and insights, but also to "sell" these truths. We want to persuade our dialogue partners to see and feel these truths as we do. Here, let me use a word that is usually forbidden in discussions about dialogue: we want to *convert* each other. I want to convert you, not away from your religion and into mine, but to the experience or discovery that has enriched my life and that I think can be added or incorporated into your life and religion. In dialogue that works,

---

[6] Edward Schillebeeckx, *The Church: The Human Story of God* (New York: Crossroad, 1990), 166.

Christians become better Christians and Buddhists become better Buddhists for having learned from each other.

So, two of the defining virtues necessary to practice inter-religious dialogue are *honesty and humility*. We must be honest about what we believe and what we hold to be true and valuable. That means that we can't water down what we are convinced about, even though it may be hard for the others to hear it. But at the same time, we have to be humble about what we are honest about; that is, what is so preciously true for us is not the whole of Truth. And we may not have correctly or clearly grasped the truth that has been given to us. There is always more to learn. If we forget that, we not only incapacitate ourselves for dialogue, we also make the truth that we do have into an idol. And that can be dangerous. Idols want to be the "only show in town." Not only do idols and their followers refuse to talk with those who hold other views, but they generally want to remove and replace them. And all too often, as we have seen throughout the religious history of humankind, they do so violently.

So, for me as a follower of Buddha, to meet and talk with followers of other religions is not simply a profitable pastime. It is a moral obligation. The religious families of humanity can address the horrendous sufferings that unnecessarily afflict so many of earth's creatures only if they act together, only if they learn from one another in a shared ethical commitment. And they will find success in this interreligious endeavor only if they approach one another with honesty and humility, with the eagerness to witness to the truth they have discovered and to be challenged by the truth they have yet to discover.

A Christian Response: Roger

Paul, you see an excess of suffering, violence, and environmental degradation impelling us toward a fundamental human and spiritual solidarity. You beautifully inject human affectivity into my more formal analysis of dialogue. I want therefore to pick up the drift of your statement and move it forward by contrasting interfaith dialogue with religious debate.

Like dialogue, debate will take different forms when different subject matters are on the table and different parties seek different outcomes. But generally, debate refers to a form of contention, a fight for the truth often between opposing positions. Its goal is to reach the truth by showing the other side to be false or inadequate by reasonable analysis and coherent argument. Debate works its way through the different construals of evidence; its dialectic reaches for clarity by narrowing the field of vision and making distinctions more precise. Debate thus unfolds in an atmosphere of competing ideas, and the goal is to arrive at a formulation of the truth at the expense of the other side. Debate is precisely a zero-sum game pitting clarity against fuzzy concepts. The goal is to win and thus produce a loser. Religion cannot mean "everything goes."

Insight can be gained into the character of religious dialogue by contrasting it with religious debate: dialogue is a form of religious interchange whose subject matter and goals of engagement differ from debate.

The subject matter of religion (and the guiding object of spiritual commitment) is transcendent. It cannot be known with the clarity and precision that allows it to act as a first principle from which other truths can be deduced and compared. Religious awe, a mixture of unknowing and being certain, produces a form of knowledge that is both individually intimate and socially mediated. Faith's convictions are deep, complex, and unclear because their objects cannot be defined but only clung to. Thus the real but non-categorical knowledge of faith cannot be deployed as principles for debate or axioms in argument. Their transcendent reference cannot be controlled by language but always exceeds it and overflows, thus leaving room for different perceptions and convictions that may also be true.

For you, Paul, the principal goal of dialogue is to repair a damaged human condition and restore it to existential unity before the mystery of transcendent reality and the sanctity of human life. The religions construe ultimate reality differently. The goal of human communion can only be achieved when it is postulated at the start that all stand before absolute Mystery as seekers. The goal of dialogue is not to reduce Mystery to a plain view; it is not to get all to agree. Religious pluralism is the natural condition of humanity. But the mystery of transcendence should unite human beings, not divide, because all share in it. The transcendence of ultimate reality unites by drawing all humans into itself. Just as debate distorts transcendence by implicit and often noisy claims of possessing it, dialogue recognizes that we are already united in an honest, humble, and quiet quest for the truth that all participate in by degrees.

It Seems to Us

After talking through what each of us has so far had to say on the topic of this chapter, we realized that, from our personal Christian and Buddhist viewpoints, we are very much on the same page. In fact, this may be the chapter in which it is easiest for us to speak with one, though differently inflected, voice.

That's encouraging—because the topic of this chapter, interreligious dialogue, is what this book is about. We imagine this book to be the basket in which we collect what we hope will be the nutritious fruit of a conversation between two friends who, though they continue to be members of the same religious tradition, presently draw their spiritual sustenance from two different sources. It is encouraging to confirm that we agree on what we want to do and on what is necessary to do it well.

What follows in this common statement offers nothing essentially new to what has preceded in this chapter. We hope, however, that it will highlight what seem to us to be some of the prerequisites—or as philosophers put it, "the conditions for the possibility"—of the kind of dialogue that will clarify and vivify the visions of Buddha and Jesus.

Historical consciousness—dialogical consciousness. First of all, we recognize that we share a common context: for both of us what cultural historians call *historical consciousness* provides the foundation, the urgency, and the guidelines for a fruitful dialogue of religions. Sifting and simplifying the multiple ways philosophers and anthropologists speak about this consciousness born of the Enlightenment, we might describe it as the sobering awareness and acceptance that everything we know, and every attempt to communicate what we know, is *historically conditioned* or *socially constructed*. To reuse the metaphor that Paul suggests in this chapter, we never have direct vision of the world; rather (now it is Saint Paul speaking), we're always looking at reality "through a glass darkly" (1 Cor 13:12)—or through a socially-historically constructed telescope or set of glasses.

For those imbued with, or burdened with, historical consciousness (whether they use that term or not), two conclusions
bear directly on the necessity and the nature of interreligious
dialogue. Historical consciousness means, whether we like it or
not, that *everything* we know or claim to be true is construed in
a *limited* and particular way. We may be convinced that what we
know is true, but we also are convinced that it is not the whole
Truth and that it is one of many other assertions of what is true.
If there is one ultimate Truth, for us historically conditioned
human creatures, it can be known only partially and multiply.

This makes a dialogue among religions necessary, for if the
truth that has been revealed to or discovered by each religion is
always limited, then, as we already heard from Edward Schillebeeckx, there will be more truth in many religions than in any
one of them alone. Therefore, too, if religious people, by their
very nature as religious people, want to deepen and expand their
grasp of God or ultimate Truth, they are going to have to talk
with and learn from people in other religious communities.

But such dialogue will be, paradoxically, a conversation or an
exploration in which no one makes *absolute claims* about his or
her own religion, and everyone makes *universal claims* about his
or her religion. To assert that my religion contains the only or
the final truth for all other religions will strangle dialogue right
from the start. But unless I try to show you why I think my truth
can also be helpful for your truth, we won't have anything to
talk about. If dialogue requires *listening* on my part, it requires
witnessing on yours—and vice versa.

So historical consciousness establishes the importance, even
the necessity, of something theologians, for the past decade or
so, have started to realize: For Christian theologians to do their
job properly, they cannot limit their study to Christianity. We
strongly and enthusiastically agree that all theology, in some way
or at some point, must be *comparative* theology. Sometimes this
will be a comparison with a specific other, and at other times it
will be reflection that takes other faith traditions into account.
Baldly stated, I cannot really know my God unless I ask you
about your God.

But we want to point out and stress that the first steps in such
comparative theology or interreligious exploration will have a
certain objective quality. Given the ever-lurking danger (especially

if one lives in a country that considers itself *the* world power) that we will read our own convictions or expectations into what we find to be "true" in another religion, we have to do the hard, careful, academic work needed to get the data right. We have to try to understand the others as they understand themselves. The first phases of the dialogue will have the character of what might be called an us-them relationship. We are objects of study to each other. We want to pay each other the respect of recognizing and honoring who we are and how we differ.

If it is not personal, it is not dialogical. But it can't stop there. Any dialogue that calls itself religious and that speaks out of a religious tradition—even when it begins as or wants to define itself as objective or academic or theological—will eventually and necessarily lead to what we described in the previous chapter as *spirituality*. It will lead participants to examine and speak about how they have *experienced* that which gives meaning to their lives and grounds their being in the world. Interreligious dialogue, in what it requires and makes possible, is not really a dialogue between religions; it a conversation between spiritual persons—people who within their particular practices feel they have touched or have been touched by God or Dharma, and who, through their conversation, want to share and deepen their experiences.

So if dialogue requires "head work" in serious study, it leads to and demands "heart work." Interreligious dialogue really doesn't happen until heart speaks to heart. This means that although dialogue will generally require books and texts and ritual practices, it reaches its ideal and richest possibilities when it becomes a *conversation between friends.* Two or more people who are very, very different in how they nurture and live their spiritualties but who deeply care for each other, and who therefore seek not to convert each other but to foster the well-being of each other—here we have dialogue at its heart-filled and heartfelt best. Friends talking to each other. The "us-them" relationship has become "I-Thou."

Here is another and more deeply felt reason, we realized, why in the dialogue no religion can or will announce that it is "the best," or "superior" or the "fulfillment of all other religions." Friends don't talk to each other that way. They don't because they can't.

What we do have and can have in common. In our conversations about this chapter we also came to realize that we share not just a historical consciousness as the context for dialogue but also what we might call a pluralist consciousness. Amid the sometimes cacophonous and edgy discussions among representatives of the differing theologies of religions (Are you an exclusivist, inclusivist, pluralist, or particularist?) we confess that, despite or with the help of our many critics, we are still abiding but chastened pluralists. (Perhaps Paul is less chastened than Roger.) That means that as pluralists we believe—better, we trust—that, first, there is an ultimate Reality or holy Mystery that is the source or ground of *both* the evident and incorrigible *diversity* of religions and of their latent *commonality* and potential *interconnectedness*. And, second, because of this incomprehensible holy Mystery, no religion can hold itself up as superior or final over all others.

We make this pluralist confession clearly and, we hope, humbly, not primarily because we are Western children of the Enlightenment (although that is certainly a factor), but because we are disciples of Jesus and Buddha. Both of them made universal claims that lend themselves to meta-narratives: that there is a God who loves and is present to all creatures and an "unborn, unbecome, unmade, unconditioned" Reality that provides "escape" to liberation for us all (Udana 8,3).

We add to our confession and agreement, finally, that we are *ethical* pluralists. We recognize that the conversation among the many religious communities will take different shapes and serve different purposes—academic, mystical, neighborly, and ethical. But we also agree, between ourselves and with Hans Küng, Eboo Patel, and many others, that there is an ethical and global urgency—perhaps priority—for a dialogue of religious believers that will bring them and the wisdom and energy of their traditions together to confront crises of human and environmental suffering due to violence and injustice. As we will explore in the coming chapters, we believe that the primary intent or goal of such a globally responsible interreligious dialogue needs to be the *reconciliation* of nations, peoples, and religions. Dialogue will thus move us from an "I-Thou" consciousness of friendship to a "we" consciousness of solidarity.

For us, therefore, interreligious dialogue is urgent and necessary not just to *know* more of the Truth and so to deepen a mystical spirituality, but also to *do* more of the truth and so deepen a prophetic, world-engaged spirituality—a dialogical spirituality that transforms self and the world.

3.

What Did Buddha and Jesus Teach?

In this chapter we seek to make our starting points clear: the core teachings of Jesus and Buddha revolve, respectively, around the rule of God and enlightenment for all. Recognizing that these messages are irreducibly different, we also affirm that they are nonexclusive, noncompetitive, and therefore importantly, even urgently, complementary.

A Buddhist Perspective: Paul

The question we are trying to answer in this chapter—what was the heart of the good news that Buddha and Jesus announced?— is as impossible as it is important. For such a question there is no one answer for all times. While there are indeed pivotal, essential, unchangeable ingredients to the transforming messages of Jesus and Buddha, these ingredients will always be assembled and understood differently for different cultures and times.

So let me suggest a way of summarizing Buddha's core message that I think is both faithful to Buddhist tradition and tuned to the needs and language of our present day: To the people of his time and of all times, Gautama the Buddha announces that *peace is possible now.* He knows that this is true for everyone because he discovered it to be true for himself. It is really and truly possible for all human beings—as long as their basic needs of food and shelter are met—to attain a level of inner peace that will sustain them no matter what happens in their lives.

As the Dhammapada, one of the oldest and most revered of Buddhist scriptures, puts it tersely and dauntingly: "The *bhikku* [the serious practitioner of Buddha's message], peaceful and well-concentrated, is called 'one at peace'" (vs. 378); "The wise person can become an island no flood will overwhelm" (25).

Peace is possible now is the message that Buddha announced in his very first sermon on the Four Noble Truths. But the first of these truths makes it clear that Buddha's promise of peace was as honestly realistic as it was daringly optimistic. The opening line of Buddha's sermon is this: "Life is full of suffering [*dukkha*]." This is Buddha's hard-nosed realism; there is no way to live life and avoid pain, disappointment, loss, and frustration. There is no place we can go, there is no thing we can do that will fully protect us from, or make us entirely immune to, things or people or events that hurt us. Although Buddha would not have put it this way, he would, I think, have agreed with Forrest Gump: "Shit happens." And we can't stop it from happening.

But *we can deal with it*. And here enters Buddha's optimism, his good news. No matter what kind of suffering happens, no matter how much of it there is, there is always a way in which we can deal with it so that it does not diminish or destroy our abiding peace. The peace that Buddha offers is stronger than any kind or amount of suffering. In fact, if we follow Buddha's directives and advice seriously and persistently, there can come a point in our lives in which we still feel the pains and disappointments of life, but they will no longer be felt as suffering. They will happen. We will feel them. But they won't be able to unsettle our lives, our fundamental peace-full-ness.

And this can be the case *in this life*—before we die. This is perhaps one of the most sobering and delightfully challenging aspects of Buddha's teachings for Christians: We don't have to wait till heaven, till the next life, in order to be truly and fully "saved." It can happen now—just as Jesus insisted that the reign of God can happen right now. It is already here. We can be healed, saved, given a new lease on life, before this life is over. In fact, if we follow Buddha's advice, embodied in the Eightfold Path, we can be saved today.

Buddha's diagnosis and remedy for the problem of suffering. Such optimism about finding a solution for the problem of suffering is rooted in Buddha's diagnosis of the deeper causes of suffering. The Second Noble Truth announces that *tanha*—translated "craving" or "grasping"—is the origin of all our sufferings. Why does *tanha* cause *dukkha*? Simple. Because it is trying to do the impossible—to hold on to things that can't be held on to. They can't be held on to because they are *impermanent*. Impermanence—the teaching that everything, absolutely everything (even God!), is part of a process of constant change through constant interconnecting—is one of the core truths that Buddha woke up to under the Bodhi tree. Suffering, therefore, is basically the frustration anyone would feel when trying to contain water in a sieve or trying to catch a bird in flight.

But if the problem is craving or clinging, what can we do about it? Here Buddha's diagnosis goes deeper. And here is where it might differ somewhat from Christian diagnoses. At first, what Buddhists call *craving* and what Christians call *sin* may seem to be pointing to the same problem. After all, Christians understand sin as selfishness, trying to hold on to things just for oneself. But when we take up the further question of why we are sinful, or why we crave, there seem to be major differences between Christian and Buddhist responses. For Christians, we are caught in selfish craving because we are *fallen*. Our human nature is a fallen nature. Somewhere, somehow, early in humanity's history, things got messed up. And the mess is something we're born into—or born with. This, we are told, is what the foundational Christian doctrine of *original sin* is trying to get at. We are sinful by nature, by fallen nature.

Buddha's diagnosis is quite different. The fundamental problem that humanity faces—the underlying reason why people keep causing themselves and others so much suffering because of so much craving and clinging—is not that we are corrupt and sinful by nature. Rather, it is because we are *ignorant* about who and what we really are. Our problem is not an inherent sinfulness but an inherited ignorance. We've inherited the ignorance from all the karma that preceded us. (We will take a closer look at karma in coming chapters.) But—and here is the really good news—if ignorance is our fundamental problem, we are dealing with a fixable problem. This problem is not *within* us as part of our human nature. Rather, it's *around* us, like a surrounding darkness. But darkness can be dispelled by light. We can be en-*lightened*. The antidote for the ignorance that causes suffering is to wake up to what we really are.

So, what are we really? This we will be exploring in the chapters dealing with the nature of the Ultimate and of the human self. For the moment, following especially Tibetan and Zen teachings, we can say that our true nature, our real nature, is Buddha-nature. Our real self is not our individual self. Our individual small minds are really part of a big Mind. As my Buddhist teacher puts it, we are the Space that contains and expresses everything—a larger conscious, compassionate, interconnecting Reality that is the source of our fundamental safety and peace.

Once we start to realize or wake up to what we really are, we realize that we don't have to cling to or hold on to anything because, as it were, we are already held. Once we wake up to our Buddha-nature, once we realize the Space in which and out of which we live and move and have our being, then nothing, no matter how much it hurts or disappoints or frustrates, can destroy the strength of our inner Peace, of our ability both to endure and to respond to whatever happens.

We look into all this, again and more deeply, in Chapter 7.

Buddha offers an orthopraxis rather than an orthodoxy. The question that now naturally and perhaps hesitantly arises is this: How can we wake up to what we really are? How in the world—in *this* world, *right now*—can we achieve enlightenment? Buddha offers an answer in his Fourth Noble Truth: by following the Eightfold Path. Here we have another pivotal, glowing piece of Buddha's good news. Not only does he promise that we can deal with suffering and find Peace, but he also clearly lays out how to do that.

We've already touched on the Eightfold Path in Chapter 1. It is especially important for Christians, I think, to note that in offering the Eightfold Path as the means to overcoming ignorance and achieving peace, Buddha is not telling us what we have to *believe*. He's telling us what we have *to do*. This is why I'm describing Buddha's good news as primarily a call to orthopraxis rather than to orthodoxy—right acting rather than right believing. Here we may have a certain difference between what Jesus and Buddha called for. Good news based on orthopraxis carries two implications for what it means to follow Buddha:

1. A call to acting a certain way as the avenue to achieving peace has the character of an experiment. Try this and see what happens. If it doesn't work, if it doesn't produce the kind of peace that can deal with any form of suffering—then chuck it and try something else. Buddha's good news is extremely pragmatic. If it doesn't work, it's either not true at all, or it's not true for your particular situation and conditioning.

2. Buddha's preference for right acting over right believing is not intended to diminish the importance of right believing. Rather, he is offering us a way, or a method, of arriving at right beliefs that is rooted in our own experience and not in his, or anyone else's, authority. In calling us to try out the Eightfold Path, he is promising us that if we *act* a certain way, we will *feel* a certain way. And what we feel and what we experience in our own awareness and intelligence will tell us what is true. By acting a certain way, we will begin to experience ourselves and our world differently. Acting leads to knowing. Behavior leads to belief. We will *know* the truth by *doing* the truth. For Buddha, we don't first believe the truth and then practice it. We first practice it, and then we believe it.

An orthopraxis of mindfulness and compassion. How might we summarize the right practice to which the Eightfold Path calls us? Picking up on the brief description of the Eightfold Path in Chapter 1, and reflecting the instructions I have received in my Tibetan practice, I think we can focus right practice in two essential ingredients: mindfulness and compassion. Without these two ways of living, we cannot wake up to what we really are.

Mindfulness, as we will see in greater detail in Chapter 9, is the ongoing effort not to let our thoughts and feelings get the best of us. Our problem is not that we have thoughts and feelings, but rather that we take them too seriously; we think they are giving us the full and final word about who we and others really are. When this happens, we don't have thoughts and feelings. They have us.

So Buddha's good news calls us to develop our "mindfulness muscles." We do this especially in the "gym" of our daily meditation. We are *mind-ful* of all our thinking and judging and feeling and reacting; we observe what's going on. And we *don't cling to* thoughts or emotions. We let them be. And we let them go. By not holding on to them, they can't hold on to us. And in this process we can get behind, or see through, our thoughts to an awareness or a feeling of the Reality that contains us and that we are. Mindfulness cleans the condensation on the windshield so that we can see what is really there. Just how this all works, I can't say. That it does, I can say. Thich Nhat Hanh calls it "the miracle of mindfulness."

Compassion is both what happens when we are mindful and also a way of practicing mindfulness. Compassion is mindfulness directed to other people and sentient beings. We don't let the thoughts we have of them define them. We don't allow the feelings they stir up in us to determine who they really are. In doing this, we come to feel and understand that they too are held in the Space or Spirit that interconnects us all. In extending compassion to them, we feel the Space. In being mindful of the Space, we naturally feel compassion. This is what Buddhists mean when they announce that Wisdom generates Compassion, and Compassion reveals Wisdom.

So this is the good news of Buddha: it is really and truly possible to wake up to a Reality that grounds us in Peace (Wisdom) and calls us to care about others (Compassion).

A Christian Response: Roger

Paul, your brief but exquisite representation of Buddha's teaching shows its metaphysical depth. Despite its practical character, for the way to peace is through practice, it also reflects the universal condition of the human. This prods me to go back to my largely historical representation of Jesus's teaching and to open up some of its metaphysical underpinnings and projections.

The God who rules is the loving creator God we met in Chapter 1. The God of infinite energy who is "larger" than the universe is personal, loving, attentive to each creature, and intends the flourishing of all. Followers of Buddha and Jesus will have to talk about the latent suppositions of their straightforward depictions of a way of life.

The personal character of the God who creates, sustains, and rules implies a moral universe. The scenario is not persons in an impersonal world, but a material universe suffused with moral or intentional underpinning. Enlightenment should enable discernment of cosmic intention, concern, and love beneath nature's objectively random and sometimes destructive ways. God is the within of all things, their source of energy and life.

At the heart of this universal morality Jesus locates justice, and he teaches this in forceful ways. The rich man who lacked nothing but ignored the poor man at his door died into a lonesome and punishing suffering; the poor man who succumbed neglected and unattended at the rich man's gate was born anew into comfort and fulfillment. Jesus's parable is a blunt statement that the universal human desire for equity in a world of innocent suffering has a transcendent warranty, a personal Dharma.

Jesus's teaching, according to his tradition, imagines things narratively in time; the cyclical rhythm of the seasons exists within the rule of God that is not affected by them. The realization of God's rule lies up ahead, maybe as something always possible, maybe close at hand, maybe breaking in with this or that event, maybe in fragments here and now, but absolutely in the end. In no case, however, is it programmed organically or teleologically; it is not automatic as a necessary development of nature; it is promised as the result of God's power and fidelity and always mediated by historical events.

The rule of God may be available now, but to tap into it requires practice in the form of action rather than the practice of meditation. The rule of God is a historical project. Here is another item about which followers of Buddha and Jesus have to talk. We cannot drive a wedge between meditation and social activity. The followers of each can understand the language of a path of life. Buddha invited people into a path leading to enlightenment that then overflows in service. Jesus invites followers to do as he does: teach, heal, bear witness, promote change in the death-dealing structures of life, and pray. Living within the rule of God entails living a life of discipleship of one who is enlightened and connected.

A Christian Perspective: Roger

Over the centuries countless essays have been written to introduce Jesus of Nazareth. The Gospels, practically speaking, are the sole source for recreating Jesus's ministry. But they can be enhanced by historical reconstruction of Jesus's context. In the last couple of centuries historians have also tried to get behind later embellished interpretations of him in the Gospels in order to represent how his ministry appeared to his contemporaries. This historical approach is helpful because it allows comparison with Gautama Siddhartha. Although the Gospels do not provide a detailed record of Jesus's activities, they yield a fairly clear but broad portrait of his ministry and the content of his message. This introduction to Jesus focuses on the rule of God that centered the many facets of his ministry.

Jesus of Nazareth. Jesus was born a few years before the beginning of the first millennium and died around the year 30 CE in what is today Israel or Palestine. The Gospels provide no physical description of his person. The stories surrounding his infancy are generally considered theologically motivated legends. Jesus learned his religious heritage as a Jew from Nazareth in Galilee. He was referred to as a carpenter (Mk 6:3). Many think that he became a disciple of John the Baptist before striking out on his own. John preached religious repentance and conversion and symbolized them with a rite of ritual cleansing (Mk 1:4ff.). The messages of the two men are similar in some respects and different in others.

One can discern how Jesus appeared to his fellow Jews by the way he fitted the known roles of teacher, healer, and prophet. As an itinerant teacher Jesus went from town to town in Galilee preaching to people in parable and sayings. Such teachers were generally poor and detached from accumulated possessions; they concentrated on deeper matters of the spirit and illustrated their message by example. A healer was a role that people were familiar with in Jesus's time. Jesus did not use medicines[1] but relied on the spiritual power of faith and an appeal to God's Spirit. His healings are depicted both as routine activity among crowds who pressed in around him and occasionally as wondrous events. As a prophet Jesus criticized various social and religious practices

---

[1] He sometimes used visible rituals or demonstrative gestures to dramatize what he was doing. A good example appears in Mark's Gospel, when Jesus used spittle to heal a man who was deaf and had a speech impediment (Mk 7:31–37).

in the name of the standard of God's word and values known through his Jewish tradition. His criticisms ranged from indictment of "this generation" to stinging criticism of certain groups within Judaism. His preaching was not timid. He provoked some; he occasioned conflict with certain parties; and his ministry led to his death.

It is not certain how long Jesus's ministry lasted, somewhere between one year and three. But in the end he so antagonized either the religious leaders of Israel or the Romans who were occupying the land, or both, that they reacted. This led to his execution as a threat to public order and other religious charges. After his death his followers became convinced that God had raised him from death and received him into God's own sphere. This faith conviction empowered the formation of a Jesus movement that gradually evolved into a Christian church independent of Judaism.

The rule of God. This phrase describes the very heart of Jesus's teaching. Its comprehensive meaning requires that it be carefully studied in its relation to Jewish tradition and in Jesus's usage. This account of the content of the rule of God simplifies the many different facets of this image but does not betray the basic meaning. What the "rule of God" refers to may be paraphrased as the way things would be on earth if they coincided with the intent of the creator God and the way things will be at the end of time.

Jesus's view of God reflects his Jewish tradition. Because God is creator of the world, Jesus refers to God as both caring for every creature and ruling the world like a king. Kingship in Judaism had none of the negative connotations it might have today in democratic cultures. Jesus's God is both creator and heavenly father; God is sovereign and personally attentive to history. In his ministry Jesus related to God both as divine power and one to whom one prayed using interpersonal language. When Jesus taught his disciples to pray, he gave them some typical words and phrases. He said that one should honor the transcendence and holiness of God and then ask that God's rule be established in this world in the same way that it is in heaven (Mt 6:9–13). From this one can discern some of the different connotations of the rule of God. The world as it is does not reflect the order the creator intended, but the prayer that Jesus taught asks that God act to establish it. The rule of God points to an expansive idea, the way things should be in contrast to the way they are, and therefore as a standard for criticism that can help change things.

Aspects of God's rule. Jesus spoke about the rule of God using various rhetorical devices, and he demonstrated its values by his actions. He told parables that illustrated God's rule. These brief vignettes frequently make a point about the rule of God by sharp contrast to human expectations. Describing some of these parables illustrates how creatively they suggest that things could be different. Imagine these stories being told to different people in groups of various sizes.

Jesus spoke of a rich "fool" who stored up all his wealth in barns to finance a long and leisurely retirement and then suddenly died (Lk 12:16–21). The story dramatizes that human life unfolds within a sphere of transcendence that encompasses the whole of existence. The man was a fool because he ignored his relation to God and thought only of immediate temporal comfort.

Jesus told the story of the younger of two sons of a landowner. He asked for his share of the inheritance, went off and squandered it, and ended up in a subhuman situation. When he gained the courage and humility to return home, he found his father waiting for him with outsized acceptance and love (Lk 15:11–32). God is like this father who restored the young man to dignity as though he had been dead and now was alive again. The story depicts a personal, loving, and forgiving God who unconditionally embraces every single human life.

Jesus told his fellow Jews the story of one of their enemies, a Samaritan, who went out of his way to take care of a Jew who had been robbed, beaten, and left for dead by thieves (Lk 10:29–37). The story displays an ethics of love that is not ethnically limited but universal, an ethics that seeks out those in need, even enemies, and makes them neighbors.

Jesus told the story of a rich man living in luxury with a diseased beggar lying outside his gate; the rich man died and was punished in an afterlife; the poor man was comforted in heaven (Lk 16:19–31). This simple story affirms that morality and justice structure the universe; the impersonal and destructive passage of time does not describe the inner substance of reality. Justice means the equal worth before God of each human being and the human imperative to respect it.

Jesus told the story of the end of time, when those who have actively loved others will be rewarded and those who ignored others in need will be punished (Mt 25:31–46). This story, with its perspective of finality, sorts things out in terms of ultimate importance.

The rule of God has all these qualities that together emphatically change a spontaneous and superficial appreciation of things. It reproves absolute attention to immediate satisfaction. It rejects the idea of an impersonal universe that offers no forgiveness. It condemns a pragmatic individualist ethic unconcerned with society. It transcends a worldview that aims for no future at all or one of absolute emptiness. In contrast, the rule of God offers a universe sustained by a personal power of love, a friendly source of being who accepts and energizes people to love all others out of gratitude, and who offers humanity a promise of eternal life.

The significance of God's rule. There are two distinct but overlapping ways of appreciating the rule of God that Jesus taught. The first way is analytical, as in the preceding paragraphs. Jesus communicated the rule of God in many indirect ways, through his parables, sayings, and actions that reflected its values. The first approach collects the many testimonies of his ministry and tries to fit them together into a complex whole. The second approach recognizes at the start that the rule of God is not a clear idea corresponding to a definable object but instead expresses a religious experience of God's being the almighty creator God who is also a personal lover of human beings and whose desire is that each one flourish and in the end be saved. The rule of God points to the deeper foundation of all reality that cannot be clearly imagined. Although it only appears in fragments, it still contradicts the ordinary assessment of things. It manifests itself in Jesus's ministry, which thus provides ideals to be striven for, a basis for critique of destructive human behavior, and grounds for hope in an absolute future.

The rule of God proposes a utopia, an idealistic conception of reality. It sets forth ideals for human striving and virtues that are worth cultivating for oneself and for others in society. The rule of God is not a set of commandments but a comprehensive vision of reality that grounds the character of human existence, personally and as a community of persons. This framework actualizes itself in concrete persons, actions, and situations as exemplified in Jesus's stories and in his own story.

The rule of God as just described sets the context for an ethics. It does not provide a set of rules to decide complex cases; it is not a categorical imperative that can be expressed in maxims. But the rule of God carries an ethical edge. It gives human beings leverage to recognize that this or that is wrong when it attacks or undermines the value of human lives, or when society fails to be concerned about whole groups of people who are squeezed out of the workings of community.

The rule of God also supplies human existence with the grounds for hope in an absolute future. It responds to the questions of whence, where, and whither with a premise of creation and a promise of eternal life on the basis of the power of a personal creator God. Such a promise engenders a second kind of empowerment beyond the power of being itself. It gives humans something to live for in the future, a goal. And this goal promises meaning for each person and for each person's actions. In other words, the rule of God challenges the rule of death and promises eternal meaning for what human beings are and do. It directly addresses the question of human suffering.

Jesus's relevance for all. That which opens up the possibility that Jesus can be a universally relevant and reconciling mediator and not a competitive religious figure lies in the exegetical consensus that historically Jesus did not preach himself but the rule of God. Jesus's mission and being were oriented toward making God's values, the will and the rule of God, operative in the world, in personal lives and in society.

This exocentric interpretation of Jesus can be found in the hymn to Jesus Christ in Philippians 2:6–11. Jesus emptied himself and took on the form of a servant or slave relative to the rule of God. This is frequently called kenotic Christology, a term drawn from this text. In theology Paul Tillich has adopted a version of this strictly dialectical Christology: Jesus is the Messiah or Christ because he surrenders his own person to the absolute and ultimate reality of the creator God, ground of being.

The strictly theocentric character of Jesus's ministry requires a christological interpretation that preserves the humanity of

Jesus and his being filled with the power of the Spirit of God the creator. This tension allows the Christian to find the creator God who was at work in Jesus analogously at work in other religions precisely as immanent, loving, accompanying, and provident energy. Jesus does not appear to be a divisive barrier between religions, except where religion sanctions human behaviors that run counter to the values of God's rule, and these appear as frequently in Christianity as they do in most other major religions.

A Buddhist Response: Paul

I must say, Roger, that your summary of what Jesus taught contrasts starkly—but I hope promisingly—with what I think Buddha taught. The differences revolve around Jesus's notion of the rule of God.

If you had just focused on Jesus's experience of "a personal, loving, and forgiving God who unconditionally embraces every single human life," then, as we shall see in Chapter 5, we could explore some illuminating analogies between God as love and the Mahayana teachings on Emptiness and Interbeing. But if Jesus's main concern, as you say, was not just God but the rule of God, then I believe we have something that is really unique to Jesus, that is, something for which there is not a direct analogue in Buddha's message.

The rule of God, as you describe it so clearly, means that Jesus's God wants to change not only hearts but social structures. The world as it is—as it was in Palestine under Roman oppression—is *not* the way God wants the world to be. As you and other liberation theologians make clear, for Jesus, as a good Jewish prophet, a society consistent with God's rule will be built not only on love but on justice—justice especially for those who have been stepped on and pushed aside.

So the God of Jesus is up to something in history. History is going—or can go—somewhere, toward a world that can be better tomorrow than it is today. Therefore, Christians can hope. Indeed, they *must* hope. And they have to act in order to bring about this hoped-for, changed world.

I hear very little of such a message from Gautama. The intent of his teachings was primarily to change hearts and minds, not society. He wasn't concerned about history going anywhere.

Yes, he surely realized that enlightened minds would produce an enlightened society, but he wanted to transform the way people saw and experienced the world so that they would not cling to their thoughts and desires about the world. Yes, his message that everyone could be enlightened was an indirect criticism of the caste system and gender identities of the time. But that was not his main intent. The notion of justice does not even figure into his preaching. He was so concerned with living in the moment that he warned against the distracting dangers of hoping for the future.

So, he never got into trouble with the powers that be, as Jesus did. He did not antagonize or provoke kings or princes the way Jesus and other Jewish prophets did. Thus, the differences in their deaths—Jesus dying the victim of a political execution, Buddha having eaten poisonous mushrooms (according to some traditions) and succumbing to old age.

Are these differences contradictory, illustrating the frequent contrasting of the "prophetic-historical" religions of the West and the "mystical-personal" spiritualities of the East? Or are they fundamentally complementary, in need of each other? We will be exploring those questions especially in Chapters 10 and 11. For the moment, we have to note and take seriously the apparent contrasts between Jesus's central concern for the rule of God and Buddha's for Enlightenment.

It Seems to Us

On the question of what Gautama and Jesus taught, one of the first things that we agreed on was the importance of getting it straight—that is, the importance of doing our historical and hermeneutical homework as best we can in an effort to understand the original impact of these two teachers. Yes, we both recognize that the prospect of arriving at a clear, final, universally recognized picture of what the historical Jesus and Gautama said, what they did, and what they thought of themselves is beyond our reach. The Gospels and the early lives of Buddha are, one might say, impressionist paintings rather than clearly defined photographs. They're interpretations, not historical records.

But we also agreed that if the task of knowing the historical Jesus or Gautama can never be done perfectly and finally, it is still possible and necessary to do it partially and as best we can. That's what Roger's phrasing "the original impact" is getting at. With the help of historians and scholars we can know how and why Jesus and Gautama upset, inspired, and made a difference in people's lives; we can determine what must have been key elements in their message, their vision; we can know what people of their time thought of them and why they followed these two teachers. A firm hold on this original impact and intent of their messages will provide us with needed leverage over the interpretations that were made of them through the centuries. Needless to say, we can be sure that both Gautama and Jesus have not been happy with many of the things that have been taught and done in their names.

Irreducibly different. And when we take up our hermeneutical tools and try, as best we can, to bring into focus what Jesus and Gautama taught, we find that their messages are *not the same.* Indeed, they are remarkably and irreducibly different. These stark differences are embodied in what we can call the core content— or better, the core intent—of their messages. For Jesus, that was the rule of God. For Gautama, it was the enlightenment of all.

The rule of God was for Jesus a social reality. Certainly, it called for a change of individual hearts. But it aimed at a new way of organizing and living in this world that would be both the result and the facilitator of such a change of heart. As Roger made clear in this statement, Jesus believed in and experienced a God who was intensely personal and who had a plan for creation and so was "up to something in this world." The rule of God was Jesus's vision of what this earth would look like if humans lived according to God's intention. It would certainly be a world very different from the violent, oppressed, and poverty-laden land in which he lived.

Having realized his own enlightenment, Buddha's intent was to make enlightenment a possibility for everyone. His main concern was to transform the awareness of each individual. If he could remove the ignorance in the mind of each, there would necessarily be less greed and less hatred in the lives of all. Yes, Buddha, after his enlightenment, wanted to form a *sangha,* a community of his followers. But the purpose of coming together was the transformation, the waking up, of each individual. Let that happen right now, in the lives of each, and the future will, as it were, take care of itself.

We recognized that the differences between the *social* rule of God and the *individual* enlightenment of all led to even more marked differences in what went on in the lives of Jesus and Gautama. We suggest that perhaps those differences can be emblematically captured in an event in Jesus's life that does not seem to have a counterpart in Gautama's life: the cleansing of the Temple (Mk 11:15–19). For Jesus, as for all Jewish prophets, the God of love was a God of justice; so yes, for them the universe does bend—or better, can and must be made to bend—toward justice. Prayer and meditation, though necessary, are not enough. This world will not change, the rule of God will not be realized, without the prophetic actions of God's people—actions that seem to be spurred on not only by compassion but by anger. If these actions can be, and need to be, forceful, confrontative, disruptive, they are also nonviolent. Such seem to have been the actions of Jesus in the scene at the Temple. And, as we know, the disruption of the Temple led to the crucifixion on Golgotha.

In noting that an incident like Jesus's prophetic action at the Temple does not appear in the life of Gautama, we are not suggesting that it should have. For the moment we want only to recognize differences. Buddha had his own program for transforming suffering (with an analysis of private property as the cause of poverty that bears socialist coloring).[2] But it did not include the announcing of a God who called for justice and for active confrontation with the pharaoh or emperor or landowner. In the coming chapters (especially Chapters 10 and 11) we will take these differences very seriously.

Jesus and Buddha are coinciding opposites. We expect that these (and other) "remarkable and irreducible" differences in the messages of Jesus and Buddha will turn out to be what Nicholas of Cusa calls a "coinciding of opposites." This is part of our understanding of Christ and Buddha as nonexclusive and noncompetitive. That means that their messages, no matter how head-buttingly opposite they may appear to be, will or can prove

---

[2] *Aggannya-Sitta* (Dighami Kaya 27).

to be coinciding—complementary rather than contradictory. At this juncture, we cannot say we know that for sure. But the following four reasons make us suspect that this is what we will discover as we carry on our discussions in the rest of this book.

1. It would be difficult to deny, we think, that however stunningly diverse the messages of Jesus and Gautama are, what motivates the messengers is the same: negatively, the desire to remove, or deal with, unnecessary suffering; positively, to promote full human flourishing. We believe that this shared motivation—really, this shared goal—can therefore serve as a criterion for assessing not only the veracity but also the complementarity of their teachings. Even if the content of each's message seems to contradict the other, if both messages are effective in enabling people to deal with their sufferings and so to promote human and environmental well-being, then there has to be something in each message from which the other can learn.

2. Besides having a common motivation, the messages of Gautama and Jesus have also produced common ethical fruits: radical love/compassion for others, for all sentient beings or all of God's creatures. Buddha could endorse Jesus's admonition: "By this everyone will know that you are my disciples, if you love one another" (Jn 13:35). This would suggest that both teachers and students have much to learn from each other about their different ways of achieving and practicing such a capacity to love.

3. The evidence is quite clear that both Gautama and Jesus considered their messages to be more important than themselves. We can imagine, therefore, that whatever Jesus encountered that helped promote the rule of God, or whatever for Buddha enabled enlightenment, would have been warmly acknowledged by each of them—even though it might be something not clearly contained in their original teachings. They were the kind of teachers, we suspect, always ready to learn—and they would want their followers to do the same.

4. Finally, and more theologically, in light of the pluralist confession that we made last chapter, we do believe (*trust*

would be the better word) that despite the insuperable and incorrigible differences that do exist in the messages and self-understanding of Jesus and Gautama, they are, both of them, *mediators of absolute Mystery and Truth*. Yes, we recognize that these words and symbols are more familiar to Christians and Westerners than to Asian Buddhists. But we believe that they can be functionally analogous for Buddhists. The Buddha and the Christ can be understood and experienced as very different fingers pointing to the same moon (or perhaps to different parts of the same moon).

In the rest of our conversation we explore how the irreducible differences in the message of Gautama and Jesus might be mutually challenging and life-giving. At this point we can list some of the sharpest "opposites" that we hope will coincide: How is ultimate Mystery personal yet beyond personality—intimately present to but always exceeding what is happening in our lives? How might the absolute end of history be contained in its eternal now? If history bends toward justice, how might compassion make it amenably bendable? Can one be both angry and accepting before the sufferings of injustice? Can one speak of a priority for either personal or social transformation?

We expect our conversations to be as rewarding as they promise to be challenging.

4.

Who Were Buddha and Jesus?

After their deaths, Siddhartha was recognized as the Buddha and Jesus as the Messiah or Christ. Every Buddhist and Christian lives within the interpretive context of who these historical persons really were and are. So we will talk about the complex meanings that have grown up around being followers of Buddha and Jesus.

A Christian Perspective: Roger

The stories of Jesus of Nazareth and Siddhartha Gautama did not end at their deaths. Both of them gained followers, and as the movements progressed over time, they became subject to extensive and cumulative interpretations. In the case of Jesus, in a relatively short time after his death many of his followers recognized that God had raised Jesus from death. The bases for the interpretations of Jesus lay in his resurrection and what he communicated to people. The interpretations also resonated with the various ways in which Jesus introduced God into people's lives. This experience was called salvation, and it will be necessary to examine what it means to call Jesus savior. All of this locates Jesus at the center of a Christian spirituality of following Jesus; it is there that the identity of Jesus appears.

Jesus's resurrection. After Jesus's death and the faith experience that God raised him from death, a Jesus movement arose, and interpretations of the sacred character of Jesus gradually developed from within it. All the interpretations of Jesus that followed depend upon a conviction that Jesus was raised by God from death, so understanding those interpretations has to start there.

The resurrection of Jesus refers to a transcendent "event," a reality that transpired on the other side of history. It refers to Jesus being drawn up into the power and life of God. Practically speaking, it is not possible to represent the process of resurrection in sensible or empirical terms as a physical event of history in a way that is plausible. There were no recorded witnesses to the resurrection of Jesus. Rather, the New Testament explains the conviction that God raised Jesus by encounters with Jesus's being alive and interacting with his disciples in vivid visitations that emphasize the realism of Jesus's victory over death. Resurrection refers to the passage to a state of being within God's loving being on the other side of finitude and time. It compares with nirvanic fulfillment and includes cessation of all earthy suffering.

Many exegetes read the stories of Jesus's appearances not as the historical causes of the belief in Jesus's resurrection, but as ways of expressing the faith that Jesus is risen. This invites theories that explain how it came to pass that disciples, who were first dispirited at Jesus's violent death, turned around to affirm that he was alive in God's sphere. Understanding what changed their minds becomes important for understanding the language of resurrection. But such a question cannot be separated from the larger question of the destiny of all human life. Jews in Jesus's time already believed in resurrection in different ways. For Christians, the conviction that Jesus is risen extends beyond his own person to include the potentiality of human existence itself. The disciples' faith in Jesus's resurrection is also hope in their own resurrection. Faith in Jesus's resurrection coheres with what Jesus taught about God, and it promises fulfillment to human existence as such. Resurrection gradually appeared to the disciples as an objective promise of God that bestows meaning and transformation with its acceptance.

The development of Christologies. Jesus communicated to his disciples physical, psychological, spiritual, religious, and human wholeness that was of divine provenance. People who encountered Jesus knew he was connected with, sent by, and even bore God into their midst. Conviction about Jesus's resurrection confirmed these experiences. Even during his ministry people interpreted him in various ways. But after his death and resurrection a new variety of conceptions of how God was at work in Jesus grew along with the Jesus movement itself. A rough sense of these developing Christologies can be gained by analyzing the New Testament writings according to their community provenance and date of composition. Each community bore witness to Jesus of Nazareth as the Messiah or Christ, but always in somewhat different terms drawn from the Jewish scriptures and its own situation. For example, Jesus offered God's forgiveness of sin; he welcomed all and healed the wounded; he promised eternal life; he communicated the rule of God; he was God's Prophet, God's Wisdom, God's revealing Word.

These developments continued after the New Testament texts were written and reached an apogee in the fourth century when the Council of Nicaea (325) declared that Jesus was divine because the Word of God incarnate in Jesus was not less than God. So clear was this stress on Jesus's divinity that it had to be balanced by the Council of Chalcedon (451), which declared that Jesus was both truly human and truly divine. It provided language to affirm these convictions of faith but gave no explanation of how it could be true. These two doctrines are considered classic statements through the centuries and across most Christian communities.

But development of different understandings of Jesus Christ and what he accomplished for humankind did not end with these public markers. It continues through the churches in the way Jesus is preached; it takes on local accents; theologians reflect on the beliefs of different communities in the light of the varying cultures in which the church exists. Behind all the interpretations, however, lies the experience of salvation.

Mediator of God. All the positive interpretations of Jesus rest upon an experience of Jesus mediating God's presence to people. The term *salvation* can be understood generically as indicating that Jesus communicates God in a way that makes people whole (or healed, or healthy) or eternally fulfilled in their being. Because the term *salvation* is so basic to the Christian language of being related to God in a new way, it always takes on specific meanings according to context. People in common recognized Jesus as one who communicated God's salvation to them, but this was expressed in a variety of metaphors, conceptions, and titles. For example, the title Christ or Messiah both associated him with God and interpreted how God worked through him. Today the language of salvation has lost some traction in the secularized technological cultures of the West, and it needs constant reinterpretation.

One conception of how Jesus saves connects salvation with the nature and function of revelation. In general, human beings cannot directly perceive God, so any specific conception of God must rely on some earthly mediation. Thus, the Christian response to the question of what God is like receives the response that "God is like Jesus."[1] In this framework Jesus reveals God to be personal, not a big human person in the sky, but in such a way that the absolute divine power that creates and grounds all being is personal, intelligent, knowing, understanding, willing, and desiring what is good for God's creatures. This means that all beings, in themselves and in their specific relationships and actions, stand in relation to a ground of being that is personal. The universe is suffused with intelligence and affective attention. Individual beings have a value that is guaranteed by a creating power that personally cares about them. Persons are more than individuals; they are subjects called to respond to an all-encompassing personal attentiveness. In the light of Jesus's resurrection each person is not only a product of chance and fate but one who has an absolute future. The projects of human freedom are consciously attended to and valued by the absolute power of being. All positive relationships bear a promise of permanency. To think of Jesus as a parable of God, a person who in his teaching and actions reveals the character of absolute being, transforms every facet of human experience with transcendent depth, value, and promise.

This example of developing one of the traditional ways of interpreting who Jesus is by what Jesus does for the person who relates to him in faith does not by any means exhaust the various

---

[1] Juan Luis Segundo, *The Christ of the Ignatian Exercises* (Maryknoll, NY: Orbis Books, 1987), 23–24.

ways in which Jesus is conceived to be savior. But it shows that understanding who Jesus is transpires on a spiritual level deeper than the words and concepts that are used. Spiritual interpretation recognizes Jesus as communicating God in response to the question of a person's being.

Locating Jesus in the Christian imagination. This reflection on Jesus as revealer of God leads to the question of how Jesus relates to other mediators of ultimate reality. One has to respond to that question in terms of history and development of doctrine; the response in today's historically and pluralistically conscious cultures cannot be stated in terms dictated solely by a classical or universally normative consciousness. The question today cannot be, What is the one absolutely true religion before which all others are lacking? The question has to be asked by each religion in open terms that respect religious pluralism: How can we understand our true religious beliefs in such a way that they preserve as well the truths of other religions?[2] The response to that question has to build upon an interpretation that places Jesus of Nazareth at the center of Christian spirituality as the revealer of who God is, and at the same time allows God to be revealed in other historical mediations. This will encourage a Christian spirituality of following Jesus that allows for other valid and valuable spiritualities and opens the way for interreligious spiritual dialogue and communication.

Some theological distinctions can facilitate a shift of understanding from a universalistic perspective to one that is attentive to historical particularity and limitation. *Theocentrism* and *christocentrism* refer to two very different ways of framing an understanding of the Christian vision. In the first, theocentrism, God pure and simple, as creator of all reality, prior to the differentiations of trinitarian theology, stands at the center of all things. This means that correspondingly the Christian believer

---

[2] Edward Schillebeeckx phrases the question in this way in terms of Christianity: "The problem is . . . how can Christianity maintain its own identity and uniqueness and at the same time attach a positive value to the difference of religions in a non-discriminatory sense?" See Edward Schillebeeckx, *Church: The Human Story of God* (New York: Crossroad, 1990), 165.

appreciates reality primarily, but not exclusively, in terms of the creator God. Who saves? The creator God. By contrast, christocentrism puts Christ, or more accurately the Word of God as incarnate and manifested in Jesus, at the center of reality. In this view of things the Christian appreciates Jesus Christ at the center of all reality so that reality itself is "christic" or bearing the character of God incarnate in Jesus. A comparison of these two views shows that the first approaches the question of salvation in terms of revelation and knowledge; it sees Jesus as a revealer of the creator God. The second view transforms Christian revelation into a cosmology; the New Testament depicts an incarnation that transforms the world.

Another distinction helps one thread a way through these alternatives while hopefully preserving the value of each. A "christomorphic" conception of Christian faith is one that takes as its object God, as in theocentrism, but relies on Jesus of Nazareth to shape the "form" or morphology of its faith. This correlates nicely with the New Testament conception of Jesus as revealer of God. It also describes fairly closely the transition of Christian faith from Jewish faith without in any way dismissing its ancestor. Jesus became a new Jewish lens for re-viewing the content of Jewish faith. This distinction does not "demote" other religions but simply adds a new revelation of the ultimate reality that they share. This is not a competitive assertion; it is important to see that it does not demote Jesus in Christian spirituality. It does not subtract from the developed doctrines about Jesus, but in fact demands them or something analogous to them to explain how Jesus could be a revelation of God.

This view of who Jesus was provides relief for Christian spirituality in our time by freeing it from the absolutism and competitiveness that are behind many of the Christian excesses of the past, from anti-Semitism and the crusades to a more general religious imperialism. It does this in two ways: first, it reads the relationship of the Christian to God as mediated by Jesus in open terms that encourage a positive view of other religions and of the founders of such spiritual movements like the Buddha: they are not competitors but fellow travelers. Second, and more particularly, it encourages religions to look for "functional analogies" between religions.[3] The term is almost self-explanatory in a situation of seeking transcendent reality. Jesus and Buddha both open up the human imagination to the immanent experience of ultimate reality.

A Buddhist Response: Paul

As I read your account, Roger, I happily recognized that we are very much on the same page in our understandings of how Jesus and Gautama were experienced and interpreted in their early communities of disciples—except for one central issue that may cast a shadow over our shared page.

There was, for me, an amazing lineup of similarities—or, as you phrased them, "functional analogies"—in the process by which Jesus and Gautama were interpreted and "glorified" after their deaths; in the way both of us understand salvation as an experience that enables people to feel whole or fulfilled; in the conclusion that therefore we could affirm both Jesus and Buddha as saviors; in the recognition that both of them "saved," mainly by revealing and teaching; and finally, in our agreement that Christians and Buddhists can affirm the uniqueness of their saviors/teachers without denying the validity of others. For both of us, therefore, Jesus and Buddha are not, as you nicely put it, "competitors but fellow travelers."

But there was one piece of your picture of Jesus where analogies for me did not seem to function so fruitfully and noncompetitively. And that had to do with what Christians consider the bedrock of their following of Jesus: the resurrection.

Now I know that you reminded us that the resurrection of Jesus cannot be represented in "empirical terms as a physical event of history." But as a Buddhist, I have trouble following

---

[3] Perry Schmidt-Leukel, "Buddha and Christ as Mediators of the Transcendent: A Christian Perspective," in *Buddhism and Christianity in Dialogue: The Gerald Weisfeld Lectures 2004*, ed. PSL (Norwich, Norfolk: SCM Press 2005), 170. Schmidt-Leukel uses the phrase "functional equivalencies," which may be better represented by the phrase "functional analogies."

you when you tell me that in his resurrection Jesus became part of "the other side of history" or "the other side of finitude and time." If, as you teasingly hint, Jesus's resurrection might be compared to "nirvanic fulfillment," I don't know what the "other side of finitude" would mean. For Buddhists, there is no other side of finitude; nirvana is found *on this side* or *within* finitude. The resurrected Jesus would not have had to go anywhere. Resurrection would mean a deeper way of being present, and available, in this world.

So I wonder whether you think there might be any functional analogies between the Mahayana doctrine of Trikaya (that I describe later in this chapter) and Christian belief in Jesus's resurrection. As Buddha was recognized to be one with the Dharma (ultimate reality) and so is now able to be enjoyed and experienced by his followers in his "enjoyment body," so Jesus was so identified with God that he can now be enjoyed spiritually by his followers in his resurrected body.

This might help answer your question about how to "understand what changed their [the disciples] minds" and enabled them to experience the risen Jesus. As Mahayana/Tibetan Buddhists continue to experience Buddha through their various forms of meditational and devotional practices, so Christians continue to experience Jesus in their practices, especially the Eucharist.

So my basic question is this: Does the resurrection set Jesus apart from (and above) other revealers and saviors? Or is resurrection something that can be found, analogously, in other religions?

At the end of my statement I write that, for Buddhists, "all are called to become what Buddha was and is." I have one more, and very related, question. Are Christians called to be what Jesus was and is?

A Buddhist Perspective: Paul

Neither Jesus nor Gautama was given at birth the names by which future generations would know them. If either of them as young men had been in a crowd, and someone had called out "Hey, Buddha" or "Hey, Christ," neither of them would have responded. These names came later—for Jesus, after his death on the cross; for Gautama, it seems that the renaming process began already in his lifetime but then really took off after he died of eating poisonous mushrooms (or, in some stories, pork). For both, the names that really identified them, the names that truly indicated who they were and what they could do, had to be discovered later. And it was a discovery that took place more in others than in themselves.

Buddha is more a response than a name. And that's why we can say that the term *Buddha* is really more a response than it is a name. (I think the same can be said of *Christ.*) His first disciples did not have to be told by Gautama or by anyone else that this is how they were to address him. Rather, *they* came up with and gave this name to Gautama. It was a result of the way he affected them and the way they found themselves responding to him. This is a process that we can identify in most of the religions of the world that owe their origins to a central figure. Especially after the founder moved on, after he had affected them as he did—and continued to so affect them after his death—that they, as it were, scratched their heads and found themselves asking: "Who was this man? What must he have been in order to have touched and transformed us the way he did?" "Buddha" was one of the answers they gave to that question.[4]

Naturally, the name Buddha, as well as all the other titles that they heaped upon Gautama, were, as we like to say today, *culturally conditioned.* They came out of a repertoire of images or stories or symbols that were part of the still relatively young Hindu tradition. To try to understand and express what Buddha must have been in order to so inspire and redirect them, his followers, as it were, rummaged through their cultural and religious closets in order to see what best fit him—or what didn't fit him because he so transcended it. They came up with many names—Master of the Dharma, Tathagata (he who has arrived or "made it"), Lord of the Caravan, Great Seer.

But the name that stuck, the name that became the name of the religion that grew out of his teachings, was Buddha. Its

---

[4] Since men generally wrote the history, we know of few female founders of religions. Today the Wiccan spiritualities are trying to remedy that lack.

meaning is as simple as it is profound: he was truly a human being who *woke up,* whose eyes were opened, who was fully able to see what was the truth about the world and the human condition. At the time of Gautama, there were many spiritual seekers, all of them trying to wake up and discover the truth of all truths. Gautama, his followers concluded, did it. Given their beliefs in rebirth, they also concluded that it must have taken him many, many previous lives. Finally, in their own lifetimes, they met someone who "arrived," who was fully awake. Of course, they would follow him. And after his death, they would tell the world all about him.

A savior who saves by teaching. The name Savior was not one of the titles that Gautama's followers gave him. That would have been impossible since the image of a savior was not part of their cultural equipment (as it was in the Greek world of early Christianity). But I believe we can apply the term carefully—or, as Roger suggests, in a functionally analogous way—to Buddha. That means that the image of a savior can serve the same function in two different religions; that is, to point to someone who enables people to figure out what life is all about and to live accordingly in a way that promotes the well-being of everyone. Insofar as both Gautama and Jesus did this, they can be called saviors (as the early followers of Jesus did, but the followers of Gautama did not).

And here, with this image of savior, I believe we can note a significant difference in the way early Christians and Buddhists understood *how* Jesus and Gautama saved. As we review the records in the New Testament, many of the Jesus-followers understood Jesus to have saved them insofar as his death and resurrection *fixed* something, that is, the rift or rupture between God and humanity. Jesus, in dying and rising, changed the basic or the ontological structures of reality and made possible a new kind of relationship between the Divine and the world. Because of Jesus, God could relate to the world in a way that, without Jesus, would have been impossible.

For Buddhists, Gautama saves primarily by *teaching.* He didn't have to fix anything or change the way things worked. Rather, he had to teach and make clear what was already the case, what was already possible—the way things can work if only people would wake up and see what is available. If people would take seriously his teachings contained in the Four Noble Truths and the Eightfold Path (as laid out in the previous chapter), they too could wake up. And in waking up, their lives would be changed. They would be liberated. They would be saved.

His followers believed that Gautama could teach the truth about how things really work because he had discovered the truth himself. It wasn't given to him as a birthright; he wasn't chosen from ordinary human beings to have the truth revealed to him. Rather, he had to roll up his sleeves, leave the comforts of his palace and family, and go in search of it. And it took him some six years—of trial and error, including rigorous but ultimately futile penances—before the big breakthrough under the Bodhi tree. This dogged, persistent searching—which, as mentioned, his followers believed was the culmination of searching in previous lives—finally paid off.

This hard-won but confidently achieved truth is what transformed Gautama into Buddha and what he passed on to others. But this passing on was not a matter of having faith in Buddha or trusting in his word. Gautama, now Buddha, required, indeed demanded, that his followers, yes, trust him, but then test this trust in their own experience. If the truth that he proclaimed didn't work for them as it basically worked for him, they couldn't be his followers.

But what called forth trust in his followers, what persuaded them to put his teachings to the test, was the way the truth that he discovered was so clearly, powerfully, beautifully embodied in Buddha himself. As one of the early Buddhist scriptures reports, Buddha could announce to his followers, "If you see me, you see the Dharma" (the fullness of truth).[5] And they did! (Which leads one to suspect that it was originally Buddha's followers who spoke this sentence and then put it on his lips.) To use a Christian concept, we can say, quite literally, that Buddha *incarnated* the truth that he preached. He enfleshed it, embodied it, gave it visible, historical expression. We might even go so far as to say that Buddha *was* the Truth.

---

[5] Samyutta Nikaya 22:87.

And as the course of Buddhist history moved on, this is exactly what his followers did. They identified Buddha with Truth. They glorified him.

Buddha glorified. The earliest followers of Buddhism (whose teachings are today carried on in Theravada tradition) certainly extolled Buddha as an extraordinary human being in what he discovered and how he taught. But they also insisted that he was nothing more than a human being. To draw comparisons with Christianity, Buddha, though extolled, was never deified. He was never identified with one of the primary deities of Hinduism. (That happened later, and the identification was done by Hindus when they called Buddha an avatar of Vishnu.)

But as Buddhist scholars have noted, though Buddha was never deified, he was *glorified*. That is, the process of extolling or making him special continued in subsequent centuries after his death to the point that he was given a kind of super-human status or power. This took place then, and continues today, in the school of Mahayana Buddhism (represented especially in the traditions of Zen and Tibet). This process of glorification was generated by many cultural and historical circumstances. One of them, I suggest, was the simple but powerfully evident fact that Gautama-become-the-Buddha continued to have the same power of promoting enlightenment among subsequent generations of followers that he did among the first. Somehow, in a mysterious but real way, he continued to be present or available within the Sangha, his ongoing community of monks, nuns, and laypeople. To understand and to preserve this presence of Buddha among them, his followers gave him further titles and attributes. In fact, they went on to affirm that while there was only one Gautama, there could be, and there have been, many Buddhas, that is, others who carry on his enlightening, saving role.

One of the most evident and continuously meaningful ways in which Mahayana Buddhists elevated Buddha with further attributes is the Trikaya—or the teachings about Buddha's "Three Bodies." *Kaya* or "body" is here understood as a mode of being, a way of being present and active. Buddha is said to possess and to operate with three *kayas* or bodies:

1. The *Nirmanakaya* is his physical body in which he achieved his enlightenment, in which he was born, and

which passed away after his death. Relics of this body are said to be preserved in countless stupas throughout the Buddhist world.

2. With the image of Buddha's *Dharmakaya*, Buddhists recognize that Dharma, or ultimate reality, or ultimate truth, *is* Buddha's body. Or, Dharma is embodied as Buddha. This teaching or symbol is the effort of the Mahayanists to express the perfect oneness between Buddha and what was for them the Ultimate, the Dharma. As Christians reported Jesus to have said, "The Father and I are one" (Jn 10:30), Buddhists can announce that "Buddha and the Dharma are one."

3. The *Sambhogakaya* is, literally, Buddha's "enjoyment body" or "body of bliss." Though it has been understood in varying ways, it signifies for many Buddhists the body by which Buddha continues to be enjoyed by his followers, the body by which he (and other Buddhas) is present and active in this finite world. Here we might, cautiously, note similarities with the "risen body" of Jesus through which his followers continued to "enjoy" him.

In my own Tibetan Buddhist practice, Gautama the Buddha is considered a benefactor—one who fully embodies the wisdom and the compassion that are given to us in our very being (called our Buddha-nature). In meditation we visualize his image right before us, embracing us with his love, showing us what we ourselves can become. Such meditations are almost identical with the devotion to the Sacred Heart of Jesus that I practiced in the seminary back in the 1960s and 1970s. Where this Tibetan practice, however, differs from Christian devotion to the Sacred Heart is that at the end of the meditation, we are instructed to let all the images go and to allow ourselves to fuse with Buddha and become what he was. All are called to become what Buddha was and is.

In this summary of what Gautama was and became for his followers, there are remarkable similarities, I feel, with what Jesus was for his disciples. But there are also challenging differences. Both similarities and differences call for further explorations in the Christian-Buddhist dialogue.

A Christian Response: Roger

I am impressed by what you call the remarkable similarities between what Gautama and Jesus were and became for their disciples. The differences of course are complete and obvious; great diversity emerges between the two religions and within them. This makes the analogies more surprising. It is hard to resist the desire to cut through the differences in the appraisals of Buddha and Jesus and try to find *a basic structure* that will in some degree represent both developments. The following four points, while falling far short of a general theory of religion, are an attempt to describe what happened in these cases.

Mediation. The ultimate reality to which all spirituality relates and the transcendent ground of each religion, if they are truly Mystery, are not accessible to direct human perception. Thus, all contact with and conceptions of ultimate reality are mediated. That means some person, place, thing, or event becomes the vehicle for supplying specific ideas and content in the formation of human conceptions of what remains ultimate Mystery.

Mediators. Jesus and Buddha may be considered mediators because they function as vehicles of such a mediation. Paul shows well that this was a historical process; people discovered the Buddha in Gautama in the events of his leading people toward enlightenment. Jesus was called God's anointed one (Christ) and savior because he communicated God's loving embrace to people. Mediation points to the events in which Gautama and Jesus opened up to people an experience of transcendent, life-giving power.

Continual mediating. If the response dried up, there would have been no Buddhism and, with regard to Jesus, no Jesus movement and later Christianity. In one respect this observation is merely descriptive, but it also indicates the depth and realism of the spiritual experience required for the birth of a movement. The Buddha and the Christ represent life-changing existential relationships that define people, sustain them, enliven them, and make them whole. Buddha and Christ represent ongoing interrelationships between a community of human beings and transcendent Mystery.

Decisive interpretation. I say *decisive* to offset any idea that interpretation had not been going on from the beginning. To be aware of something is to interpret it. Interpretation here, however, refers to deliberate action by a community to respond to the questions Who is Jesus? Who is Gautama? in such a way that they can function as savior and the Buddha. Such comprehensive questions have a history of answers; the many interpretations of Jesus as the Christ are matched by the many Buddhist interpretations of Gautama. But the history of those interpretations makes a point. The fact of the many interpretations shows how mysterious is the bond among the mediator, what he mediates, and the community of persons who are constituted by the ongoing mediation. This is a living historical reality of intersubjectivity that cannot adequately be captured in a formula but can be truly and realistically symbolized in many different concepts and metaphors.

This framework may be helpful, not in bringing Christian and Buddhist spiritual experiences together, but in seeing functional analogies and thereby increasing appreciation of both.

It Seems to Us

We are impressed with the parallelism of how interpretation of Gautama and Jesus developed after their historical careers. Each taught spiritual truth that was accessible within his tradition; each made an impression on those around him; each became subject of appreciations that increasingly magnified his identity and led to or over the threshold of his being in various senses divine. Each became the driving force of religious movements. Each provided a focal point of a lens through which all reality is perceived, understood, and judged. So, although we write for a Christian audience, it seems to us that we should represent Jesus comparatively. We present each of these figures as possessing the potential of being a mediation for understanding ultimate reality. This can only be done in subtle and tensive language.[6] But it

---

[6] *Tensive* refers to the quality of the words we use to characterize ultimate Mystery. The words indicate something about the object to which they refer, but we know that Mystery in itself must transcend the imaginative impression given by the words. *Tensive* says that the Reality both is and is not what we say about it.

is facilitated by the fact that we remain on the spiritual level of followers of Jesus and Buddha and make no theological claims.

Four basic principles. In our conversations we found that we frequently appealed to basic principles to anchor our observations. These four principles are offered, first of all, on the level of common sense; they are not doctrines. They may be looked upon as working principles that are meant to open up and guide our thinking.

The first principle stipulates the framework for these reflections as *noncompetitive*. In the context of dialogue or of our "we-consciousness," our thinking turns to both Buddha and Jesus as resources for directing our lives. It is true that the traditions that arose around these figures built cumulative interpretations that made ready communication between them next to impossible. But going back to their own teachings helps to make access across religious lines easier. The first encounter with the source of the other faith, therefore, does not regard that person from an exclusive bias but reads with a positive, inclusive expectation of learning something about ultimate reality and truth that will have a bearing on my life.

The second principle flows from the noncompetitive framework in which interreligious dialogue should take place. The principle may be stated like this: we should interpret the source of our own spirituality in a way that remains *faithful to our tradition,* but in a way that also tries to *accommodate the spirituality of the other tradition.* When Edward Schillebeeckx spoke of the problem of interpreting Jesus as the Christ in a situation of religious pluralism, he invoked this principle in the terms of the question to be asked: "How can Christianity maintain its own identity and uniqueness and at the same time attach a positive value to the difference of religions in a non-discriminatory sense?"[7] Noncompetitiveness and solidarity facilitate this effort. For example, a Buddhist can, and many do, interpret Jesus as an enlightened teacher. A person does not have to be a Buddhist to be a Buddha, and for many, Jesus was truly awakened. Christian theology offers an example in the other direction when it

---

[7] Schillebeeckx, *Church,* 165. Schillebeeckx is not alone in so formulating a Christian approach to Jesus. Appreciations of Jesus's own teaching encourage it.

does not limit the range of God's saving grace to the sphere of Christianity. Most critical theologians today recognize that God's saving grace operates universally and potentially can raise up genuine revealers of God.

The third principle recognizes *the authority of the teacher who is not one's own,* an authority proved by the worldwide movements that relate to Buddha and Jesus. The principle may be stated this way: The person or identity of the teacher should be regarded as representative of many or of all. In other words, what is exemplified in the teacher should be appreciated as a potentiality that all might identify with and aspire to. For example, Jesus, the resurrected one, is the firstborn of many. Jesus reveals that resurrection is the destiny of all human beings. Or, for example, Gautama is one of many potential and actual Buddhas. The title is not such that it applies exclusively to the Buddha of flesh and blood in history. This does not undermine the uniqueness of Jesus and Gautama as the persons they actually were, nor does it deprive them of their dignity, authority, or influence. The noncompetitive framework should not be regarded as diminishing these figures. The disciple is not greater than the master, but all disciples should emulate the master. This noncompetitive lens provides a framework in which the massive following of Buddha and Jesus ratifies their teaching authority and their relevance for all human beings.

A fourth principle, labeled *functional analogy,* flows from the universal or classic quality exhibited by Gautama and Jesus. Analogy signifies similarity within differences, sometimes great differences, for example, mother-care across species. But we are looking at this similarity not in terms of being or nature but in terms of function: what they do and how they affect people. We want to remain on this level of practical spirituality. This existential level, that is, the level of personal encounter in history with Gautama as Buddha and Jesus as Christ, opens up considerations that foster mutual understanding and enrichment.

Functional Christology in dialogue with Buddha. These principles allow us to speak about the identity of Jesus in a comparative context. The principles are noncompetitiveness, accommodation, universal relevance, and functional analogy. We can use these principles to formulate interpretive language about Jesus. But we won't do this in terms of Buddha-nature, or

Bodhisattva, or Son of God, or Word of God, or "being," but in terms of how they functioned in their teaching, a function that did not end with their deaths but directly affects people today.

Buddha and Jesus show that the world is potentially diaphanous to ultimate reality. The source and ground of being was manifest in their lives in analogous ways. They both spoke of ultimate reality or truth and the paths to encounter it. They did not need to escape from this world in order to represent transcendence; they found it within themselves and in the dynamics of human life. Ultimacy revealed itself within them. This means that transcendent reality is at the same time immanent to the world. Both Buddha and Jesus, as understood by their followers, represent ultimate reality or the really real as an all-encompassing ungrounded power of being immanent to all things and on which everything is dependent. These statements evidently manifest or reflect our Western, Christian context, but we trust that they will be functionally analogous for Buddhists.

Jesus is risen. One reason why Jesus's disciples affirmed that Jesus was raised by God stems from his continual influence in their lives—not just his teachings, not just his memory, but his person. This is the affirmation carried by the apparition stories in the Gospels. Moreover, what Christians believe of Jesus they hope for themselves and for all people. The universality of this relevance can be discerned in functionally analogous interpretations of Buddha. He is not a figure relegated to the past; Buddha is experienced as contemporaneous with his believers today. The Buddha takes on a "body" or a manner of being in the present within the lives of his followers.

Jesus is Savior. The New Testament is not sparing in its many interpretations of what it means when we say that Jesus is Savior. In different ways these metaphors all mean that when people encountered Jesus they found that he introduced God into their lives in a way that brought them healing, wholeness, and complete ratification of their being. Jesus reveals and makes present God's power for human flourishing. We think the historical Buddha did something analogous for his disciples during his lifetime, not by pointing to God but by enabling people to awaken to the power of Emptiness. And the Buddha today, living within his followers as a model of Buddha-nature and a source of illumination and awakening, resonates with the way Christians experience Jesus.

Jesus is divine. The language of divinity applied to Jesus arose in a gradual deepening of the interpretation of what is entailed in the experience of the salvation from God that he mediated. This language is not simple and straightforward; it took centuries to reach its classic formulation, and it was always complicated, cautious, and nuanced. It never meant to compromise the fact that Jesus was a human being like all others; when it did, it was contested. The reason people affirmed the divinity of Jesus was because they encountered salvation from God in him. And the reason why Jesus could mediate God's salvation was because God was at work in him. This was chiefly expressed in scripture as his being empowered by God as Spirit. The principles of universality and functional analogy allow Christians to understand what went on in the event of Gautama in relation to the Jesus event. The power of Buddha-nature, Dharma, and Emptiness appear functionally analogous to our own Spirit language. We see in this Buddhist language ultimate reality as vibrant energy that illumines and power that awakens human life.

Who is Jesus of Nazareth in relation to Buddha? Going back to the sources of our traditions has allowed us not only to moderate some of the interpretations that have raised walls between these two sets of spiritual disciples. It has also expanded the vision of both so that the revelation of ultimate reality and of human existence standing before and within it has been expanded. Both Buddha and Jesus make ultimate reality or the really real present and discernable with different accents.

5.

Ultimate Reality

In this chapter we engage what is perhaps the most salient difference between our two traditions: Companions of Jesus are theists; companions of Buddha are non-theists. This difference, however, yields functional analogies in the way Buddhists and Christians speak about and seek to be in harmony with what is for them Ultimate.

A Buddhist Perspective: Paul

You can't blame the many Christians who have called Buddhists atheists. Buddhism does seem to be—to sharpen the name-calling—a godless religion. Buddhists don't believe in God. They don't want to talk about God. They're one of the few religions that don't recognize a supreme Being. But that doesn't make them atheists.

Non-theists are not atheists. There's a big difference, I suggest, between non-theists and atheists. Buddhists are certainly the former; I don't think they're the latter. Atheists deny God in the sense that they deny that there is anything more to the universe than the matter and energy that we identify and explore through science and empirical investigation. That's it. Nothing more. What you see, literally, is what you get. If you can't observe or measure it (and to do that you may need a telescope, microscope, or mathematical formula), it isn't worth your while. Many atheists are missionaries. Recently, they've been called the

New Atheists; they want to convert others to atheism because of their conviction that to believe in God causes many more problems than it solves.

Non-theists trust that there is more to reality that just the material, observable, measurable world. There is something more, something ultimate, before, within, or outside of what we see in the universe. Or as some put it, matter is not just matter. It may contain, or it is, something more. But they don't want to call, or imagine, or think about that something more as God—that is, as the God or Theos or Jahweh or Allah in whom monotheists believe.

This, I believe, is how we can best describe most Buddhists. They are non-theists because the image of God as a supreme, transcendent Person who creates the world out of nothing just doesn't fit what Buddha discovered under the Bodhi tree. This is what Buddhists are most interested in. This is their Ultimate Concern; this for them is what is Really Real. And it doesn't seem to bear much resemblance at all to the Ultimate Concern of Christians, God.

Well, then, what does it resemble? Buddhists have a very clear—but really unclear—answer: no-thing. What Buddhists are after is similar to nothing, to "no thing" that exists in this observable, relative world. *Nirvana,* a word they often use in order to point to what Buddha discovered, literally means "to blow out a flame." Nirvana is "no-flame." Perhaps more than any other religion, Buddhists insist that their Ultimate Concern cannot be defined or even described in words; it cannot be attained through concepts or thinking. Anything we say about it must be qualified, corrected, taken back. As the cliche has it, all words about nirvana are fingers pointing to the moon, never the moon itself.

Does that mean we can't talk about the Buddhist Ultimate? Certainly not, for Buddhists, like all religious people, do their share of talking. But for them, all talk about nirvana, or about what counts most, has to begin with and lead to *experience.* Enlightenment, the discovery of nirvana, is an experience before it is a word, or it is an experience that both arises from and then goes beyond words. But for Buddhists, enlightenment is not *just* an experience, something that occurs within my subjectivity. It is an experience *of* something real, of that which is Really Real.

So this is where we can begin our efforts to further describe what is ultimate, or Really Real, for Buddhists. If nirvana is primarily an experience, we can ask how the experience feels. Or, what happens to an individual who begins to wake up and experience enlightenment? And here, Buddhists have responses that give us more to work with than simply being told that nirvana is a no-thing that blows us away. Amid all the schools of Buddhism, there is broad agreement that to experience enlightenment is to be imbued with Wisdom and Compassion. If these are qualities of the experience of nirvana, I think we can say that they are qualities or characteristics of nirvana. Wisdom has to do with what we know or are conscious of. Compassion describes how we act. Unpacking what they mean will help us, I hope, to appreciate what the Really Real is for Buddhists.

The Really Real: Wisdom. When Buddhists tell us that anyone who is enlightened—or who begins the process of waking up—will be gifted with Wisdom, they are really informing us that to be enlightened is to be "wise to the world." We "wise up" to just how the world really works, so that we can harmonize our own actions to the way things work (that's where compassion enters the picture) and thus achieve peace and happiness. Therefore, when it comes to describing the Really Real, Buddhists seem to prefer to use verbs, or maybe adverbs, rather than nouns. Though they can't say what the Really Real is, they do talk a good bit about how it works or acts. So the Really Real, rather than being a "thing," is more like an energy that acts in specific ways.

This brings us to one of the primary names—or better, "pointing fingers"—that Mahayanist Buddhist use for the Really Real: *Sunyata* or *Emptiness*. This is similar to one of the recurrent images that my Tibetan teachers use: *Space* or *Vast Spaciousness*. Both of these symbols or pointers indicate two things: (1) the Really Real is devoid of individual identity, or substantial being, or specific location; it can't be identified as "this or that," "here or there," and (2) the Really Real is all pervasive, all embracing. If there is no place where it can be located, neither is there a place in which it is not present. "No where" means "now here." Not having an identity of its own it, as it were, infuses the identity of everything.

A Christian friend of mine once heard this kind of explanation of the Buddhist Ultimate and declared, "Why, it is similar to the way Paul Tillich speaks of God: as the ground of being." To which his Buddhist teacher snapped in reply: "No Ground! No Ground! If there's a Ground, it's groundless." My own teacher would be comfortable with this description of the Really Real: the Groundless Ground of being, or the Vast Space that contains, and is, all.

But to appreciate properly what Sunyata or Emptiness *is,* we have to ask what it *does.* We're using a noun to get to a verb. Emptiness is a reality that is an activity. That's what the Mahayanist teachers are getting at when they explain that Emptiness is another way of talking about one of the pivotal pieces in Gautama's original message: *the law of dependent origination.* Part of Gautama's awakening was his realization that nothing, absolutely nothing, exists by or of or unto itself. Everything, absolutely everything—and if you want to talk about God, this includes God—exists through relationships with something else. Nothing simply "is." Everything "is with." We don't first exist and then relate; rather, our "we" comes out of relationships. And because "being" arises out of "being with," everything is in process, in constant change through constant relating. We are not "beings." We are "becomings" in the network of myriad becomings.

If Emptiness for Buddhists is another name for dependent origination, then Emptiness, we can say, is another name for everything that is. This sounds like pantheism—making the world into God or the Ultimate. But it's not. It's what philosophers call *non-duality.* This deep-reaching, penetrating non-duality between what is Absolute and what is Relative is contained in the Mahayanist and Tibetan teachings about Emptiness and Form. The teaching is simple yet mysteriously profound: Emptiness (the Groundless Ground of everything) is Form (the finite world in its multiple forms). But the reverse is also true: Form is Emptiness. They're different, but each includes the other. We can't have one without the other. Their relationship is non-dual; they are not "two" in the sense of one here and the other there. But neither are they one, in the sense that their difference disappears.

So for Buddhists, while Emptiness or the Really Real is different from the finite world, it is not really "other" than the finite world. Emptiness is not out there; it's in here, right here. This means that the Ultimate for Buddhists doesn't create the world and then "come down to" or "step into" it. Rather, the world co-inheres with the Infinite. Rather than entering the world, the Infinite abides *in* it and so manifests itself *out of* the world.

What we're talking about—non-duality—is as mysterious as it is beautiful. I think we can compare it to the mystery of what Christians call the hypostatic union between the divine and the human natures in Jesus Christ. Jesus Christ is said to exist as "two natures in one person." So, we have both two and one, a fusing of divinity and humanity without confusing them. But Buddhists would say this about the deeper, mostly undiscovered, nature of the whole world, not just of Jesus.

At this point Christians will naturally pose a question like this: Is this non-dual Emptiness personal? To think about that question, we have to talk about the other characteristic of Enlightenment: *Compassion*.

The Really Real: Compassion. We're back to asking how it *feels* to be enlightened. Or, what happens to a person when he or she begins to wake up to what Buddha woke up to? Again, there is unanimous agreement among the differing schools of Buddhism that once we begin to "wise up" to the Emptiness or interconnectedness of everything, we will—necessarily, naturally, spontaneously—feel *compassion* for everything (including ourselves). For an enlightened person, one is not possible without the other. We cannot really be wise without being compassionate. One produces the other; one naturally becomes the other; one cannot exist without the other. The well-worn cliche fits perfectly: Wisdom and compassion are two sides of the same coin. If we have only one of them, we don't have the coin of enlightenment.

This all makes perfect, logical sense: if emptiness describes the way things *are*, compassion expresses the way things *act*. Experientially, compassion refers to the human experience of interconnectedness. But the interconnectedness of Interbeing is itself compassionate. We don't just experience it that way; it is that way. When things interconnect, they express compassion—or concern, or love—for each other (either consciously or unconsciously). Compassion is simply being "in sync" with the interconnectedness of the universe—promoting that interconnectedness, allowing its energy to flow freely and creatively through us. Or, as it is taught in my Tibetan tradition, to be fully alive, to be truly in sync with the universe, we must "give and take" compassion; we must *both* receive it and *extend* it. And when we extend compassion to other sentient beings and receive it from them, we are extending and receiving it from and to the very Groundless Ground of our being.

This is why, in the differing forms of Mahayana Buddhism, there is a paradoxical interplay between being a Buddha and being a bodhisattva. While a Buddha represents the achievement of wisdom, a bodhisattva embodies compassion for all beings. The famous story of a group of people lost and dying in the desert heat makes clear what a bodhisattva is. Four members of the contingent come upon a high wall. They are able to climb up and behold on the other side a beautiful, lush oasis. Three of them, in their thirst, jump over and plunge into the sparkling pool. One goes back to tell the others. That's the bodhisattva. That's a real enlightened being who feels compassion for others even more urgently than his or her own thirst.

So if one cannot be a Buddha without also being a bodhisattva, if one cannot be wise without also being compassionate, if Sunyata or Emptiness means not just *non-substantial* but *interrelated*, then we can, I think, draw this conclusion: Indeed, Emptiness or the Really Real for Buddhists is certainly not a person, as Christians generally think of God as a person. But this does not mean that the Really Real is impersonal! Insofar as it is imbued with, or generative of, the interconnecting energy of compassion and love, it is *personal*. Not a person but a personal presence, a field of love-energy, or—to use a Christian symbol—an all-pervading spirit of Love.

Maybe that's what the author of John's Gospel was getting at when he defined the God of Jesus: "God is love" (1 Jn 4:8).

A Christian Response: Roger

Paul, your account of the large framework that shapes the Buddhist conception of ultimate reality offers new perspectives from which a follower of Jesus can reflect on Christian teaching. The languages differ from their roots upward. But a Christian can appreciate the kind of human experiences that lie behind Buddhist concepts, and this allows me to find functional analogies that provide a new accent for Christian speech. Christian tradition has its own brand of non-duality, emptiness, and utterly transcendent personhood. For example, far from being the image of God, human beings often fashion God in their own image instead of striving to become conformed to the God revealed in Jesus.

The non-duality of creation. Creation in an objective sense refers to every finite thing. Because God creates continually by holding reality in being, everything is always being created and thus a creation. *Creation* in an active sense means "God creating," actively supplying the continual energy that is the power of being. But the idea of God creating out of nothing breaks open every sensible image of the dynamic character of being. All finite beings are like waves riding upon the watery Spirit-power of God. Christians relate to God by imagining God "up there," "out there," but God is the "within" of all finite beings continually communicating to them autonomous identity. Images fail to depict this paradoxical worldly condition between pantheism and independent existence.

The emptiness of the creator. The paradox continues when we Christians try to imagine God, and Buddhism can help us here. Thomas Aquinas learned from Aristotle the difference between an actual being and its essential form or kind of being. For example, an individual tree shares a common form of being with the rest of its species. Each finite unit of being is limited and shaped by its form of being. This distinction allowed Thomas to define but not imagine God by contrast as pure, uninhibited, utterly free, and infinite power of being without any limiting form. Without form, limitation, boundary, control, or restriction, God as the pure power of being breaks open every definition. God as pure energy with no definition is no-thing; God is a pure emptiness that is not negative but unimaginably creative dynamism and vitality.

The transcendent personality of God. At this point the Christian has to be very careful in assigning qualities or attributes to God lest they appear to limit God. The predication must be transformed into a dynamic verb and projected in an infinite way. So Christians hesitatingly say God is Love and Compassion, but the words don't catch up to the infinite activity. Still, the qualities transform faith in the creator God into a source of hope in the positive character of being and of each creature's history.

Human existence as active hope to become an image of God. We live today with an acute sense of time; our lives are short within the history of creation. We are in motion from beginning to end, and we seek to live a meaningful story in the face of various forces of negativity. This meaning arises partly out of consciously participating in God's creativity and partly out of a hope for being united with that creativity in the end.

A Christian Perspective: Roger

A Christian communicating with other Christians does not encounter great problems in speaking about the character of God. The long common tradition beginning with the Hebrew scriptures, extending through the teachings of Jesus, and the steady practice of interpreting God to successive cultures, provides a vast storehouse of images. But in a respectful dialogue with a spirituality that reads ultimate reality in a non-theistic and impersonal language, one cannot take one's own language for granted. Dialogue requires consideration of each concept against the background of a larger canvas of experience. My reflection moves from Jesus's straightforward teaching to the many problems it faces today. These problems provide places where one can adjust the language in a way that internalizes the problem and allows it to generate light. Philosophy and theology do not provide the context for understanding these reflections; such reflections arise existentially within human beings facing the absolute mystery of themselves and their world and trying to understand them in terms of a transcendent protector, covenantal advocate, wise creator, father, and empowering presence.

Jesus's language of ultimate reality. The symbol *God* summarizes Jesus's view of ultimate reality. Jesus represented God as the lover of the people God created, a forgiving father, the transcendent advocate of justice, the uncompromising champion of the poor and lowly, critic of social injustices, and guarantor of ultimate meaning and value.

Jesus's personalism finds pointed expression in God as Father. When he teaches followers how to pray, he says they should address God as Father; the holy one of the transcendent sphere is loving Father. The story of the Prodigal Son (Lk 15:11–32) displays this personal love for each creature in dramatic terms. God represents infinite compassion and forgiveness, always there to be turned to.

God is the personal basis of justice in the universe. This justice pervades everything and functions at different levels. God rewards loyal commitment and effort, and God condemns refusal to assume responsibility and deliberate failure to be compassionate (Mt 25:14–30). God, as Jesus represents God's rule, pays attention to social injustice and is concerned especially with the marginalized and other victims of society. Jesus taught that all reality is based on a cosmic justice; God presides over a just universe. The poor man who suffers innocently in this world will reap his rewards in the next. So too will the rich person who ignores the poor (Lk 16:19–31).

The personal God who created the universe is also the God of an absolute future. Jesus taught that time would end in the final rule of God over all things (Lk 14:12–24). The resurrection of Jesus is the promise of this future held out to all. God is a God of absolute fulfillment for all and of all reality.

What is God? The Hebrew scriptures and, in the New Testament, the Gospels use spontaneous anthropomorphic language to speak of God and God's work in the world. Most people are satisfied with such talk. At the same time, representing the God of Jesus to today's developed societies and cultures requires responding to new penetrating questions arising from a variety of sources. For example, scientific knowledge of reality seems hostile to many conceptions of God. The being of the universe of which God is creator is an unimaginably old and vast fluid becoming, so that God as an individual person outside and above it seems to be an impossible idea.

We cannot take for granted that we already know what the idea of God refers to. Conventional language is challenged on every side. There are many examples. We say God is personal, but we cannot think of God as a big person standing outside and above the universe. The analogy for thinking about God has

been human persons, but what are the grounds for anthropomorphically projecting on God what we experience in ourselves?
Human suffering in Buddhism is something to be overcome, but
in a Christian context the massive and pervasive character of
suffering in nature and in society calls into question standard
ideas about God's power or goodness. Finally, in a situation of
religious pluralism, which idea of ultimate reality is true? The
plurality seems to discredit all of them. Addressing these points
of interpretation does not aim at mounting a defense against
them but at allowing these questions to help shape an idea of
how God can be understood today.

The issue should not be confused with the question of whether
or not God exists. The difficulty is prior and deeper than God's
existence and goes to the very idea of God. What does the word
God call up in our mind, especially when we recognize that all
knowledge has an imaginative residue and that God transcends
all such constructs?

One way of entering this question would examine a theory of
knowledge that includes a critical account of faith, believing, and
the process of formulating conceptions of transcendent reality. A
more concrete, practical, and accessible way is to reflect on the
meaning of the word *God* in four contexts or areas of concern
that raise issues for traditional ideas of God. These are science
and nature, humanity, social divisions, and religious pluralism.

Aspects of God as ultimate reality. Reflection quickly reveals
that the ultimate reality that is God cannot be depicted as a person. Science presents us with an unimaginably large, dynamic,
and creative mass of matter and energy that, despite appearances,
is fluid and constantly moving. The creator God of this universe
thus emerges as an immanent reservoir and source of energy;
God's transcendence is also immanent, and God's ultimacy is a
present reality. That God creates out of nothing means that no
finite being is separable from the infinite font of the power of
being that is God: no finite being has within itself its own power
of being. Ultimate reality is the non-dual, always-immanent
presence everywhere of the Groundless Ground of being. In the
context of science, God is the pure energy of the act of being and
simultaneously the ground and source of that power of being.

The natural and spontaneous tendency to speak about God
in human terms reflects the necessity of projecting an image of

God in terms of the highest form of being known: ourselves. How could the ultimate ground of being be less than what has evolved into self-conscious, intelligent, and free spirit? The immanent power of being must be free, intelligent, intentional, willing, and loving, while at the same time not being a limited person or having a restricted sphere of consciousness. God, then, is personal without being a person, and it is impossible to think that the creator does not love what the creator creates. God can be discerned in the human because humanity is the product of God's being and energy through the long route of evolution. Behind karma lies transcendent intentionality; good karma leads to a good outcome because ultimate intentionality sustains the whole of reality as a moral universe.

Human beings recoil from human suffering: physical, psychological, personal, social, and spiritual. Systemic economic destitution of people is called evil because deprivation kills as effectively as disease. The suffering referred to here diminishes being and tends toward its destruction and annihilation. Suffering thus enters into human consciousness as an experience of contrast, as what should not be, and as the urge to resist it. Suffering that tends to destroy the integrity of reality is evil. This dynamism allows God to appear within the dynamics of suffering and evil obliquely as the source of the desire that spontaneously recognizes and repels evil. Christian spirituality ascribes to God's love, a quality of the power of being, the fundamental dynamism of everything; God's love impels being toward increase and flourishing. This natural tendency comes from God. Thus God appears against the grain in the experience of suffering and evil as the ground of the possible good and the source of energy to pursue it.

God, as ultimate reality, thus appears in a desire or hope of finally overcoming suffering. God is at the other end, in front of a moral demand for justice that arises within political, economic and social injustice. The elementary desire for justice, for oneself and for others, reflects an built-in longing for a moral universe. And this basic longing, in turn, finds grounding in a subjective, intentional, and personal God.

The plurality of religions does not reflect negatively on ultimate reality; it simply reveals from a corporate human perspective that ultimate reality is truly transcendent. To be ultimate reality, God must be the God above all the gods, those local "ultimates" that idolatrously evoke only self-serving awe or reverence. Each authentic representation of God is expansive, providing only a small aperture upon the truly transcendent; many representations reveal more about ultimate reality than one can. When authentic transcendence does break into human consciousness it will inevitably show that the many religions do not compete with one another, or, when they do, they are falsely construed. Each one is a part of humanity's being drawn into the transcendence of God. The creator God in the end has to be conceived as a transcendent principle of reconciliation.

Ultimate reality in Jesus's teaching today. Jesus taught that the unspeakably transcendent ultimate reality symbolized by YAHWEH was indeed a loving and provident Father. This personal God of love is the ground beneath and the guarantor behind justice in personal relationships and in the structure of the universe. This teaching has been and always will be received in ever new and different cultures; it is thus interpreted and appropriated in contexts that give the teaching of the past a new analogous meaning. The most radical cultural reinterpretation of Jesus's revelation of ultimate reality occurred in the West during the course of the Enlightenment. The illuminati recognized that Jesus's teaching developed by taking on new cultural accretions over centuries, and they wished to cut through understandings that were particular to a past time in order to retrieve the original, universally relevant, classic, and normative truth. Today we know that no such pure form exists. All we can do is transpose Jesus's teaching addressed to his culture in terms that are proportionate to our scientific, critical, humanitarian, socially conscious, and religiously pluralistic culture.

Jesus's plain speech about God tells us today that, despite the unimaginable size and age of our universe and the relentless impersonal processes of *samsara*, the world's trajectory is sustained by personal intentionality and love. This means that despite the randomness and the laws governing linear history, the world as we know it has a destination, not teleologically predetermined, but an end consisting of being received into God's sphere. This is no arbitrary projection, because human beings can only imagine ultimate reality in terms of a universe that has itself produced self-consciousness, reflection, and freedom. The world as given is constituted in conflict, injustice, suffering, failure, and death; human existence is driven by greed, possessive clinging, and illusion. But fragmentary joy and fulfillment are experienced within these larger confines. The resistance to which these negatives give rise testifies to a hope for and a trust in an ultimate reality that encompasses and overcomes these negativities. Suffering does not crush faith but stimulates and nourishes it. Religious pluralism, which from the narrowest point of view may look like a negative, testifies to the transcendent character of this ultimate personal reality. The infinite character of the transcendent One is large enough to go around; no one person, no single mediation, no particular community can possess ultimacy to its advantage over others. Ultimate reality's love is for all, making it a transcendent source for reconciliation. Any religion closed to reconciliation does not in that measure reflect God. Yet God, the lover of all, will gather together all human beings into one family at the end of time.

A Buddhist Response: Paul

I must say, Roger, that in your description of the Christian God, you sounded a bit like a Buddhist trying to describe the non-duality of Emptiness and Form. The God of Jesus can today be understood as "an immanent reservoir and source of energy . . . the non-dual always-immanent presence everywhere of the Groundless Ground of being." I was especially inspired by your non-dualistic interpretation of the traditional Christian doctrine of *creatio ex nihilo.*

But I wonder if you might go even further. I have discovered (I think I have) that this conversation with Buddhists is offering Christians an opportunity to explore a more mystical, unitive, and non-dual experience of, and therefore understanding of, the Reality we call God.

What I'm asking is this: If God, as you describe in your statement, is truly immanent and involved in the world, can Christians say that the world is just as truly immanent and involved in God? Does the non-dual relationship of God and world really go *both ways?* Is the world as much a part of God as God is a part of the world? Or, to use an image from the Acts of the Apostles, if we "live and move and have our being in God" (Acts 17:28), can we also say that "God lives and moves and has God's being in us"?

What I'm getting at is what might be called—excuse the technical lingo—an *asymmetrical reciprocity* between God and the world. Through my Buddhist practice and study I've come to feel and affirm a real reciprocity between God and creation, a real give and take, a real co-dependence on each other. But the need or the dependence is asymmetrical, vastly different on each side. The world needs God/Emptiness in order to "receive" its very being. God/Emptiness needs the world/form in order to actualize or express God's very being. Neither can be or exist without the other, but for very different reasons. Maybe Christians could even say that while God definitely creates the world, the world also helps to create God because God can't be God without some creation (just as Emptiness can't be Emptiness without Form).

This leads to further possible insights into the non-duality of what you call God's "intentionality." You really challenge Buddhists with your declaration: "Behind karma lies transcendent intentionality." But if God has an intention, it is, as you admit, "not teleologically predetermined." God's intention has to be worked out *together with creation*. God's intention, therefore, is more a direction than a goal. Christians will say that God intends a world of greater justice; Buddhists might say one of greater compassion. But just what that world will be or just what that means has to be determined through the interaction of God and creation, Emptiness and Form.

As a Buddhist, I feel a bit uneasy about your talk of the world moving toward an "absolute future." It is one thing to say that there is directionality in the world and that the world is going, or can go, somewhere. It is a vastly different thing to believe that it will "end" or "arrive" somewhere. It is one thing to be on a journey; it is quite another to have a final stop for that journey. As a Buddhist, I have difficulties with final stops or endpoints.

It Seems to Us

We do not see a straight-out antithesis between the representations of ultimate reality in the spirituality of followers of Buddha and Jesus. Several reasons lead to this conclusion. One is that the basic idea of a person is significantly different for a follower of Buddha and a follower of Jesus. The Christian considers the human person as enjoying a "substantial" identity over against a Buddhist reckoning of change as subverting an ontologically durable personhood. Relative to ultimate reality, a Christian may with some evidence think that what Buddhists are denying in God is really a limiting form of being that precludes the ultimacy of Emptiness. Christians too criticize as anthropomorphic the idea of God being a person like the individuals we know.

Critical appreciation of God will resort to other metaphors: God is the pure act of being, or the power of being, or the energy that sustains all reality. And whatever metaphor one chooses, God's transcendence requires that we radically deny that the language in any way reduces God to the form of finite beings. It appears to us that Thich Nhat Hanh is doing something similar when he insists that Emptiness points to a Groundless Ground of all being in such a way that it cannot be less than personal reality.[1] Emptiness begins to appear like a fullness of energy unrestricted by any limiting form of being. Thus the followers of Buddha and Jesus have a lot more sharing to do before they can be satisfied with a flat contradiction on the character of ultimate reality. It may be much more useful to reject the absoluteness of popular ideas and begin working through experiences toward a more moderate center.

Can we introduce some commonly held principles that may lead beyond the popular conceptions that often block mutual understanding? We do not want to collapse these two visions into each other but to soften what are often imagined to be contradictions into tensions between different aspects of our experiences that do not cancel each other out but allow learning on both sides.

First, human beings do not, as a rule, enjoy direct, unmediated, or intuitive knowledge of ultimate reality. Ultimacy refers to that which goes beyond the power of human beings to know directly. Many symbols point in the direction of ultimate reality, but language about the ultimate should not be interpreted

[1] Thich Nhat Hanh, *Going Home: Jesus and Buddha as Brothers* (New York: Riverhead Books, 1999), 44.

as dealing with everyday things. *Nirvana, Emptiness, Ground of being,* or *God* cannot be reduced to an imaginative picture.

Second, Christians have a strong tradition of negations built into their language about God. Because the terms we use to refer to God are drawn from everyday experience of finite things, what we affirm about God must be denied as applying to God in the way we imagine. We know what God is not rather than directly or positively what God is. This has to slow down our rush to find contradictions in the range of assertions about ultimate reality.

Third, it follows that although we can remain confident that what we say about ultimate reality is true, we do not really know exactly how it applies, or refers, or corresponds to the transcendent sphere. Those who are most practiced in the spiritual life are the most patient with a sense of the unknown that surrounds the objects of our belief.

Fourth, to complicate things still further, no matter how careful and abstract we become in speaking of the ultimately real, no matter how firmly the negation influences our positive affirmations, words always leave what may be called an "imaginative residue." All our concepts are accompanied by an implicit sensible image that helps connect them with the world outside us, and these inevitably tend to distort, if not falsify, their application to the transcendent dimension of reality. Christian language about God often seems to refer to a "big" "man" in the "sky." Few would say that is what they mean, yet the imaginative dimension of language and of human thought feed that impression.

Fifth, thinking more positively, how should we or can we describe how language about ultimacy works in a realist way that does not collapse the whole enterprise into subjectivism? We have been using the popular Buddhist image of the finger pointing to the moon. It has the merit of inviting dynamic activity on the part of the knower: look at the finger, no, not the finger, but where it is pointing! Christians call this dynamism mystagogy, that is, something that draws a person into mystery. Spiritual language offers statements that draw the imagination and the mind into an open unlimited sphere of encounter that sheds all particular and anthropomorphic dimensions.

Are these observations helpful in understanding theism and non-theism? Before Christians interpret the Buddhist stance on

God, it is important to acknowledge that all Buddhists do not share an identical view on this subject. That said, Christians should recognize that the Buddhist position of non-theism is not atheist. There is a complete difference between not affirming a personal God, with the specific sense that Buddhists give the term, and affirming that God does not exist. Also, Christians can appreciate a reluctance to see the power of the universe, symbolized as Emptiness or nirvana, reduced to the being of an individual person. More positively Emptiness as the ungrounded abyss of energy unlimited by form, yet inseparable from forms, bears functional analogies to the unimaginable designation of God by Thomas Aquinas as the "pure dynamism" of being itself.

For their part, Buddhists may be able to recognize the critical conception of God as the Pure Act of being (Aquinas), or the Ground of Being (Tillich), or absolute Mystery (Rahner) as coming closer to the positive energy that bears no limiting form and thus approaches Emptiness. But it may be more important that Buddhists teach Christians to beware of the anthropomorphism that almost completely envelops their God talk. This touches a whole range of issues in the spiritual domain of human existence. The imaginative projection of God as a big person or a powerful old man affects every aspect of how people relate to God with often deleterious effects that range from bargaining with God to expectations of God's intervention to solve human problems.

This attempt at a conversation between Buddhist non-theism and Christian theism does not resolve the many tensions that run across the thresholds of the distinct faiths. Christians should never cease praying to a personal God—although with the help of their dialogue with Buddhists, they may find new and quite different ways to pray. Theism and non-theism remain two very different conceptions of ultimate reality. But, as we've seen, there are bridge concepts that allow mutual understanding and cross-pollination. And religious dialogue includes mutual criticism of ordinary religious language.

So, recognizing that all religious language is meant both to stimulate and communicate religious experience, recognizing also both the inadequacy and the vitality of religious language, and trusting that there are functional and complementary analogies between Buddhist and Christian linguistic fingers pointing to the same but always elusive moon—how might we summarize what we think Christians can learn from Buddhists on the question of ultimate reality?

After much discussion, here's our answer: Buddhists can remind Christians of their inherent but often neglected experience and understanding of the *unitive, non-dual, immanent presence of God in the world.*

In his initial statement and in his response to Paul, Roger, dipping deeply and discreetly into the resources of Christian thinking, made it clear that, to the happy surprise of many Christians, "Christian tradition has its own brand of non-duality." In our conversations about this chapter Paul marveled at how much Roger's images of God's presence and action in the world reflected the language his Tibetan teachers use to describe the experience of a Spaciousness that pervades all reality and is "primordially aware" and "unconfinedly compassionate." Aquinas's notion of God is that of "Being Itself" that is empty of "any limiting form . . . pure energy with no definition . . . no-thing . . . pure emptiness that is not negative but unimaginably creative dynamism and vitality . . . God the within of all finite being . . . finite beings like waves riding the watery Spirit-power of God." And then Roger's Christian confession: While mysteriously personal, "God is not *a* person."

This is orthodox Christian non-duality mirroring Buddhist non-duality. We both agreed, from our own pastoral experience, that for many Christians to hear of this non-dual God, who is a personal Activity rather than an active Person, who does not "come down" but "steps forth," and who is an incomprehensible Mystery beyond and within all anthropomorphic images—such an immanent, unitive God would be liberating and energizing.

But if both of us resonate with the need for Christians, stimulated in their conversation with Buddhists, to retrieve their non-dual, co-inhering, personal-but-not-person God, we had to note tensions in our understandings of the extent and implications of Christian non-duality. They revolve around the question of how much God *needs* the (a) world in order to be God. Can Christians recognize that a non-dual God cannot *intervene* in the world but, as Aquinas asserted, must always act *through secondary causes*—that is, *through* and *in* and *as* finite beings? Instead of intervening, God *co-appears*. Miracles can still happen, but instead of being purely divine, they would be divine-human productions. Non-duality, it seems, means that the world is the godding of God. Can Christians affirm or recognize that?

Also, what are the implications of a reciprocal non-duality for Christian understandings of *evil*? A co-inhering God understood as the energy of Interbeing would not be totally other relative to what looks like evil. Within the reciprocity of God-World or Emptiness-Form, the unnecessary suffering that we call evil is real, but it does not have an existence of its own—neither in some ontological setting distinct from divine Interbeing nor in the human heart. The very real suffering that is evil is included in Interbeing, held in God. We couldn't reach unanimous clarity on this issue but recognized it as a productive question in our Buddhist-Christian dialogue.

The same applies to Paul's Buddhist response to Roger's affirmation of the centrality of *justice* in Christian ethics and spirituality. Recently, Buddhists have admitted that they have much to learn from the Christian-Jewish insistence on the necessity of structural, systemic justice if the world is going to move closer to Jesus's vision of the rule of God. But Paul the Buddhist wants to hold a certain priority of compassion over concern for justice. For Buddhists, it is compassion that makes justice *necessary*; and it is compassion that makes justice *possible*.

Finally, the question of *finality* stirred some of the most felt differences between Christian Roger and Buddhist Paul. Roger spoke often about creation being able to move toward an absolute end—a final destination in which the end point is both continuous with and different from the steps leading to it. Given their teaching on impermanence, Buddhists have no problem with things being different, but never finally so. Differences or end points can be reached, but they keep coming. Eschatology, we concluded, is one of the most difficult, and therefore most productive, issues in the Buddhist-Christian conversation.

But our final "finally" is a point of agreement: Buddhists and Christians, we suspect, will both urge that our ability to speak about what concerns us ultimately—both speaking within or across the boundaries of our communities—does and must arise out of our own experiences of God or of enlightenment. Although we talk very differently about what we experience—Abba or Sunyata—the personal-practical effects of the experiences seem to be analogous: a *groundedness* that produces peace and freedom of heart and a *connectedness* that produces compassion or love for all our sentient neighbors. The spirituality by which Christians and Buddhists deepen this peace and compassion is the source and guide for their interreligious dialogue.

6.

Where Did the World Come From— And Where Is It Going?

The title offers a fairly wide horizon for this particular exchange. Moreover, Buddhist and Christian worldviews contain radically different visions. We will stay with basic concepts. While occasionally some agreements may look as though they imply a single-focused picture, in reality, they remain double vision.

A Christian Perspective: Roger

The Christian Bible begins with stories of God creating all things, and it ends with a book of visions about the end of time. The Nicene Creed, which sums up the teachings of scripture, begins with belief in one God, creator of heaven and earth, and it ends with belief in the resurrection of the dead and life everlasting. The teachings about creation by God and an endtime in which God draws all things back into God's sphere are the two bookends of the whole Christian library. They define the large frame in which Christianity begins and ends the story of the universe, and they situate the great picture of all reality: in the beginning, when reality was void and without order, "the Spirit of God was moving over the face of the waters" (Gn 1:2). The specific teachings and doctrines of Christianity are all situated within the context of a vast worldview.

Before taking up the questions of this chapter, a brief caveat is appropriate: Because I have to be brief, I have to simplify some complex issues. The Christian teachings on creation first appeared in the straightforward anthropomorphic language of the psalms and the mythic accounts of Genesis. Although we have just contended that God, as the transcendent creator of all that exists, cannot realistically be described as a "person," the language of the Bible does just that. Everyday language expressing religious experience aims at proclaiming faith and not at analytical precision.

Early ideas of God creating were reworked in philosophical terms of classic Greek and Roman philosophy. What may have been imagined in the Genesis accounts as an act of artistry giving shape to formless matter and instilling order into chaos was later refined into the idea of creation out of nothing at all. In the tradition of understanding the end of time, the eschatological language of the Bible about a God who brings all things to completion commingled with teleological language drawn from philosophy. Teleology suggests programmed development, for example, from a seed to a specific, full-grown plant. Did God program the universe to attain a predetermined fulfillment? Now creation theology has entered into dialogue with scientific modes of describing the origins of the universe in which randomness plays a large role. The result is that a Christian language based on expressions of faith from scripture has to be attentive to both philosophy and the new scientific picture of the universe. For example, we have to relate an understanding of God creating with evolutionary development.

The following discussion of the Christian conception of creation and the end of time in three points provides a concise worldview. The first idea calls attention to the different kinds of language reflecting different kinds of knowledge that are involved in understanding the world today from a religious perspective. With that as a kind of preface, the next point states plainly the Christian teaching on creation and its significance for today. The third describes the Christian teaching on the end of history and its implications for Christian life.

Speaking about all reality in two languages. Language in this case refers to a set of premises and presuppositions about the kind of knowledge that is being communicated. Where does this knowledge come from? How should this wisdom be interpreted? Trying to understand the Christian teaching on creation today must reckon with at least two different kinds of language, religious and scientific. Christian religion speaks of God who is creator without an empirical historical account of how that creation unfolded; science has produced a story of the beginning of the universe and the emergence of our world without any reference to God. How do these two interpretations of reality relate to each other?

Religious language gives an account of people's faith; it expresses religious convictions that come from a person's community. These convictions can be traced back to a core experience of a transcendent source of finite reality. Such experiences of faith have their roots in a recognition that is available to all, namely, that each person is absolutely dependent on something beyond the self for his or her being. People do not have within themselves the reasons for their own being. But since each person is a conscious part of the universe itself, what is said of the person may be applied to other persons and to the world itself. The doctrine of creation is revealed through a primal structure of human experience and its consciousness of dependence.

A scientific account of reality has emerged from a different source. Science rests on controlled observations and analysis of empirical data. Science looks for explanations that come from the way things happen in the external world of observation. It measures success in true knowledge gained by further appeal to external criteria. Something is true when it works, when it can be practically verified. Truth is measured by the pragmatic predictability of a formula's results. Comparison illustrates the gap between these two ways of thinking. The idea of scientifically verifying the existence or the character of ultimate reality makes little sense if an ultimate transcends all empirical evidence. But if a conception of ultimate reality has no bearing on the working of the world, it becomes irrelevant.

These two stories of "creation," sometimes thought to be contradictory, are held together within the consciousness of present-day Christians. They are clearly different stories and should not be confused. Because each has merit in its own sphere, they interact within the thinking of people who appreciate both of them. Each affects the imagination: the vague images of an ultimate source of all things; the unimaginable image of evolution over a huge amount of time and space. The point is not to resolve this tension but to recognize the indeterminate character of answers to religious questions.

Monotheism and its implications. Where did the idea of monotheism first arise? This question would have many historical answers among different historical faiths. The Hebrew scriptures include early witness to faith in one local God among many tribal gods. A philosophical response would stress subjective tendencies to recognize that the whole of all being requires a single ultimate source or cause that is truly ultimate. Intuition would grasp that there can only be one supreme being, and this true God must be above all gods to be the genuine source and basis of all reality.

Two insights and a conclusion are crucial for the Christian idea of creation. One is that creation does not refer to a specific act of God bringing reality into being at the dawn of time. Such an act cannot be imagined because God the actor is transcendent, because creation out of nothing is unimaginable, and because "action" of God is the permanent condition of finite reality. It is not an act of God but rather God providing the ground of being. Creation refers to God being the source of being itself. God is the continually acting ground of whatever exists. This makes the understanding of creation more like an understanding of the structural condition of reality than of a single act of an agent. The other insight is that God creates out of nothing. God does not work with preexisting stuff. This means that "nothing" lies between creatures and God's continual action of creating the universe. The combination of these two insights yields a striking conclusion. God should not be seen only as outside and over against the reality God creates. Rather, God is the "within" of all reality sustaining its being, and all finite reality radically depends on God's power at every moment for its being. This amounts to "non-duality"; reality itself is not autonomous but only exists by the power of God as Spirit or the effectiveness of God.

Two corollaries flow from this basic conception of creation by God. One consists of the unity of our created universe. Science confirms this intuition, although it can imagine other universes. The unity of things that flows from a single creator raises up a primal interrelation among all beings. The unitary flow of life entailed in the process of evolution runs parallel to the different experience of a larger union of all things within the power of the creator God.

The other corollary, bolstered by science, says that humanity is a part of the world. This can be phrased more strongly with the statement that human beings are the material world conscious of itself. Human beings appear to themselves as standing back from or over the world. In reality, humans are instances of worldly matter that is free in its self-consciousness. This means that human consciousness provides a window for reading the dynamics of matter, nature, and being itself. This suggests that the experience of dependence felt by humans correlates with the condition of reality.

Eschatology and its implications. There is no way to gain positive knowledge about the end of time, with special reference to the ultimate destiny of human beings. This is a matter of absolute transcendence and can only be an object of faith. Eschatology, then, is faith's construal of how God will bring about the end of all things. This is not primarily a teleological doctrine that discerns a goal built into the nature of things, even though early Greek Christians believed that all reality emerged from God and was destined by an inner orientation to return to God in the end. But in the scriptures eschatology correlates more closely with God's sovereignty as creator and is not a doctrine about nature. The one who continually creates will bring reality to its rightful end. God stands not just behind or beneath reality, God is also up ahead of all that is as the power of its completion. God will bring all things to their just condition according to God's inscrutable plan.

Teleology has certainly been employed to interpret eschatology and to structure the Christian vision. It offers a fruitful analogy for understanding human nature as intrinsically oriented from within toward the goal of returning to and being with God. But as beautiful as the vision provided by teleology is, science cannot find it operative in the evolution of the universe as seen from the perspective of the rise of life and of *Homo sapiens*. Contingency and randomness are constitutive marks of the evolution of life; the emergence of life does not seem to be programmed along a steady axis. Evolution provides another check on anthropomorphism. But science cannot rule out a deeper logic beneath what seems to be a gradual progression out of the past toward more complex forms of life in the future.

The Christian belief in the resurrection of Jesus is the key to Christian eschatology. It is a matter of faith in a revelation of life everlasting. The resurrection of the body of Jesus is not to be understood literally as a revivification of a corpse. The doctrine means that the *person* Jesus was raised.[1] In the culture of the New Testament writings it would have been difficult for people to affirm the reality of the resurrection of the person Jesus without his body.

At the same time the notion of the resurrection of the body is suggestive. It affirms the continuity of the whole person, Jesus, with what is assumed into absolute Being. Resurrection of the body thus affirms continuity between life in this world and life in the end time. Those whom God draws up into absolute Being are not bare identities but specific persons who have defined themselves though decisions and actions. This, in turn, gives human freedom a project to co-create values in this world that will last in eternity.

A Buddhist Response: Paul

Your opening reflections in this chapter, Roger, reminded me of something that I deeply believe but often don't recognize: The dialogue between religion and science is just as important (maybe more so) as the dialogue between the religions. The Dalai Lama once said that "if scientific analysis were conclusively to demonstrate certain claims in Buddhism to be false, then we must accept the findings of science and abandon those claims."[2] This is one of the advantages of a non-dualistic understanding of God/Interbeing and the world; it has helped me manage a more satisfying dialogue between my faith and science.

---

[1] There is more to be said here. Can an identity forged by bodily existence in a temporal story preserve its identity without its body? What is an eternal body? When do we stop asking questions and admit inability to know?

[2] Dalai Lama, *The Universe in a Single Atom: The Convergence of Science and Spirituality* (New York: Crown Publishing Group, 2006), 3.

Even more than the previous chapter, this one makes clear to me how non-dualistic is your Christian faith in a creator God. You said clearly that "God creates out of nothing. . . . This means that 'nothing' lies between creatures and God's continual action of creating" and that therefore creation is not something that happened "at the dawn of time" but is continually going on. I almost applauded when you explicitly drew the conclusion I wanted to draw: "This amounts to 'non-duality.'" Here, as Christian and Buddhist, we're on the same page.

Well, almost on the same page. Again, I find myself wondering whether your non-duality between God and creation goes as far as Buddhist non-duality between Emptiness and Form. Can you as a Christian say that creation (some creation if not this one) is as eternal as is God—or that there never was a God without creation? More explicitly, if as a Christian you can say that "God is the continually acting ground of whatever exists," as a Buddhist I would like to add, "And creation, or this relative and finite world, is the necessary ground with which God exists." Can that make sense for Christian belief and spirituality? As I have said before, I do believe that Buddhism is inviting Christians into a deeper, non-dualistic, unitive, and mystical experience of God, one in which God/Spirit and I are interacting energies making up one ongoing, creative activity.

But for me as a Buddhist-Christian, it is an activity that doesn't have, or can't have, a final end point. So, I am a bit perplexed when you tell me that as a Christian you believe that "God will bring about the end of all things." The Buddhist in me asks, Why would God want to do that?

Certainly, for Buddhists, all things do end insofar as each of them is impermanent. But why should there be an end to the process by which transient beings are constantly being brought forth? Transience means that every *thing* has an end, but that there is no end to *everything*, for the ever-changing, interconnecting energy carries on. Therefore, every end is a beginning. No end is only an end.

This means that, yes, we can expect things to come to completion or "to get better." We can expect (hope) that we can come closer to realizing the rule of God. But completion will never be final, will never be "the end." The rule of God will never come once and for all.

A Buddhist Perspective: Paul

What is often said about the Buddhist view of God is also said about its view of creation; that is, it doesn't have one. But it's not simply that Buddhists do not have a doctrine of creation similar to what we find in Christianity. Most Buddhists, I suspect, would have to voice their grave reservations about, if not outright rejection of, four ingredients that are essential to the traditional Christian teaching on creation: It took place *in time* (or at the very beginning of time) as the *free act of a creative agent* coming forth *out of nothing;* and it is headed toward *a transformative end point.* For Buddhists, there is always has been a world, a universe. It wasn't created by a creator.

Creativity rather than creator. But if Buddhists deny, or don't affirm, a *creator of* the world, they do, I think we can say, affirm or recognize *creativity in* the world. Creativity pervades the whole system, the whole process. It is going on everywhere, all the time. Such creativity is implied in two of the most fundamental and all-pervasive teachings of Buddhism: impermanence *(anicca)* and dependent-origination *(pratitya-samutpada).* To say that nothing is permanent, that everything changes, that nothing remains what it is—this is to recognize that everything can be, and will be, different from what it is right now. The world is constantly producing *newness*. That's pretty creative.

This newness, this constant generation of differences, is really the energy that keeps the whole thing going. This is the meaning of *dependent-origination,* or profound, pervasive *interconnectivity.* Things are constantly interconnecting; otherwise they simply couldn't be. That's what we were getting at earlier in saying that the world consists not of *beings* but of *beings-with*. And that means, as we noted, that we can't really say that the world *is.* Rather, it's *becoming*. Thus, one of the most fundamental things Buddhists can say about the world is this: It is all interconnected. *Therefore* it is all changing. (Which is pretty much what any biologist or physicist nowadays would also tell us.)

For many people, this may sound like bad news: You can't keep anything. For most of us, I suspect, it's really good news: You're never, ever stuck. Things can always—*always*—be different. Or, as it says on a Buddhist tee-shirt I have seen: Impermanence makes everything possible.

Eternal creativity. If Buddhists don't have much to say about when this inherently creative world got started and where it is headed, they do have something more to say (at least for Christian ears like mine) about the inner workings of this creativity. This has to do with another central teaching found in most Mahayana and Vajrayana (Tibetan) schools of Buddhism: the reality of, and especially the relationship between, Emptiness and Form. As we discussed in Chapter 3, Sunyata (Emptiness) is one of Buddhism's primary "fingers pointing to the moon." It is the Buddhist pointer to what Christians/Westerners would call the Ultimate. But the sonorous verses of the *Prajnaparamita Sutra,* which resound through Zen and Tibetan meditation halls around the world, tell us that:

> Form is Emptiness, Emptiness is form.
> Emptiness is not separate from form, form is
>   not separate from Emptiness.
> Whatever is form is Emptiness, whatever is
>   Emptiness is form.

It is what we have been calling the non-duality between Emptiness and form, between the Infinite and the finite. This non-duality implies, or *is*, creativity. Emptiness by its very nature brings forth—or generates, gives expression to—the infinitude of forms that make up the relative world. Philosophically, this means that Emptiness has a certain ontological priority over forms. Emptiness, as it were, comes first. Forms are second. But not really, because there is no Emptiness without form. There never was a time when there was "a first" without "a second." Which means that what is "second" is not really second. What is "second" or derivative is simultaneous with what is "first" or generative. While there is Emptiness and form (Infinite and finite), there is no first or second. That's how deeply *creativity* can be identified with Emptiness. There was never a moment when "first" was not creating "second."

If this last paragraph is rather abstract and murky, it can take on sobering clarity when we venture to make connections with Christian understandings of God as Creator. Carrying on the task of comparative spirituality that is the nature of this conversation and of this book, can we say that just as there can never be Emptiness without form, so there can never be God without creation? If creativity is as essentially a part of God as it is of Emptiness, then just as God is eternal, so is creation. Now we see why many Buddhists have trouble with the Christian notion of creation having a beginning—and, as we shall see shortly, an end.

Buddhists can also ask Christians (and Jews and Muslims) this connected question: If Christians really take creativity as something essential to God—insofar as a loving God has to have something to love—then don't they have to admit that God has no choice but to create? Creation is not, strictly speaking, a free choice for God. This doesn't mean that God is forced to create. Rather, it means that it is the very nature of God to create, to pour forth God's self, and to bring forth that which God can love and be. If God did not create, God would not be God. Please understand, this is not language that Buddhists would be comfortable in using. But it is language that Christians have to think about if they take their conversation with Buddhists seriously.

Reciprocal creativity. I have found that my conversation with Buddha and Buddhists challenges my Christian understanding of the world even more uncomfortably and creatively. What I'm getting at has to do with the third verse of the lines from the *Prajnaparamita Sutra*: "Whatever is form is Emptiness and whatever is Emptiness is form." This implies what we can call a *reciprocal causal relationship* between Emptiness and form, or between God and the world. It's not just that Emptiness/God is doing all the creating. If, indeed, "form is Emptiness," then "form" is also sharing in the creating. The creativity is, as it were, a joint effort. Emptiness/God is not simply *the cause* while form/world is the effect. There is a non-dual relationship between cause and effect. Both are cause, and both are effect, but in different ways.

For Emptiness or the Divine to exercise its creativity, it has to do so in and as form, or in or as the world. This means that form is determining—better, co-determining—how the creativity of Emptiness/God expresses itself. There is real reciprocity between Emptiness and Form, between creator and created. They work together, as it were, in the ongoing process of creation or existence. And yet, the reciprocal relationship is not the same on each side. Form, as it were, depends on Emptiness much more than Emptiness depends on form. Thus we speak of an "asymmetrical reciprocity."

So if form also determines what happens in the world, this means that there is no predetermined plan for the world. What happens—that is, the "something new" that comes about—is the result of the interaction of Emptiness and form, of God and the world, not just of Emptiness or God alone. This would still allow us, I think, to speak of a general direction for the history of the world. In Buddhist terms such a potential or purpose would be the goal of every reputable bodhisattva: to promote ever more awakening, more wisdom, and more compassion, and so, less suffering. That, Christians could say, is what God is "up to" in the course of history. But what actually happens—or how this big picture of is filled in and realized—will be determined by the particular, un-predetermined and totally free ways in which Emptiness and form, God and finite beings, interact in the actual course of time.

All this would both affirm and deepen the Christian or Jewish claim that we are co-creators with God. But it would assign a much bigger role to the finite co-creators. Emptiness or God "depends" on form or creatures, not for its existence, but for its activity. While forms or finite beings can never threaten the reality of Emptiness, they can co-determine what results or is manifested out of Emptiness. So, in Christian language, God and human beings need each other for the interaction that keeps the dynamic process of creation/creativity going. Can Christians recognize such a dependency of God on creatures?

The world is going nowhere. Therefore it's all "now-here." For Buddhists, the world isn't going anywhere. Buddhism, therefore, doesn't have an eschatology—teachings on what's going to happen at the end of the world. For Christians, it seems essential to believe and to hope that this familiar, messy world is going to come to an end, and the end is going to be the beginning of a transformed state of existence in another "world" called heaven. Such a belief appears to be integral to the expectation of Christ's "second coming."

For most Buddhists such absolute, eschatological finality does not seem to be important. Yes, there are teachings about *kalpas,* different periods in the course of time that mark a pendulum-swing between deterioration and improvement. And there is widespread devotion to the Maitreya Buddha, the Buddha of the future who will come to the rescue at a time when the teachings of Gautama Buddha have been neglected. But there is never a final end, the end of all ends. Rather, if one world or period passes, there will always be another. Impermanence constantly gives way to newness.

A hint, however, of what Christians might call a Buddhist eschatology is found in the notion and ideal of the *bodhisattva*. Bodhisattvas are those who have reached the end of the process toward enlightenment. They've made it. They've attained nirvana. It's over! But it isn't. To reach the end of enlightenment is to return to the ordinary, messy, hectic reality of daily life in this world, wherever one happens to be living. For the bodhisattva, to reach the end of nirvana is to return to *samsara*. To reach the end is to return to the now. But it is to return to the now in a different state. Because one has "arrived" at the end, one sees and responds to the "now" differently. One finds the end in the now. One has the *wisdom* and the strength to deal with whatever is happening in the now. More, one has the *compassion* to change and transform the now—and so help others to begin the process of enlightenment, the process of finding the "end" in the "now." And in this regard, although Buddhists don't hold to a final end to the world, they do share with Christians the conviction that this world can not only be different (because of impermanence), but it can also be transformed into a world where there is greater wisdom and greater compassion in the hearts of individuals and in the structures of society.

Rather than hope for the future, live in the moment. So Buddha warns Christians not to be too preoccupied about the future—or more pointedly, not to be *too motivated by hope* of what the future will be. The danger is that we Christians can become so attached to what we think the future *should* be that we miss what it *can* be. Also, how easily we slip into discouragement and burnout when the future we hope for keeps evading us. With their insistence on being here now and living in full mindfulness and acceptance of the present moment, Buddhists are reminding Christians that for Jesus the reign of God is both "already *and* not yet," both really present *and* really to come. We Christians have been strong on the "not yet," but have we taken seriously Jesus insistence that God's reign is "already"? "The reign of God is among you" (Lk 17:21)—right now, right here. This is an even greater affirmation of the value of this world. What is going on right now is supremely valuable, for it is the only way in which or through which we can realize the future reign.

To bring about a better tomorrow we must be fully present to today.

A Christian Response: Roger

These topics of the beginning and the end of things shine a brilliant light on two very different incommensurable visions and languages about reality. No more than you do I intend to remove these differences because they contain possibilities for insight and spiritual life that should not be undermined or lost. But I will explore points where your account of Buddhism pushes Christian spirituality to expand its vision, sometimes by retrieving elements of its own tradition.

No creator, only creativity. Buddhism speaks of two truths, the one expressed in conventional language, and the other, critical and metaphysical, reaching for a deeper level of reality. Speaking of God in the Christian tradition as a person (the Bible) or as the pure actualizing energy that grounds reality (Thomas Aquinas) illustrates the distinction. Critical thinking says that God is not a person but is pure empowerment of the process of constant becoming. Ultimate reality can neither be less than personhood nor reduced to it. There is plenty of room here for conversation on a deep level.

Pure act of being is becoming. Buddhist analysis of constant temporal development, interrelatedness, and dependent origination matches the sense of historicity that characterizes modern culture. When Aquinas defined God as "the pure act of being," he was expressing something analogous to Emptiness in its infinite and unrestricted power active beneath or within everything that exists. Buddhists help Christians to probe more deeply into the fluidity of reality and, aided by the paradigm of evolution, to see that divine creativity is *the pure act of generativity and thus becoming.* In our day the depth and pervasiveness of change brings this deep understanding of reality to the surface.

Cooperative grace. Your reflection on the Buddhist idea of a reciprocal relationship between Emptiness and form reminds me of the traditional Christian concept of cooperative grace first fashioned by Augustine. His metaphysical superstructure fused the ideas of grace, divine help, and the Spirit of God; in a less interventionist way than Augustine, I imagine this language pointing to God's primary grounding of becoming. As Augustine insists, this gives rise to a dynamic interpretation of God acting in history through the agency of creatures (forms). Far from being merely possible in Christian spirituality, God has really and truly ceded dominating control over history to agents among whom only humans are conscious, free, and deliberate. Spirituality in this framework is serious business. Many Christian theologians speak of co-creation with God, not as an equal partner but as an agent of God's primary and gracious causality.

The future is now. Paul, you make an important point when you say we should not sacrifice what we can do in the present to what we should do in the future. The future is now. The past is gone, and the present never holds. The future is immediately pressing in. Reflective responsibility, a distinguishing mark of the human, functions in relation to the future. It measures the present against a wider horizon and a better future and decides. Buddhists are right; to be is to change. Accepting the present frequently hides a delusion that pretends to not make a decision. We cannot opt out of fashioning our future.

Finally, at several points you see Buddhism challenging the Christian idea of an end to reality. End here does not mean stopping; it means fulfillment or completion, not completely unlike someone whose Buddha-nature achieves enlightenment. But a deep difference separates these two imaginaries: the one is of perpetual or eternal becoming, even for the enlightened; the other is shaped like a story, a narrative in which individuals move through time to their destiny. Many crucial factors lie embedded in these two schemes, but most important for the Christian is the substantial individuality of the person over against what looks like dissolution of the self into some whole.

These categories of whence and whither the world reflect metaphysical aspects buried in following Buddha and following Jesus. They are radically different. But we can talk across them about how to act spiritually.

It Seems to Us

The metaphysical language of creation and eternal creativity has drawn the discussion away from following Buddha and following Jesus. So we must remind ourselves that each worldview provides an imaginative framework for the person of faith. A larger understanding of the world contributes much to a person's self-understanding and to the meaning of concrete decisions and actions. But worldviews developed out of concrete experiences and spiritualities. So we ask how these worldviews might influence spirituality on the ground.

Suppose that we ask a Buddhist or a Christian who is performing an everyday action: What is the significance of what are you doing? Practically, the Buddhist and the Christian will give identical answers: I am working to earn a salary to support my family in a happy life together. I do the best job I can at work. I have oriented my life by the teachings of Buddha or Jesus, but they do not distinguish me from the others on the assembly line or in the office. Yet each lives in a differently conceived metaphysical world that supplies different meaning to otherwise identical concrete actions.

In a Buddhist community individual persons who cultivate an awareness of self and world through meditation will generally come to recognize their non-dual identity with the formless power of being. They are mindful that, like individual waves relate to the water that constitutes them, they are made up of energy and connections larger than themselves. Non-substantial and non-autonomous individuals cultivate their phenomenal "selves" by realizing their connectedness to the power of creative Emptiness. We *are* by being an identifiable element of a larger abyss of energy. This sense of being as grounded in Interbeing translates very neatly into belonging to a community, one of the refuges of Buddhist existence. Individuals are part of something larger than themselves. We do not rush one-way to old age, death, and nonexistence. The Buddhist finds stability and not disruption in being one with a changing world that has never been anything else. So what are you doing? I am what I am at this time. I already am where I am meant to be. I must constantly be mindful of that.

In a Christian community individuals view themselves as creatures of God, with a substantial God-given identity. It often takes reflection to awaken an awareness of the absolute dependence on God that creation entails. Buddhists have a sense of dependence through their dependent co-arising out of nature; Christians have a sense of dependence on the direct maintenance of their existence by a creating God, and they are grateful. Does gratitude require personality to whom it responds? In any case, their freedom means responsibility for themselves and the world around the self: family, larger circles of social participation, and ideally the world. And time is short by any comparative reckoning. The sense of freedom and responsibility that goes with a more autonomous self easily translates into a desire for achievement. In idealist Christian terms of following Jesus this means: What can I do to advance the rule of God? And whereas the whither seems permanently postponed in the endless creativity of Buddhism, Christian life is headed toward a personal and corporate fulfillment. So, while the Christian is doing exactly what the Buddhist is doing, the meaning is radically different. I am carrying forward the will of God in my trajectory of life as discerned by the gifts that I've been given. In doing so I hope to contribute my part to the building up of the human community into the people of God.

These characterizations of following Buddha and following Jesus in the light of big questions about the nature of the whole of reality are so general that they may disappear into a deeper and more nuanced vision of a particular person. But they serve to illustrate a number of things that will help Buddhists and Christians understand each other. Consider the following series of tensions.

Buddhists and Christians live with different accents on the polarity of being in a community and being an autonomous individual. The community should ratify a person's individual gifts and nurture them; persons should be loyal members of the community that nurtures them.

Buddhists and Christians live differently in time. Buddhists know that the time is now, that the past and the future do not exist, and that one cannot escape the present, for the present holds all that is and each person's existence is immersed in it. Christians know that because of constant change, every moment is challenged by the possibility of doing something new that comes to it from the future and is enabled by the past. No two people will put these vectors into play in the same way; they are subject to infinite variations. A Christian may behave more like a typical Buddhist in realizing that the rule of God for Jesus was *already* as well as *not yet*. And Buddhists can resemble Christians in recognizing that impermanence gives birth to what is truly *new*. Perhaps Christian and Buddhist monks best recognize these similarities in each other.

Buddhists and Christians live in a tension between being dependent and being responsible. Both are absolutely dependent upon a formless power of being that accounts for each one's emergence out of nature to be the relative individual that each one is. They also mature into responsibility that others cannot assume for them. Morality disappears without this provision.

These polarities never collapse Buddhists and Christians into a common world. Buddhists are not Christians. But they show that being a Buddhist or a Christian in an increasingly common world makes sense. One can begin to understand how some of the values operate in each spirituality, and how they can be put in tension with seemingly opposed values to create a fuller response to self, others, world, and ultimate reality.

Saving our world from ecological catastrophe. Having explored how our very different Buddhist and Christian worldviews can still lead us to encouragingly similar but at the same time challengingly different ways of living out our lives in the world, we ask now how these differences might enable Buddhists and Christians to collaborate in saving our world from the environmental catastrophe that threatens it. How might Christians and Buddhists, from their very different views of the whence and whither of this planet, challenge and support each other in responding to what scientists tell us is one of the most dangerous and decisive stages in the evolution of earthly life? We see four areas of such converging support.

First, for differing but concurring reasons, both Christian Roger and Buddhist-Christian Paul can and must affirm the *goodness and the inherent value of this material earth*. This earth of which we are made is not a throwaway as we enter eternity; nor is it a slough-off as we realize the spaciousness of Enlightenment. In light of the teachings of Jesus and Buddha, this finite planet and the universe of which it is a minuscule part participate in and give expression to the very being and activity of what Buddhists call Emptiness and Christians call God. As the *Prajnaparamita Sutra* declares, earthy form *is* Emptiness. As Roger declared earlier, the Christian belief that "God creates out of nothing . . . means that 'nothing' lies between creatures and God's continual action of creating the universe." Buddhists therefore enable Christian theologians to affirm, even more coherently and convincingly, the metaphor of *this earth as the body of God*. We must therefore care for—which today means save—this earth not only because, if we don't, we perish with it, but also and especially because this earth *is* the sacredness of the Divine and the beauty of Interbeing.

Second, as a Christian and a Buddhist we both affirm the *real responsibility* and the *necessary role* that humans must play in restoring the earth to its original health. Both of us recognize a mutual dependency or co-responsibility between God and humans, or Emptiness and human forms. One cannot work without the other. If the job of maintaining—and today we can say, rescuing—the world is going to be accomplished, it will have to comprise the interaction and collaboration of God *and* humanity, of Emptiness *and* forms. But we also noted balancing differences between our Buddhist and Christian perspectives. In affirming that there can be no Emptiness without forms—that Emptiness, as it were, needs forms—Buddhists stress the necessity (in Christian language) of good works. Environmentalists are essential if this earth is going to make it. But Christians—now using Buddhist language—stress that these necessary forms are Emptiness, or that when we are trying to act to save the world, to carry out our ecological commitments, it is not just we who are doing the work. God/Interbeing/Spirit is what is animating, sustaining, guiding us. Grace precedes our good works. We are not all by ourselves. What seems an impossible job can work.

Third, regarding the central ecological menace of *anthropocentrism*, we recognized that Buddhists can provide a needed help for Christians. If, as we saw in the previous chapter, Buddhists might help Christians recognize that Interbeing is an appropriate, maybe essential, image for what God is and how God acts—that God is indeed Interconnecting Spirit—then interconnectedness (the Buddhist notion of dependent origination) is how

God creates. As contemporary evolutionary science has made it even clearer, it is through the interaction and collaboration of all God's creatures that continuous creation takes place. Every creature, every living and nonliving being, has a different role, but all have essential roles.

Fourth, we've already noted the apparently intractable differences between our Buddhist and Christian views on *the eschatological future*. As a Buddhist, Paul struggles with Roger's Christian declaration that "The one who continually creates will bring reality to its rightful end." For Buddhists, final ends are a problem. But in our discussions we wondered whether this might be a place where Christians offer Buddhists a helpful nudge. If Buddhists have understandable problems in expecting things to come to an absolutely final, once-and-for-all end, are they missing something in not expecting things to be able to come to different and "better" ends? If, as we've heard, the Buddhist teaching on impermanence means that everything is possible, Christians can ask: Doesn't this also mean that real improvement—difference for the better—is possible? In other words, we can and need to *hope* that the future will be better—more life-giving, more compassionate, more just—than the present. We can hope that in the future we can solve the environmental mess that we are in today. For Christians such hope is possible. And while Christians will need to heed the Buddhist admonition not to cling to such hope, they can still cherish and draw strength from hope.

7.

The Problem in Human Nature

Trying to get at the fundamental problem for which Jesus and Buddha offer remedies, we find in this chapter that Buddhists and Christians agree that humanity is in a big mess and that the mess consists of needless suffering. But they differ in their diagnoses of the problem: original sin or original ignorance.

A Christian Perspective: Roger

Formulating the basic question of human existence demands an appeal to the common experience of every person about something that envelops all humanity. From one point of view, human existence poses the basic question of itself to itself: our very being elicits wonder at who we are and what we are, as well as speculation about where we have come from and where are we going. These questions penetrate deeply. The pervasiveness of the problem can be appreciated by isolating three themes that have marked Christian language almost from the beginning. These are the mysteries of death, sin, and potential lack of overall meaning. These basic marks of human existence have preoccupied Jewish and then Christian traditions, and they are operative beneath the essential languages of faith.

Reflective consciousness. Human existence appears to be distinctive in its reflective awareness of its own consciousness of the world. Human beings are those who not only know, but know that they know. This refers to the ability to be conscious of some object and, at the same time, of oneself knowing that object in a distinctive way. We can objectify and examine our own acts of knowledge; we are aware of the acts of attending and knowing; we can remember them; and we can go back and analyze the whole process. This reflection appears in consciousness as an ability to "stand back" from our own activity, or to be above and observe it. The whole process transpires in the use of language that enables humans to encapsulate intimate experience in a public form and share it with others.

One way of characterizing this defining character of the human, for there are many, describes it as transcendent freedom. Freedom here refers to the measure of self-control or ability of self-disposition that reflective human consciousness bestows on a person as a unique individual. The term *self-consciousness* indicates a level of self-possession that in turn bestows personal identity. The idea of transcendent freedom refers to the differentiation of the self from all that is not self, that is, the world, the objects that make it up, and other human beings, who are recognized as persons like oneself. Transcendent freedom makes each person a center of consciousness in and through which the whole world is viewed. Self-conscious freedom designates the clearinghouse for the basic ideas of *me, you, others,* and *the world.* Self-consciousness is the root of the free choice that describes the way a person makes decisions and, at a higher level, assumes responsibility for his or her own life in various forms of commitment and deliberate action.

Basic human desires. The Christian tradition has never ceased analyzing the human person using simultaneously the sources of scripture and Western intellectual culture. A first premise for this analysis appears in the creation narrative where, after bringing forth all the forms of being that exist, God saw that each created reality "was good" (Gn 1:3–31). This premise suggests that a point of departure for describing the self-transcendence of human existence should be in positive terms.

From this perspective one can say that human self-transcendence is basically good, and that it harbors basic desires to be healthy, to know more, to achieve values, and to *be* integrally and absolutely. A basic desire in this context does not refer to an act directed to a specific object but to an internal tendency or drive to act in ways congruent with a being's development and fulfillment. A word about each of these fundamental desires will begin to fill out a portrait of the human.

On a biological level the human self, like other organisms, has a tendency to grow, mature, and fully actualize the potential of its form of being. This tendency manifests itself in the sphere of knowing in a most remarkably open and comprehensive way as a constant search for new knowledge. The range of human knowing is often described as infinitely open since no limits contain it. Hence the cumulative growth of human knowledge and the explosive expansion of the range of science in recent times. Expanding knowledge sets ever-new goods and values before human desire; it stimulates the will to possess more things and achieve greater goals. "The good" points to an open sphere in which individual objects attract human desire and quest. It is as if the expansive dynamism of evolution plays itself out in each individual consciousness.

Stepping back from these processes and viewing them abstractly and comprehensively as a whole yields a picture of the human and reality itself as an unrestricted process. In each person the dynamism can be construed as being driven by a desire to be, that is, to exist more fully and more completely than is possible at any single moment of time. The desire to be, this push toward a fuller form of life, implicitly aims at absolute being in contrast to annihilation. To be human involves an implicit dynamism toward absolute being.

The negation of human existence. Every adult human being becomes aware of the cycle of life, the pattern of birth, growth, and creativity that is followed by decline, old age, and death. It seems quite natural because the pattern obtains across species; individuals come and go while the species lives on or gradually develops into something new. But within the human species a desire to live and flourish has become reflectively conscious. In relation to humanity the universal pattern of life seems to contradict and even negate basic human desires. Human existence appears to be thwarted in its fundamental aspirations by sickness, ignorance, egocentrism, suffering, and death. The three categories of death, egocentrism, and meaninglessness well describe spheres where Christianity consistently has sought salvation.[1]

Death negates individual human life. With death, to all appearances, the person ceases to exist. Each person lives with the

---

[1] Paul Tillich, *The Courage to Be* (New Haven, CT: Yale University Press, 1952), 40–54.

burden of having to die and with the constant threat that this can occur at any time. It is remarkable how individuals manage to block out this threat and live free of fear—but never completely. Finitude leading to death surrounds human existence. Reckoning with death does not mean explicitly entertaining it. Rather, awareness of finitude and death subsists as an existential undertow of human life. By contrast, Christianity has been attracted from the beginning by a promise of eternal life.

Evolution seems to be driven by *egocentrism*, a vector of energy that promotes life and growth in being. The blind desire to live takes hold of the individual and becomes translated into spontaneous self-protection and self-affirmation. Each individual has within itself an inertia that resists all motion against its immediate self-concern. Saint Paul said that he could not do what he wanted but consistently did what he did not want to do. There is some potentially negative thing at work within human beings (Rom 7:19–20). In the fifth century Augustine described this in Neoplatonic terms as a weight that prevents the free human spirit from expanding and soaring; it seems to curve in on itself and to be unable to recognize value independent of the self or be spontaneously drawn toward it. The human spirit is so encumbered by custom that it resembles a person overcome by drowsiness and lethargy.[2] Luther described this as internal bondage, freedom bound from inside by self-interest.[3] Thus, the human person, a center of self-reflective consciousness, turns an expansive life force into narrow and selfish activity. The pervasive anxiety wrought by a consciousness of moral failure generates a sense of unworthiness and a fear of condemnation. Reformation Christianity saw this as the main problem of human existence.

The modern period ushered in a new crisis for human existence: *meaninglessness*. Prior to modernity, death and sin prevailed within a stable, comprehensive vision of humanity. But the new understandings mediated by science, the phenomenon of historical change, and the discovery of different cultures threatened a unified worldview. Reason began to lose its moorings. As

---

[2] Augustine, *The Confessions* 8.5.
[3] Martin Luther, *The Bondage of the Will*, ed. J. I. Parker and O. R. Johnston (Grand Rapids, MI: Baker Publishing, 2012).

constant random motion causes seasickness, so too the threat of relativism robbed coherence from accepted worldviews and left human existence without its metaphysical foundation. Human existence appears to be no more valuable than the passing flowers on a hillside. On the surface, human achievements have no lasting value or meaning. Without an absolute or an ultimate reference point, the existence of the world and each individual in it appear empty.

These three crises of human consciousness do not relate to one another in exclusive or competitive terms. They exist together and intermingle. They characterize human finitude and life in history. Human existence does not exist absolutely; it struggles for its own self-possession; it is ignorant and attains only fragmentary knowledge of reality.

Social nature. Human nature points to the dimensions of existence shared by all the individuals of the species. A relatively stable biological human nature allows us to make generalizations about human beings. But one can also isolate a somewhat more variable "social nature" consisting of socially mediated qualities that also constitute the being of individuals in different ways. The characteristics of individual human beings are compounded by another concomitant set of social conditions that surround, enter into, and intrinsically shape individual freedom. Social values and disvalues, along with patterns of behavior, reinforce the vulnerability of finite existence on a personal level and complicate the problem of human existence.

Many examples lie on the surface of social life. Societies hide sickness and death and promote an active life of chasing shallow pleasures in the moment. Reflection on death encourages seriousness and depth, the opposite of life on the surface. Consumer society and culture mirror egocentrism by feeding a desire to augment the human person by gaining more possessions. Because a society has no central nervous system or individual consciousness, it cannot be self-transcending; it is constituted as corporate egoism. Even groups dedicated to altruistic causes are self-protective. Pluralism in society fragments a given set of values that could give a unified meaning to life and dissolves a unified cultural system of meaning into privatism. In short, the social character of human existence compounds everything. People do not suffer only as individuals; they also suffer as groups according to economic class, or caste, or race, or gender, or for no reason other than being somehow different. Analogously, individual persons are not able to think independently of their group; all human thinking reflects a social location by imitation or reaction.

The loss of ultimacy. The loss of ultimacy represents a way in which the three crises of death, egocentrism, and meaninglessness might be synthesized. In each case something integral to human existence is lacking. Death exterminates the individual person; ultimately, the species itself will pass. Without some attachment to a transcendent ground of being, death undermines the ontological value of human existence. Egocentrism, in its personal and social forms, also removes the grounds for the value of human existence. All assertions of one's own being against the interests of other human beings essentially deny the inherent value of humanity as such. Self-assertion against other humans relativizes and implicitly denies the ultimate significance of humanity. The same is true of a competitive privatization of the grounds of ultimate meaning. The natural condition of human existence in history is pluralistic. The assertion of our meaning over against the convictions of others that are held in good faith implicitly abandons the possibility of the ultimate as something that is available to all. The value of human existence lies in the freedom to enter into a relationship with ultimacy. When that is denied for others, it is implicitly denied for all.

These aggressive negative behaviors represent the constant typical actions of the human species. The problem of human existence, therefore, is not a false problem of one ideology over against another. The value of human existence appears to be intrinsically questionable, especially at this particular time in history. Human beings are not and cannot of their own power become what they inherently desire to be. Further, they deny the value of the human as such when they undermine the value of other human beings. The problem of human nature is the effective loss of ultimacy and with it human worth and dignity.

A Buddhist Response: Paul

This chapter faces us with some of the starkest differences—and therefore perhaps the richest opportunities—in our Buddhist-

Christian conversation. John B. Cobb, Jr., once commented that the Buddhist teaching that most challenged his Christian beliefs was not nirvana/emptiness but *anatta*/not-self. This chapter illustrates what he meant.

Initially, as a Buddhist, I resonated with your description of how evolution has reached a level of transcendent freedom in the human species. For Buddhists, too, to be born a human is a precious gift, for no other sentient beings (as far as we know) have the "self-conscious freedom" to wake up to what they really are. But what Buddhists wake up to *sounds* or *looks* (I'm not sure it *is*) quite different from your description of a "transcendent freedom" that makes "each person a center of consciousness in and through which the whole world is viewed."

For Buddha, that is precisely the fundamental problem in our human condition: What we think we are is not what we truly are. Certainly, each person has a sense of self that is distinct from other selves. Buddhists recognize this as true on *the relative level*. We need this sense of a conscious and free self to function in the practicalities of everyday life. But as my teachers have put it, although this sense of self is *real*, it is not *true*. What we truly are is called *anatta* or not-self. This is what we are on the ultimate level. *We are not individuals*. And once we wake up to this reality, once we begin to experience ourselves not as individual beings but as interrelated becomings that are part of a big picture of Interbeing, then we will be able to function on the relative, everyday level with greater interior peace and compassion for all.

I do believe that the dialogue with Buddhists regarding the teaching of *anatta* is providing Christians with the opportunity of coming to not only a deeper but, somehow, a qualitatively different understanding of what Jesus was calling us to when he announced that we must lose ourselves in order to find ourselves (Mt 10:39). Or what he was getting at when he said that the seed must really and truly die before it can bear fruit (Jn 12:24). Or what Paul means when he talks about losing himself in Christ (Gal 2:20).

This brings me to a second key issue your statement raised for me: If egocentrism is recognized as a fundamental problem for both Christians and Buddhists, then where does it come from? Is it our innate sinfulness—which you describe as "some negative

thing at work within human beings"? Or is it our innate ignorance? Can we Christians understand sin as ignorance?

I think this question has pivotal implications for Christian
spirituality. If we understand sin as something that has gone
wrong within our constitution, then the solution will have to
come from outside. We'll have to receive it; help will, as it were,
have to be injected. But if our fundamental problem is ignorance of what we already are, then the solution will have to be
discovered within us. We'll need help to do that—which is why
Buddhists "take refuge." But *we* will have to do the discovering.
And we can, because what we are looking for we already have.
This creates a big difference, I think, in how Christians feel about
themselves and what they do to feel better.

A Buddhist Perspective: Paul

Why are we in such a mess? If we ask that question of Buddha
and of Jesus—or more accurately, of their followers who have
tried to understand them—we are going to get two different
answers. Buddhists and Christians have starkly contrasting diagnoses of why it is that humanity, throughout its history, cannot
seem to get its act together—why it is that humans seem more
proficient at producing suffering than happiness. More ana-
lytically, scholars might say that Buddhists and Christians have
starkly contrasting anthropologies—two very different views of
human nature. (Whether these differences are ultimately contradictory or complementary is a question for our conversation.)

For Christians, the mess that humanity is in has traditionally
been linked with *original sin*. From the very beginning something
went wrong, got profoundly "out of whack." The product that
God created was broken, so broken that it could no longer work
the way it was intended to work. It would have to be repaired.
This, basically, is how the story of Adam and Eve has traditionally been understood. They—human beings—are the reason
things got broken. However it happened, it wasn't God's fault.
But the results are drastic: The human condition, or human
nature, is *fallen*. Philosophers would say that, for Christians,
the problem is *ontological*. Since and because of Adam and Eve,

humans are born into a state of being that is broken, fallen, sin filled, or sin prone.

For Buddhists, the human condition is no less messy than for Christians. But for Buddhists the basic problem, or the fundamental source, of the mess is *ignorance*. Humans are not fundamentally fallen or sinful. Rather, they're fundamentally ignorant or mixed up. The crucial problem facing every human being is that we really don't know who or what we are. And not knowing what we are, we act in ways that hurt ourselves and others. Buddhists don't have an explanation for the causes of this pervasive ignorance (though we will explore that question below). They just accept it as a fact. It is there. We have to deal with it. For Buddhists, therefore, the basic problem of humanity is, in philosophical terms, *epistemological*. It is not in our *being* but in our *knowing*. Human nature isn't corrupted; rather, the human mind is clouded.

So it seems that Buddhism and Christianity offer two contrasting diagnoses of the fundamental problem. Yet both recognize that a remedy is needed. Will the remedies be as different as the diagnoses? That's the question for our next chapter. To answer it, we first have to have a clear grasp of the Buddhist diagnosis.

The problem: Ignorance of what we really are. If ignorance is our big problem, of what are we ignorant? What are we missing? The answer points us to a central teaching of the Buddha that we have already talked about, that is, his good news that we are all, really, *anattas*—not-selves. Because Buddha's teaching is apparently so strange, and therefore for Christians so difficult to grasp, I'm going to turn to a highly respected Buddhist teacher, Walpola Rahula, to lay it out for us.

In "denying the Self" as "an unchanging substance," in announcing that my "self" or my "ego" is "only a convenient name or a label" for a reality that is beyond the label, Buddha proclaimed a message that is both "unique in the history of human thought" and at the same time "frightening." Yet, if correctly understood and *felt*, it can also be a source of deep "peace and freedom." It is as radical as it is complex, for it implies neither the annihilation nor the eternal existence of the Self. Rather, it urges us to consider that what we really are is not contained in the feeling that "I AM." Our real identity is not found in our individual selves but, rather, in the bigger picture of which we are constantly changing expressions. Buddha called this bigger picture "the Unborn, Ungrown, and Unconditioned." It's this bigger, interconnected, and constantly changing reality that really matters, that surrounds and constitutes each fleeting moment of our lives. To be truly and fully and peacefully alive is not to stand out as individuals but to fit in as participants.[4]

But Buddha did not just announce that ignorance is our primary problem. He also described just how it works and how it insidiously pervades and distorts our daily lives. The ignorance that we are born into expresses itself, as it were, in the way we take our thoughts and feelings too seriously, in the way we allow them to "pull the wool over our eyes" and blind us to what we really are and to what is really going on in our lives. We think that the ideas or feelings that we form throughout the day are telling us who the people and things we encounter really are. Or, as my Buddhist teacher puts it, we *reify* our thoughts; we make *things* out of our thoughts, and we erroneously conclude that the world, including ourselves, consists of *things*. And then we cling to, we absolutize, these "thing-thoughts." That's our problem. That's how we are ignorant and miss what we and others really are.

As we will hear more in coming chapters, Buddha tells us that the trick for overcoming ignorance and getting in touch with the bigger picture is to be aware of or *mindful* of our thoughts, of how they make *things* out of *everything*. (Our very language "thingifies"!) By being mindful, we do not allow our thoughts and feelings to have the last word about what we are or about what is going on.

The results of ignorance: The three poisons. The traditional Buddhist teaching on the three poisons—delusion, greed, and hatred—explains the mess that ignorance creates. Here we have the fuller picture of how Buddhists understand the human condition. Really, it looks a lot like the Christian picture of "fallen" humanity. But the big difference—I think it is *big*—is where this mess comes from.

---

[4] Walpola Rahula, *What the Buddha Taught*, rev. and exp. ed. (New York: Grove Press, 1974 [1959]), 51, 56, 38, 66, 37.

Ignorance produces *delusion* insofar as it leads us to base our lives, and all the choices and goals we set for ourselves, on a false premise. Because we erroneously think that we are substantial, enduring, individual selves, we spend most of our energies in trying to protect, affirm, and increase our individual "me." But that is impossible. We're trying to protect and augment something that doesn't really exist. It is a bit like the delusional person who thinks he is Napoleon and spends all of his resources in trying to be—and to convince others that he is—someone he is not. Because we are ignorantly trying to be something we are not and can never be—that is, an individual, self-existing, enduring self—we end up feeling a deep-reaching, existential insecurity that seeps into every corner of our lives.

Delusion produces insecurity—or, as the Buddhist scholar David Loy puts it—a nagging, enchaining sense of *lack*.[5] We feel we are lacking what we think we need in order to be what we are not. So life becomes a frantic effort to find what we lack in order to be secure, enduring, defined individual selves. Existential insecurity becomes existential anxiety. We're constantly afraid that we're going "to lose ourselves"—not realizing that there is nothing to lose! Within the big picture, within the Space that surrounds and is us, we are already secure. As the Christian mystic Julian of Norwich puts it: "All manner of things are well," *already* well. But we can't trust that that is indeed the case.

Because we don't know or trust that, because we think that our security comes from preserving and protecting our individual selves, we are infected with the second poison of *greed*. Greed is nothing but the effort to buy a faulty insurance policy—a policy that cannot insure us and a policy for which we can never pay enough. We keep trying to acquire possessions, power, and prestige that will make clear who we are and that will secure our identity. But we can never get enough—simply because our insurance or our security can't be bought. We already have it. We already are secure, not as self-constituted individuals but as ever-changing expressions of the bigger picture.

---

[5] David Loy, *Lack and Transcendence: The Problem of Death and Life in Psychotherapy, Existentialism, and Buddhism* (Atlantic Highlands, NJ: Humanities Press, 1996).

Greed, therefore, blinds us to the difference between need and greed. Needs are what we require in order to keep the interconnected, constantly changing process of life going—food, shelter, medicine, education. Greed seeks to give permanence, stability, superiority to one little piece of the process: a permanent "me" and "mine." Greed, because it seeks an impossible goal, can only create havoc, both for us and for others. So, though the goal of greed is unreal and impossible, its effects are very real and painful (though, Buddhists add, also impermanent).

In a life animated by anxiety and driven by greed, everyone else becomes either an ally who will provide me with security, a competitor who is trying to corner the market on security, or an enemy who threatens my security. Life easily becomes an arena of *hatred,* in which, as the Latin poet Plautus puts it, "Homo homini lupus" (humans are wolves to one another)—all people competing to acquire what will give them stability, permanence, self-satisfaction. If you can contribute to my being, you're a friend. If you stand in my way, or try to exploit me for your purposes, then you are an enemy. As it turns out, maybe because we think the pie that provides security and permanence isn't big enough for everyone to get a piece, we seem to have more enemies to hate than friends to relax with.

Individual ignorance becomes social ignorance: Karma. Buddha's teaching on karma makes it clear that although our basic problem is the ignorance in our head, it produces very real problems in the world. The basic content of the doctrine of karma is simple and self-evident: every action yields unavoidable results. And the quality of the results depends on the quality of the action. More simply still, we have to deal with what you do. So, the street philosopher's dictum, "Shit happens," is, according to karma, not accurate; for humans and among humans it doesn't just *happen.* It is caused. If we are suffering, there is a cause of that suffering somewhere, somehow.

Traditionally, karma has been understood individually: My sufferings are due to what I have done in the past, often in a former life. Today, Buddhist scholars and practitioners are recognizing that Buddha's original teachings on karma can and should be understood socially: *Your* karma can become *my* karma. I am suffering because of what others have done—others who may not know me and are distant from my life. Now we're talking about *social karma* (which, as we'll see, offers multiple points of conversation with Christian liberation theologians). The karma of many deluded individuals builds up into a social reality, a culture in which everyone takes it for granted that we are all individuals competing with one another. So my ignorance, and the results of my ignorance, become part of the culture that everyone is born into and has to live in. This is why I'm caught in ignorance—because my ancestors were caught in ignorance and fashioned a world built on such ignorance.

Contemporary Buddhists, like David Loy and Sulak Sivaraksa, are exploring how the three poisons, though they originate in the human mind, take on or are embodied in social structures that exist independently of the human mind. *Delusion* surrounds us in the consumerism and advertising that constantly tell us that we cannot "be" unless we "have." *Greed* is built into *economic principles* that declare that only if everyone is selfish can everyone prosper. *Hatred* nurtures a military-industrial complex that is built on the conviction that our survival depends on conquering our enemies through weapons superior to theirs.[6]

So Buddhists are not less graphic in describing the mess that humanity is in. And although they don't have a dominant Adam and Eve story as to how it all started, they do explain how it keeps going: through an ignorance that produces a social karma into which we are all born. We *have to* deal with karma, our own and that of others. And, as we will explore in the next chapter, Buddhists are convinced that we *can* do just that.

A Christian Response: Roger

Buddha and Jesus unleashed traditions that developed elaborate interpretations of the problem of human existence. Cumulatively these reflections offer a severe negative appraisal of human nature. I cannot avoid responding to both of these estimates of the human so that a more positive account of the human in the next chapter does not appear totally gratuitous.

What is the problem? The reflection thus far has described qualities of human existence that are more or less universally

---

[6] See David Loy, "Listening to the Buddha: How Greed, Ill-Will, and Delusion Are Poisoning Our Institutions," *Transformation: Where Love Meets Social Justice* (May 12, 2014).

recognized as intrinsic to human nature as we know it. Suffering in its many forms affects all. In its most definitive form suffering culminates in death and apparent extinction. As the premise for suffering and death, ignorance forms a vast horizon for the history of our claims to knowledge; we are unfathomable to ourselves. This ignorance, along with other forces, stimulates some elementary forms of moral depravity: pride, greed, and hatred provide endemic temptations that have their effects on everyone individually and envelop whole groups. In the postmodern situation of constant fragmentation, plurality, and shattered certitudes, the Buddhist and the Christian conceptions of human inadequacy undermine any enduring meaningfulness of human existence on its own empirical terms.

None to the exclusion of the others. A single answer to the question of the encompassing problem of human existence that excludes the other candidates will not do. Each of these negativities realistically describes the human condition, human nature as it is. And each of them suggests a different focus for an opposing virtue that will set the tone for a positive spirituality. But none should be so emphasized that the full scope of our precarious situation is ignored.

Real problems intrinsic to human existence as given. Human existence is not plagued by problems that have solutions; it subsists as a mystery to itself. Deep-reaching ambiguity marks the actual nature of human existence and characterizes the coming into being of the human. The doctrine of original sin does not explain the situation but only testifies to it. We should not assume that the creators of these etiological myths did not know that they were wrestling with impenetrable mystery. Evolution excludes the idea of a historical fall. Moreover, it is not needed because these weaknesses are intrinsic to the human nature we share.

How negativity gives rise to hope. But human beings cannot rest satisfied with these characterizations of flawed human existence. The very negativity of these descriptions indicates that there is more to the story. One cannot perceive these radical tendencies of the human as defects without being aware that more is expected of human beings. Failure can be measured only by another possibility. Appreciation of their negativity could not happen without an image of what human beings could be or are called to be. Negative perception already stimulates openness to other positive potentialities—this should not be, it does not have to be, because this virtuous action is possible. Longing and hope have their negative ground in the radical fallibility of the human.

It Seems to Us

Even though Buddhists and Christians, as we have seen in this chapter, have different ways of describing the human predicament, even though they differ in their understandings of the root cause of the problem, even though they have differing remedies—both traditions resonate in agreement that *we human beings are in a big mess* that for the most part we ourselves have created and continue to create. For both of us *horrible* is the word that spontaneously issues from our Christian and Buddhist feelings when we witness the way human beings are treating each other as well as the earth and its creatures. The suffering that so many men, women, children, and millions of other sentient beings are daily enduring lay claim upon our attention and demand our response.

We are in a mess. And we have to do something about it. On that, from our Christian and our Buddhist convictions, we agree.

The story of Adam and Eve's expulsion from the Garden and the Christian notion of original sin are the Jewish and Christian attempts to make sense of this mess. The story in the book of Genesis of an original fall is what is called an *etiological myth*; it seeks to get at the causes, the basic source, of our pervasive problem. But, like all myths, we disempower it if we take it literally. Its truth lies in its meaning, not in its historical facticity. The meaning of a myth has to be interpreted, drawn out of the story. Such an interpretative effort is an ongoing task, to be renewed at different times and places throughout history.

Both of us have discovered that the dialogue with Buddhists can be for Christians a gentle jolt that opens up new possibilities for interpreting and understanding what the myth of the fall and the doctrine of original sin open up to our imaginations. It seems to us that in their analysis of the human predicament, Buddhists and Christians agree on our symptoms. But they differ in their diagnoses of the fundamental cause of this sickness. We think that, in the consideration of those differences, Christians have something to learn from Buddhists.

For both Christians and Buddhists, our sickness can be described as self-centeredness, egocentricity, or simply, selfishness—putting "me" first, and thus using others as instruments for my own advantage. This "me," of course, can be my own ego, my gender, my race, my nation. For Christians, we *sin* every time we fail to love our neighbor as ourselves—or as Augustine and Luther put it, every time our "heart turns back into itself" *(cor incurvatum in se)*. For Buddhists, we cause suffering *(dukkha)* every time we give way to greed or cling to things all for ourselves *(tanha)*. For both Jesus and Buddha, it seems, our basic human problem arises from the way everyone wants the "center" for himself or herself—the way everyone refuses to share the center.

At this point we need to make a self-evident disclosure. As two white American males we belong to a class of people for whom the problem of self-centeredness is particularly acute and dangerous. Women and marginalized minorities remind us that the issue of self-centeredness must be understood and dealt with differently by people whose selves have been disempowered or subordinated by others. One must first have a self before one can realize that it can be a problem. We can't forget that.

But if Buddhists and Christians agree that our pervasive human sickness has to do with selfishness and the way we use and abuse others—humans, animals, or the planet itself—for our own advantage, the question naturally arises: What causes this sickness? And here, as we said, Buddhist and Christian answers seem to diverge.

To summarize and focus what we have already explored in this chapter, Christians have traditionally located the root of our problem in *what we are,* while Buddhists find it in *what we think we are.* For Christians, something is wrong in our present makeup.[7] We're caught in an "internal bondage" (Luther) or, as Roger stated, there is "some negative thing at work within

---

[7] The best explanation of why we are the way we are comes from evolutionary biology. We have inherited some built-in genetic antisocial behavior patterns from our distant ancestors, for example, violence, the need to hoard possessions, territoriality, and a distrust of others. See Patrick J. Amer, *The Five Commandments of Jesus: A New Approach to Christianity* (New York: iUniverse, 2009), 23–31.

human beings." For some Christians, we have *fallen* into a place we can't get out of. For other Christians, we're painfully and unavoidably *wounded*.

For Buddhists, as Paul has pointed out, our deep, generating problem is ignorance *(avidya)*. We don't know, we've lost cognitive contact with, what we really are. And out of this primary poison of ignorance or delusion flows the other two poisons that cause so much suffering: greed and hatred.

Do these different diagnoses of our sickness and of our mess really matter? We think they do. And we suggest that Christians might learn from the Buddhist diagnosis that our problem is not so much in what we are but in what we think we are. Can original sin be better understood as original ignorance? (Maybe this is how we might interpret "the tree of the knowledge of good and evil" that Adam and Eve were forbidden to eat [Gn 3:6]; it represents a false knowledge and thus an ignorance that replaced the original knowledge given by God that "all was good.")

To understand our original sinfulness as resulting from our original ignorance would mean for Christians that we are not *fallen*, nor mortally *wounded*, but that we are *lost*. We've lost our bearings, our way, our original knowledge—the knowledge that is originally given to us in our very being and nature. Although the consequences of such ignorance can be horrendous, we both believe that such an interpretation of the Christian doctrine of original sin as original ignorance can stimulate a real, personal difference in the way Christians feel about themselves and act in the world.

If the problem is rooted in what we are, in a corruption or malfunctioning of our nature, then the repair will have to come from outside ourselves because what we have of ourselves isn't working. We have to be fixed by a fixer. But if the problem is that something is missing in our awareness, in our knowledge, then, yes, we will need help. But the help will consist in revealing what we really and truly are; we will have to be illumined by a teacher or taught by a revealer. And the remedy will consist in revealing our basic goodness rather than our basic fallenness or corruption. In removing our original ignorance, we will see our original blessing and goodness.

This is one way our Buddhist-Christian dialogue might help Christians clarify their conception of our fundamental human problem: *Original sin is original ignorance of our original blessing.* Moreover, we've found functional analogies between Christian and Buddhist viewpoints that tell us what that original blessing is. In different languages and symbols both Christians and Buddhists announce that *originally*, or *actually*, we are not separate selves or independent individuals or egos left to fend for themselves. In Christian language, to be created and held in being by God is to be loved by God; we are grounded in an all-pervasive Love. In Buddhist teachings we are part of a web of connectedness that is, as Paul's Tibetan practice declares, conscious and compassionate. We are sustained and secured in this interconnecting energy.

When we are not aware of this original blessing, or when we forget it or lose touch with it, when we feel we have to fend for ourselves and create our own well-being and safety through wealth or power or fame, we cause *dukka* (suffering) or sin for ourselves and everyone.

But if ignorance is the problem, where does it come from? Even though this is not as pressing a question for Buddhists as it is for Christians, we think Christians can help with an answer. Many Christian theologians have proposed a *sociocultural* understanding of original sin.[8] It is not a moral scar or a defect or wound that we inherit. Rather, it is the state of the world we are born into—a culture that determines that "I" or "my tribe" comes first, that success and security derive from power over others. Such ignorance, such forgetfulness, of our original blessings of interconnectedness has been building up like a snowball throughout history. Original sin, or what Buddhists call social karma, is like a virus born of human free will that continually infects most of humanity.

That makes for a mess, but, and here is the Buddhist and Christian good news, a *curable* mess. Ignorance can be removed. Enlightenment is possible. The truth can set us free. That is what we look into in the next chapter.

---

[8] See Marjorie Hewitt Suchocki, "Original Sin Revisited," *Process Studies* 20/4 (Winter 1991): 223–43.

8.

The Potential in Human Nature

After looking at the downside of human existence, we have to explore comparative views of human possibility and destiny. Again, large conceptual differences separate us. But the human experiences behind the teachings offer many possibilities for mutual understanding, appreciation, and learning. What we are living for lies at the heart of spirituality.

A Buddhist Perspective: Paul

"Can we really change human nature?" Every time I throw that question at students I know what answer to expect. Nine out of ten will respond with an immediate "No way!" Human beings, they tell me, are going to remain the same selfish, fearful, anxious creatures they have always been. Yes, there is a basic goodness within every human being. But it keeps getting covered over by the dreck of selfishness and violence. When it comes down to the last piece of pie, and I really want it, I'll more likely take it rather than share it. That's human nature, my students insist. If there's any possibility of changing it, we'll have to wait till whatever might come after death.

Buddha would disagree. After his Enlightenment experience under the Bodhi tree, the story tells us, Mara, the Evil One, threw this same assertion at him: "People will never understand or accept what you just discovered. You're not going to change them." But because of the wisdom and compassion he had just discovered, Buddha saw things differently. I don't think he would have put it in terms of changing human nature. But he was convinced that people could wake up to what human nature is in such a way that their lives, and those of others, would be very different from what they are now.

Good and evil: A 50–50 chance? As we have already seen, this doesn't mean that Buddha and Buddhism candy-coat the mess that we are in now. The three poisons of delusion, greed, and hatred—whether in the actions of individuals or in the structures of society—cause horrible suffering. They are real, devastatingly real. But as Tsoknyi Rinpoche dares to assert: As real as the three poisons are, as real as is the suffering they cause—they are not really *true*. Real but not true. Yes, he's playing with words, but he's playing in order to make a mind-boggling and life-transforming point: If we take this state of delusion and hate and greed to be the final description of what we truly are, we're making a big mistake. It doesn't have to be that way, because it *isn't* that way. Our deepest human nature, what we truly are, is Buddha-nature. And when Gautama-become-Buddha finally decided to stand up from the sacred ground on which he had experienced enlightenment, he believed that everyone—yes, everyone—can wake up to what one really is. Given the reality of karma, it might take longer for some than for others. But it is a real possibility for everyone.

And so Buddha's answer to another fundamental religious/philosophical question—Is human nature fundamentally more inclined toward evil or toward good?—would be different from that of many Christians. If as Christian and Jewish teachers tell us, there are two opposing forces within the soul of every human being—good and evil—is one naturally stronger than the other? Or to put the question even more incisively: Do good and evil have a 50–50 chance?

Buddha, I believe, would definitely answer no. Though Buddhists have not traditionally articulated this question as Western Christians might, they would affirm that human nature, in its reality and potential, is *fundamentally good*, fundamentally disposed toward wisdom over ignorance, compassion over greed, love over hatred. To realize this potential for goodness, human nature does not have to be changed or reconstructed or compelled.

It has to be awakened, clarified, rediscovered. That may take some doing, but it is a thoroughly hopeful doing.

A potential to be mystics. Trying to unpack and translate Buddha's understanding of human potential into a language that Western Christians speak, I believe we can also say that, for Buddha, all human beings have the potential to be mystics. Mysticism isn't just for the spiritual specialists. If a standard dictionary definition of mysticism is "a direct, intimate union of the soul with God through contemplation," then that basically describes what happens in enlightenment (though, as we've seen, *God* is understood as a verb, not as a noun). And Buddha was insistent that enlightenment can happen to everyone.[1] Through the following of the Eightfold Path, through some form of meditation or practice by which we transcend our usual way of thinking and simply let go into Reality, it is possible for all men and woman to experience themselves as more than themselves, that is, as a dynamic, ever-changing and always interrelating expression of what my Tibetan Buddhist teacher calls all-encompassing, all-sustaining Space. To have some sense or feeling that this is possible, that this is true, is to walk in the company of the mystics found in all religions. It's a company, Buddha assures us, that has open membership. All can join, if they wish.

A potential to be God? I believe we can talk about the Buddhist understanding of human potential in even more drastic, and perhaps somewhat dangerous, Christian language. If the Buddhist understanding of ultimate reality that we tried to summarize in Chapter 5 is basically on target (as much as any attempt to talk of ultimate mystery can be on target), then it means that human beings have the potential to be—or more accurately, to wake up to the fact that they already are—divine. Or to give the Christian envelope an even bolder Buddhist push: humans have the potential to realize that *they are God*. That doesn't mean that all of God is the individual. But it does mean that all of the person is God (or has the potential to realize that). As my Buddhist teacher declares, over and over again: "You are the Space. The Space is you. Be the Space. Let the Space be you."

---

[1] A man of his time and cultural conditioning, he needed some coaxing to recognize that women were just as eligible as men.

Here, I suggest, Buddhism is pushing the Christian envelope regarding the traditional but often neglected teaching about *theosis*—the doctrine, found especially in the Orthodox tradition, of the divinization of humanity. The early and highly respected theologian and saint, Athanasius, announced that "through the incarnation of the Word . . . God assumed humanity that we might become God"—*theosis*.[2] What does that really mean?

Buddhism can help answer that question. Just as Mahayana Buddhists do not hesitate to say that *samsara* (this finite world with all its bumps and bruises) *is* nirvana (the Ultimate), or that Emptiness *is* Form, or that the Absolute *is* the Relative, so Buddhists urge Christians to explore the possibility of announcing that God is the finite world, or that God is humanity. For Christians, this sounds like pantheism. But it is not. In announcing that Emptiness is Form or that *samsara* is nirvana, Buddhists also insist that they are different.

However difficult it is to understand and put into words this Buddhist teaching on the non-duality between Emptiness and Form, or between God and the world, Buddhists insist that humans have the capacity to *feel* it. We may not be able to explain it in words, but we can feel it in our very being. We have the potential, through our spiritual practice, to come to the feeling that no matter what happens to us and no matter what we think or feel about what is happening to us, it is the very activity of the Divine that is the source and energy of all that happens and of all that we think or feel. It is all real, and we have to deal with it. But what is more deeply true is that it is all the energy or the manifestation of Emptiness, of Spirit, of Space (different fingers pointing in the same direction). In all that is going on in our lives, both around us and within us, there is this Spirit, this Space that grounds us, that holds us, that manifests itself in us. And precisely when we feel and become aware of this Spirit/ Space that holds us and is us, then we find the capacity to deal with whatever happens, with whatever we find ourselves thinking or feeling. Holy Mystery pervades all. Therefore we can deal with all.

Buddhism, I think we can say, is nudging Christians to understand with their minds and to feel in their hearts that the unity

---

[2] Athanasius, *On the Incarnation*, para 54.

between God and the world, between divinity and humanity, is deeper, tighter, closer than they have so far imagined. The *unity* is a *oneness,* a non-dual oneness, in which two become one without ceasing to be two. They co-inhere. All this suggests, further, that what my teacher Karl Rahner said about Jesus makes all the more sense: "To say that Jesus was divine," he told us, "is to say that in him human nature reached its full potential." Few of us may reach that potential as fully as Jesus did, but, from a Buddhist perspective, that's the challenge he gives us.

Postmortem potential? If Buddhism assures us that we humans have the potential to wake up to our basic goodness, to our mystical capacity to realize and experience that in some real sense we are divine and co-inhere with the Mystery of God, what does this all mean for what we can expect, or hope for, after we die?

When Gautama was asked this question—whether the self lives on after death—he gave an answer that was as profound as it was tantalizing. Probably with a twinkle in his eyes, he warned his followers that it is not correct to say that the self lives on after death. But he immediately added that neither is it correct to say that the self does not live on. After death, the self will not be annihilated. But neither will the self be preserved.

So what goes on after death? What continues? I think Buddha would answer: nothing terribly new. The same constantly changing, interconnecting process that constitutes one's present life will go on after one's death. In this sense there is no "other place" to go after death. Whatever *eternal life* might mean and contain, it is happening right here. As many Buddhist teachers point out, there is no essential difference between life and death; both are essential parts of one bigger picture and process. Without death, life is impossible. Every death is the occasion for new life. This is not just a biological law. It's the way Emptiness or the Interconnecting Spirit works.

But after physical death the *same* bigger picture that is the life-death process will go on *differently*—to a large or small degree—because of the way one lived this life, that is, because of what one did and how far one came in waking up. Here we are entering the controversial, and rather opaque, realm of Buddhist teachings on rebirth. Whether taken literally (one's energies will be reborn in another individual's consciousness) or more metaphorically, it means that what one did isn't lost, for better or for worse. Rebirth might be understood in contemporary terms as a cosmic process of recycling, of reprocessing. Because of the way one lived, possibilities of the whole process working more compassionately, more knowingly, more "enlightenedly" will be better or worse.

But where's the "me" in all this? In line with Buddha's teaching that my "me" is neither annihilated nor perpetuated, I think a helpful answer is this: I will live on as that which Buddha taught was my real nature and my full potential. I will live on as an *anatta,* a not-self. After death there will be consciousness. But it won't be individuated consciousness, "my-consciousness." Perhaps we can say that it will be "we-consciousness"—the kind of wonderful "me"-transcending feelings that flash on us in moments of deep meditation or in the exhilarating embrace of natural beauty or of a lover.

As Jesus put it, we have to *lose* ourselves before we can *find* ourselves. While Christians have generally stressed the *finding,* Buddhists remind them that they first have to experience the *losing.* No finding without losing. And what we find after death is not going to be what we lost. (If it is, then we really haven't lost it.) What we find after death is not going to be our individual selves with our individual consciousness.

What it will be, we can't really say. It is beyond our present, individuated consciousness. So in the end, our attitude toward our after-death potential is a matter of *trust*—trusting that what worked in life will work at death. Just as in life we found that it was in dying to ourselves in compassion for and in interconnection with others that we found ever greater life and happiness, so it will also be in the final act of death. We let go, trusting that in losing we will find.

So what is trustworthy in life is trustworthy at the moment of death: Let go! Let God! Let life-death go on!

A Christian Response: Roger

Paul, I think this chapter, more than any other, encapsulates the foundation of Christian spirituality. At this crucial point I see both significant learning and pointed difference from Buddhist spirituality. I will therefore be precise but somewhat abstract and analytical in making four points responding to your depiction of how Buddhism opens up human potential. I hope that in our common statement we can flesh out the schematic character of this response.

Staying close to the Jesus story. Christian spirituality goes back to Jesus of Nazareth and cannot lose touch with the historical figure. Recall that spirituality consists holistically of one's way of life and possesses a narrative structure. Worship, meditative practice, mysticism, and regular sacramental practice all fit within the larger narrative of how we live. The basic historical paradigm for this is Jesus of Nazareth. Jesus is the historical medium for Christians to find God in history. Everything Christian has its source there. This is not meant in an exclusive or reductionist way but as a method of sorting things out and keeping them in perspective.

Strained supernaturalism. The Western Catholic tradition and language of spirituality houses categories that were useful in the past but are dysfunctional today. For example, a distinction between natural and supernatural orders protected the gratuity of saving grace for a teleological imagination. But the distinction led to contrasts, antitheses, and implied separations. The competing values of nature and supernatural grace, of free will and grace, rent the languages of spirituality, polarized Christian self-understanding, and ultimately detached spirituality from everyday life. One of the truly great contributions of Karl Rahner to Catholic theology was his bringing together creation and grace in a non-dual relationship. But he retained the language of the supernatural as an abrasive residue. We need new superstructures today.

Sacred naturalistic historicism. Christian dialogue with science, contemporary philosophy, other disciplines dealing with the human, and other faiths, in this instance Buddhism, show that spirituality cannot operate on a premise of a supernatural sphere above the natural plane of reality. For example, the maxim "grace builds on nature" implicitly renders them separable, grace added to nature. In a variety of ways these different dialogues show that we must find grace *within* nature and history by various phenomenologies of spiritual experience. For example, we cannot treat the idea of creation as a given; one must appeal to a broadly common spiritual insight into being absolutely dependent and held in existence over an abyss of non-being. This spiritual perception entails a conviction that God constitutes the sphere in which everything exists and thus is immanent to all of nature and history. Spiritual mediation means finding grace within the depths of finitude itself. Buddhism helps Christians to realize this.

Resurrection. At the same time, keeping close to the Jesus story helps the Christian to cut through the elaborate Buddhist meditation on afterlife. One can imagine innumerable ways of "survival" through the memory exercised by other humans or by God, or through the cumulative effects of one's life. But Jesus's resurrection, called "bodily" to mark his individuality, gives focus to an absolute trust that is both more plausible because it is simpler and more effective in its valuation of reality than Buddhist speculation offers.

A Christian Perspective: Roger

Some Christians may look upon Buddhism as an elaborate system of self-help. Buddhism addresses the crisis of human suffering by striving to awaken our inner Buddha-nature. Meditation gradually wears down greed, hatred, and ignorance and enables a person to let go of attachments that block an awakening of the human spirit to ultimate reality. By contrast, people usually portray Christianity as an appeal to an outside source of salvation. God transcends the world, and God's grace gratuitously enters from "outside" human nature to enable human freedom to do what it cannot do through its own power. But constructive reflection from the Christian side of things reveals striking analogies between these seemingly opposing conceptions. This brief meditation moves through stages that revolve around the narrative of Jesus in a way that can be correlated with the lives of all people.

Jesus as revelation of human nature. An earlier reflection on ultimate reality turned to Jesus as a revealer of God. God should not be conceived as an individual person hovering over all reality. One cannot accurately imagine God at all. But Abrahamic faiths are committed to the personal character of the ground and power of being. The consideration of ultimate reality shows that, in the Christian imagination shaped by the preaching of Jesus on the rule of God, the positive potential of human existence (and all reality) comes from God, the creator of heaven and earth.

This reflection turns again to Jesus, this time as a revealer of human existence. Instead of attending to Jesus's characterization of God, this reflection looks at the way Jesus related to God and thereby opened up a conception of human existence in relation to God. This comes into view by focusing attention on the logic of his life and ministry as portrayed in the Gospels. The stories of Jesus show that he appealed to and won followers, and they in turn composed the Gospels. What understanding of human nature is gained from following him? What does Jesus, as one to be followed, reveal about human potential?

Empowered by the Spirit of God. All of the Gospels, but especially those of Mark, Matthew, and Luke, represent Jesus as empowered by the Spirit of God. *Spirit* suggests a nonmaterial power and source of energy that evokes, moves, and even causes an exalted human response. Sometimes God as Spirit is conceived as an outside force coming into Jesus's life; sometimes the Spirit resides or dwells in Jesus. In both cases the Spirit of God is God and not other than God.

This understanding of God's action within people flowed into the conception of the church and God's presence to it. The Spirit of God affects each believer as saving gift. Especially in Western theology since Augustine, God's saving power, or the Holy Spirit, was the internal "help of God" that moved a person toward faith. Grace and free will were measured over against each other. Salvation could only come from God's grace or be initiated by God's Spirit; it could not come from human freedom itself. God as Spirit thus appeared to be introduced into human subjects as a power from outside human nature and freedom.

But God as Spirit can also be conceived as the power of the creator God's creating. God's Spirit is the immanent, loving, and empowering presence of God within each finite creature. No creature can exist without this immanent power that is both transcendently other in being and at the same time the power of the being of this or that creature—indeed, every creature. The creating presence of God is both immanent and essential to each being and simultaneously other than it and transcendent to it. Analogously, because the whole system of understanding is different, the Spirit of God is the Christian Buddha-nature and it belongs to each one.

In Chapter 1, spirituality was considered as the way one led one's life when measured by its relation to ultimate reality. By this definition Christian spirituality is life lived in relation to God as God is revealed in the gospel portrayals of the ministry of Jesus. Too often in this saying God is understood as an individual being out there, up there, self-contained beyond the sphere of finite being. By contrast, finding God within Jesus's ministry entails recognizing the Spirit of God as a creating and empowering source of life within Jesus's being and acting. The Spirit of God is not a creature and is other than the human person Jesus, but in a non-dual way. Human beings are creatures and not the Creator. But the theology of creation forces one to think in terms of differences held together as one. The Gospels present the Spirit of God as of the very being of Jesus. Not only is Jesus empowered by the Spirit along the way of his ministry, but the Spirit is also involved in his coming to be and his birth. This applies analogously to each creature. No creature can exist outside of the power of "the Spirit of God," because that phrase symbolizes the effective presence of God's creative power in each individual. Each person can say that the Spirit of God is the power of his or her being and inseparable from his or her continuing existence.

Within the context of the Spirit of God at work within all human life, Jesus's ministry provides specific ideas about where the Spirit of God leads. In other words, one can read concrete directions about what it means to live an integral human life by looking at Jesus as empowered by the Spirit and as a leader to be followed. The spirituality of following Jesus cannot be developed here in detail, but it can be characterized. In his commitment to the rule of God, Jesus revealed basic programmatic principles of resisting everything that prevents the flourishing of the human and of positively supporting everything that ameliorates human suffering. This was not an abstract program in Jesus's ministry; it summarizes what Jesus did in favor of concrete individuals whom he met in his ministry and what the rule of God means for human spirituality.

The cross of human suffering. Moving to the violent end of Jesus's ministry, his punishing death as a criminal quickly became the great Christian symbol for human suffering. Jesus had stood publicly and prophetically for the rule of God. This caused conflict and won him enemies. People conspired to eliminate him. His was not a natural or painless death, but a torturous execution inflicted by outside forces on an innocent person. It is hard for people today, especially Christians, to get back into the conflict-ridden context in which Jesus's ministry unfolded. By confronting situations of injustice, Jesus provoked conflict; he was captured and killed for *political reasons* in the broad sense of that term.

Christians find within that protracted event a compact symbol expressing the whole of human suffering. Jesus's death was not at first perceived as a salvific event but as a scandal. The more deeply human hopes were invested in him, the more devastating was the disappointment. Jesus preached a God of justice and life. He represented God's rule. He was God's emissary. His death, by contrast, represented the negation of his message, a triumph of his enemies, and the victory of false accusation. Jesus promised the rule of God, a sphere of justice and peace, but he died a victim of injustice in great physical suffering. His was an innocent, untimely death, an incarnation of the ultimate threat of meaninglessness.

Resurrection. Christians live in the belief that God raised Jesus from death. Jesus's death in itself has no salvific power; it is pure negativity, aside from the fidelity of Jesus's commitment to the rule of God. But God raised this typical life of suffering into eternal life. The resurrection of Jesus is a revelatory event; resurrection is offered to all human beings. One does not open up to the resurrection of Jesus as an isolated event; it bears significance for humanity as such. Belief in Jesus's resurrection thus offers a framework of hope for the fulfillment of human freedom and for a comprehensive meaning for all human existence.

This hope for an absolute future should not be conceived as a prediction about the end of human time and the human species. Jesus provided images and symbols for eternal life, but they do not amount to objective information about it. Faith in resurrection as the "end" of God's creation provides not pictures but a horizon of hope that the author of reality will be its finisher. What happened to Jesus is a promise of an absolute future: in Buddhist terms, it is an end of suffering and human nature fully awakened.

The relevance of faith in the future of reality cannot be reduced to what will happen after death. Resurrection does not happen only in the end. It also transforms human life in the present moment. Resurrection faith doubles back on the present moment; it can fill human life in this world by bestowing on it a potentially absolute meaning. Resurrection faith adds new dimensions of depth, transcendence, and promise to what appears as a superficial *samsara* in the absence of an absolute future. The horizon of fulfillment thus throws the foreground into perspective. All reality is rendered important as the penultimate of something solid (not static) that is to come. In the imagery of John's Gospel this holistic conception floods light on an otherwise dark human existence. The endless routines of the cycles of life in this world open up to the possibility of comprehensive meaning. The future promises that the present moment and the particular situation will be part of a greater permanent reality. According to Jesus's teaching, a person already shares in this future by resisting sickness, ignorance, egocentrism, suffering, and death within the human community. In the end, Jesus's resurrection reveals a God who guarantees the value of human existence despite and in the face of moral failure, suffering, death, and the seeming lack of purpose carried by random events.

Returning to the notion of spirituality that governs these reflections, the theoretical representation of a vision does not do justice to what essentially consists of a concrete way of life. This schematic outline of a conception of spirituality does not adequately represent the way Jesus's ministry unfolded or the actual commitment of his followers. Spirituality is an existential thing. Meaning may be grasped notionally in a descriptive account, but it only overcomes suffering in the practice; it only bestows participatory meaning in the action that flows from its internalization. Only a spirituality that aligns a person's life with the rule of God that Jesus represented in his ministry actually begins to engage suffering, guilt, and the prospects of death and meaninglessness.

Overcoming death, sin, and meaninglessness. This phrase expresses the inner potential of human existence negatively in relation to the question of the human discussed in the previous chapter. A positive response to the question of human nature lies in creation theology and the language of God as Spirit as the story of Jesus communicates this to the Christian imagination.

More specifically, the language of God as Spirit translates the immanent loving power of the creator God into words whose meaning can be experienced in human living. Creation does not refer to a single act of God in the beginning but to God's Spirit constantly sustaining reality through time. This understanding relates directly to spirituality. It overcomes a dualistic Deism that places God outside the workings of the world; it makes God the inner dynamism of existence that is directly present to human life.

Life that consciously draws its power from a spiritual conviction of the Spirit of God within itself has the potential to experience an inner freedom from the ultimate annihilation of death. People touched by the Spirit of God within can experience new creative energy in the recognition of God's affirmation of them with all their moral failures. Encounter with the Spirit of God provides the ground for an overarching meaning for human existence. God as Spirit embraces the whole of reality and, as personal, relates to each individual. God as Spirit thus promises that existence is meaningful from within the randomness of evolution and the arbitrariness of history. The potential of human nature, then, lies in human freedom itself, not autonomously, but in conjunction with the power of God as Spirit within.

A Buddhist Response: Paul

I'm happy to confess, Roger, that your section "Jesus as Empowered by the Spirit of God" confirmed for me that *Spirit* is the Christian symbol that can best connect with the non-dual nature of the Mahayana Buddhist experience of Emptiness or Interbeing. Your descriptions of Jesus's experience of the Spirit as "the immanent, loving, and empowering presence of God within each finite creature" that is both "immanent" and "simultaneously other" resonated for me with what I have learned from my Tibetan teachers about the compassionate Space—the "love essence"—that holds and constitutes what we are.[3] This is a Spirit or Space or Energy that is just as much *one with* as it

---

[3] Tsoknyi Rinpoche, *Open Heart, Open Mind: Awakening the Power of Essence Love* (New York: Harmony Books, 2012), 60–76.

is *more than* creation. I was delighted to hear you say that "the Spirit of God is the Christian Buddha-nature." As Buddhists are called to wake up to their innate Buddha-nature, Christians are called to wake up to their innate divinity. Salvation, therefore, is not a "repair job" but a repossessing of what we already are.

But the question I raised in the previous chapter still lingers: Does the Christian non-duality that you recognize between Spirit and creation go both ways? Can Christians say that the Spirit needs us (or needs Jesus) similarly to the way we need the Spirit? Is there real, though asymmetrical, reciprocity between Spirit and world?

Although *Spirit* is functionally analogous to the "love essence" of Interbeing, that character of love that marks the energy of being, there are aspects of your description of the Spirit manifested in Jesus that profoundly challenge me as a Buddhist. They have to do with the reality of the cross in Jesus's life. As you made clear, the crucifixion expressed the conflict that Jesus's Spirit-inspired message created between him and the political-economic powers of the time. It seems that the reality of conflict necessarily brought about by Jesus's response to the Spirit is telling us that in order to be in tune with the Spirit (or our Buddha-nature), we are going to have to be out of tune with the way the world is being run. There is something countercultural in the Spirit that Jesus wakes up to. The Spirit as present in Jesus, therefore, calls humans to be political beings—engaged in the complexities, the ambiguities, the "dirtiness" of political and economic realities.

Finally, what you said about the resurrection and life after death helped clarify for me what you mean by your Christian "hope for an absolute future." We don't have any objective information about what is to come, but we can hope that after death "the present moment and the particular situation will be part of a greater permanent reality." As I tried to make clear in my section, for me as a Buddhist, that "greater permanent reality" will not necessarily have to include my personal consciousness as Paul Knitter. After my death it will no longer be I who live, but the Christ-Spirit (Interbeing) that lives and carries on with the fruit (karma) of my life. My consciousness returns, as it were, to Spirit consciousness. Can this make sense for Christians?

It Seems to Us

In the end we have to try to represent how we assess the positive potential of human nature as followers of Jesus after hearing a decidedly different appraisal of human existence from the Buddhist tradition. This topic is impossibly large, abstract, and deep. It has been intellectually examined for millennia; both faith traditions provide insight and teachings that far exceed what one can discern from Gautama's or Jesus's teaching alone. But from our conversation we can highlight certain convictions and hopes around three dimensions of human potential: its basic character, its possible achievements, and its destiny.

The character of human existence. The discussion in the last chapter showed that a good deal of evidence points to a negative view of human nature. Christians accounted for that with the doctrine of original sin. But many today believe that that doctrine itself has caused enormous human damage by its negative appraisal of the human, its inducement of unwarranted guilt, and its overall effects on human practice. Although an evolutionary view of the world rules out a historical fall of the race, the mythic story of a first sin still bears deep symbolic meaning. But it cannot be allowed to define a framework in which good and evil, grace and sin, exist apart from each other to form a dualism that spawns a duel between equal powers.

We found that we share some basic attitudes and broad conceptions of some fundamental things here: something remarkable because we spoke to each other out of different conceptual backgrounds. Roger tends to think of the economy of grace and salvation not as an add-on, not as something on top of or built upon a system of nature or arising later, but as a given, constituent part of what we are. Moreover, the nature of the human cannot be conceived as a static, permanent, and non-developing essence but presents itself as a temporal changing economy. Roger thinks the saving love of God characterizes the immanent active power of a creating God; this in turn is what saves (it is sometimes called *grace* and sometimes God's *Spirit*). These terms all refer to the inner ground of all reality that is positive in character: "God saw everything that he had made, and indeed it was very good" (Gn 1:31).

This conflating of Christian terms together allows a startlingly hopeful view of the human in the face of all the problems discussed in the last chapter. Despite aspects of the phenomenal world, God is the *within* of all things; God the Creator loves creation; God is a positive energy for new being and new life; though never overt, God is accessible presence. Absolute Mystery envelops, embraces, sustains, empowers, inspires, illumines, energizes, and encourages human beings, and promises a new future.

By the principles of universality and functional analogy the Christian has to expect that, if this view corresponds with reality, there will be analogous appraisals of the human and equally positive language about human life in other faith traditions. And so it is. Paul speaks of how Dharma affirms the goodness of human nature. All human beings exist within the power of Interbeing or Emptiness; it is the energy that constitutes being. It suffuses nature; it constitutes, sustains, and energizes human beings; being connected with it militates against egocentrism, greed, clinging, and hatred. All share a common Buddha-nature; each person exists within the energy of the whole; all potentially manifest outwardly the energy that constitutes all reality.

Of course these terms, like those that make up Christian language, all have distinguishable histories and meanings. But they also fit into a worldview in which the character of the human is good and is "saved" always because the world and all that it contains subsists within the power of positive and affirming creative energy. Salvation does not come from outside creation, for the power of being is not outside creation. It is the power of gratuitous love—or what Paul's Tibetan teachers call "love essence"—in which all creation exists and can be responded to when we become awakened to it and drawn into it. The antitheses between creation and salvation, nature and grace, God's initiative and human initiative tend to block appreciation of the positive dynamics of the power of being that sustains all reality.

The possible achievements of the human. After complaining about the abstract character of the Christian debates on the relation between nature and grace, we may have fallen into the same trap. Let's see whether we can more concretely deal with the positive potential of human nature in terms of achievements. Jesus and Gautama provide some specific teaching here.

The question of the possible achievements of the human may be regarded by some as misplaced. It should be phrased in terms of purpose and goals. Roger notes that for Christians the ultimate purpose of life is life with God in blessedness. Aristotle's generic response to the purpose of beings is their fulfillment or happiness. Christian eschatology readily appropriates this idea while insisting on God's agency in bringing it about. Paul's Buddhist lens is more concrete: The purpose of life is awakening or illumination; the goal is to overcome suffering by conquering ignorance, greed, egoism, clinging, and hatred along the path to nirvana. But both of us are interested in spirituality *in this world* and what human potential contributes to life together. Jesus has a positive response to this question, and Gautama reinforces it.

Jesus's teaching is so overt and obvious that it frequently gets lost in abstruse debates about human nature. Jesus preached the coming rule of God, and he mediated it with his ministry of healing and prophetic criticism. The rule of God represents what the world should be according to the intention of the Creator. Generally, his ministry was directed toward human flourishing, with a special attention for those who were lost, poor, left out, marginalized, sinners, despised, weak, or vulnerable. But his message was not simply directed to these victims; it specifically addressed those with power to say that in the rule of God the helpless are *their* concern because they are the concern of all.

The Christian finds resonances of this social responsibility in the message of Gautama. One of its most powerful symbols is found in the story of his turn, after his Enlightenment, to the service of others. This value or ideal of the bodhisattva, dedication to the flourishing of other human beings, counters every conception of human achievement that is individualist or narcissistic and replaces it with service to others and to society.

These ideas describe the ideals we set for ourselves and the way we actually live. Jesus enlisted disciples and sent them out to do what he did. In a spirituality of being a follower of Jesus, how does that translate into behavior today? We think that Jesus's views and his enjoining others to take up his ministry are not reserved for leaders. All participate in society and all contribute their small creative acts to the ongoing life of the community. This vision fits nicely into an evolutionary context where the whole is moving forward in time, and the movement develops its character from the millions of contributions from the participants. Each has his or her role to play. It is not too strong to say that in this Christian vision people are called to be co-creators in the sense of instruments of the rule of God. This way of thinking has direct bearing on spirituality. We will take them up again later under the theme of contemplation and action.

In the face of death. We compared our views of the other side of human potential, that is, its ultimate destiny. Paul's appreciation of Buddhist views on life after death differ from Roger's more traditional views of eternal life. Roger hopes for a continuity of self-consciousness, an assumption of individuality into a sphere that preserves and, one would hope, polishes the rough edges of sin and imperfection. Gregory of Nyssa uses the term *purify.* Of course, it is impossible to conceive of a purely individual salvation, and there can be no perfect happiness while other human beings are suffering. The logic, then, runs from human potential toward completion; that is, if what one does in and with one's life does not find a place in eternity, the work may have ultimate meaning in its effects, but personal fulfillment has been lost. In this vision the power of being is personal, so that personality and inter-personality defines the ultimate character of reality itself.

In contrast to Roger's claim that the simplicity of a hope for personal and self-conscious life renders life more fecund, Paul wonders whether a non-subjective or non-personal immortality might have greater plausibility for many today. Does not non-personal immortality correspond more faithfully to Jesus's call for self-emptying and, just so, Saint Paul's interpretation of Jesus as God's *kenosis*? Paul's Buddhist accents are aligned with Saint Paul's linking of the risen Christ with the Spirit of God. Nothing is lost, but individuality becomes taken up into the dynamic and productive energy of Emptiness or Interbeing. In Christian language, it will no longer be I who live, but the Christ-Spirit (Interbeing) that lives and carries on with the fruit (karma) of my life. I "let go" and my consciousness returns, as it were, to the dynamic Spirit from which it arose. Can this make sense for Christians? This question represents one of several dividing lines between these two faiths that perhaps should not be resolved.

It is important, however, to recognize the source of this free-ranging speculation. We agree that we do not know what the future looks like or what lies on the other side of death. We speak out of a positive hope for the future in the light of the symbols of great traditions that have provided meaning for billions of people and still quicken the imagination. Given the inexhaustible marvel of creation, it seems unreasonable for either the Buddhist or the Christian ultimately to be pessimistic.

9.

Words vs. Silence in Spiritual Practice

Words prayed to a personal God play a central role in the spirituality of a companion of Jesus, and non-conceptual silence within an interconnecting Mystery does the same for a companion of Buddha. In this chapter we explore what Buddhists and Christians can learn from each other in their recognition that both words and silence are necessary.

A Buddhist Perspective: Paul

On the question of the role of words in spiritual practice, I think it is fair to say that for Buddhists, silence always has the last word—and very often the first. Buddhism is based on Gautama's original experience—an experience passed on through the centuries—of awakening. And to be awakened (or to start the process thereof) is, as we have heard frequently in these pages, to be the recipient of an experience that is as *real* as it is *ineffable*. *Ineffable* is from the Latin *in-effabile*, literally "not speakable." And if it is not speakable, that's because it is "not thinkable." For Gautama and all his followers, Buddhism begins with a "Wow!" experience immediately followed by "What the heck was that?"

Something undeniable, something absolutely real, happens, or starts to happen, in us. But because of the way it feels, or because of what it does to us, we know, from the start, that we can never figure out just what it is. We sense that it is utterly real, definitely true, but at the same time, utterly mysterious, not graspable, not "pin-down-able." Or it is so beautiful and powerful that it constantly gets beyond us, always seems out of reach. It so deeply and thoroughly affects our feeling that it eludes our thinking. Buddhists would certainly affirm Paul Tillich's description of ultimate reality as "infinitely apprehensible, yet never entirely comprehensible."[1]

Therefore, one of the most salient Buddhist virtues is what we might call verbal humility. Or, they are verbally diffident. They are wary of words, knowing that although words may be unavoidable, they are usually inappropriate and always inadequate. This is simply because the more the experience of awakening begins to dawn and become real, the more we will feel that it comes out of and leads back to silence. Silence—that space beyond words and beyond thoughts—is felt as the abode of awakening, the birth room and the living room of the consciousness of Emptiness or Interbeing.

What the Buddhists are attesting to isn't anything different from what Christian or Western theologians and philosophers have also, in their better moments, recognized. Saint Thomas Aquinas tells us that "the divine substance surpasses every form that our intellect reaches."[2] Saint Augustine is more direct and demanding: "If you think you understand God, it is not God."[3] And Ludwig Wittgenstein, from his more contemporary and philosophical perch, draws this conclusion: "Whereof one cannot speak, thereof one must be silent."[4]

To wake up we have to shut up. This primacy of silence, or this verbal diffidence, is based on two Buddhist teachings that we've already heard a good bit about. One is more *philosophical*, the other, *psychological*. Philosophically, especially for Mahayana Buddhists, reality or the world that we are living in is made up of two different but vitally intertwined aspects: the Ultimate (or Emptiness) and the relative (or forms). The Ultimate is what is going on, but it is going on *in* and *through* and *as* all the forms—something like the electricity that becomes manifest when it

---

[1] Paul Tillich. *What Is Religion?* (New York: Harper-Collins, 1973), 15.

[2] *Summa contra Gentiles* 1.14.3; *De Causis* 6.

[3] *De Vera Religione* 36.67.

[4] *Tractatus Logico-Philosophicus* 7.

lights up a bulb. What we are seeing is the electrified bulb, not the electricity in itself. Through the forms we know the Ultimate, but we never know the Ultimate fully. All of our knowledge that comes through the forms of language or thoughts is *relative,* or inadequate, limited.

But according to Buddhist psychology, not only is all our knowledge through forms inadequate, it is also *mischievous.* This is the Buddhist teaching on ignorance. Our ignorance—our failure to "get it" or to understand correctly—arises out of our built-in and inherited (through karma) tendency to take our thoughts and our words too seriously, or better, too absolutely. We keep assuming that our thoughts about ourselves, or our feelings about others, or our spontaneous reactions to particular situations are telling us what is really going on. They're not! To wake up to what is truly going on, we have to move beyond our thoughts and feelings to the Interbeing or spacious Emptiness that is their source and reality. Now, if this is what we humans-caught-in-ignorance are doing with all the passing people and events of our daily lives, this is also what we find ourselves doing when it comes to trying to understand the Ultimate or the Divine. In Buddhist terms, we *cling* to our religious words and ideas. In Christian terms, we turn them into *idols.*

Therefore, throughout Buddhist scriptures we find constant warning signs about language. There's the one we have already heard: Don't confuse the finger pointing to the moon with the moon itself. Even more demanding, words are rafts that are meant to help us get to the other, enlightened side of the river. Once we arrive, we are to throw away the raft. Most drastically of all, Zen Buddhists scandalize us in suggesting that, once we've awakened, if we meet the Buddha, we are better off killing him. His words and teachings, evidently, will only get in the way.

What I believe these Buddhist admonitions are suggesting to Christians is that if we want to arrive at Enlightenment and wake up to the reality of the Divine, we are going to have to find some way, some method or procedure, by which we turn off the open faucet of our thinking in order to allow the divine Interbeing to seep in by osmosis. Or to change images, Buddhists are telling Christians that if our destination is to know and experience God, then there is no way to get there from here. If we try to go the usual way, by land with our normal ways of traveling, we will never get there. We have to go, as it were, by air—by a very different way of traveling or navigating that leaves the solid earth of words and ideas behind.

So, if we want to wake up, we have to shut up.

The sacrament of silence. Silence, therefore, plays a central, necessary role for most Buddhist practices. The differing schools of Buddhism offer a panoply of diverse methods of meditation, all of them geared to help us shut out our usual, discursive way of knowing and experiencing. All of them, in one way or another, are aids to enable us to turn off the spigot of our usual way of thinking and apprehending. Meditation is for Buddhists a "silencer."

For Christians this suggests that the silence that is practiced in meditation is for Buddhists what Christians might call a sacrament. The traditional definition of *sacrament* is "an outward sign that produces grace." And the different sacramental signs, theologians explain, consist of both *matter* (a gesture like breaking bread or pouring water) and *form* (words to explain the gesture). More simply and less theologically, a sacrament is a symbolic activity by which we feel the abiding and loving presence of God's Spirit. Now, for Buddhists that's a basic description of the practice of silence in meditation, with one big difference. There's the element of *matter*: usually a very particular way of sitting, of holding your hands, of setting your gaze, and especially of watching your breath. As the Zen Buddhists put it, you sit, just sit. But—and here's the difference—for this Buddhist sacrament of silence, there is no *form*—no words, no thoughts, no commentary.

This, I believe, is what Buddhists can remind Christians of: We need a sacrament different from all our other sacraments— a sacrament, or an outward practice, that will enable us to get beyond words and thinking. If we don't have such a sacrament— that is, such a regular practice of silence—our spirituality may be missing something very helpful, maybe something essential. Buddhists are suggesting to Christians that they need to add to their sacramental repertoire the sacrament of silence. This is a sacrament you don't have to go to church to receive (although I would guess that most church services would be greatly enhanced if they made greater use of the sacrament of silence).

Silence needs words—words need silence. But as far as I can judge, although Buddhists urge us to throw away our rafts or even to kill the Buddha, they never do. For most Buddhists words continue to play an important role, maybe an essential role. But it's a very precisely defined essential role. Buddhists use language as a helpful—again, perhaps necessary—tool for *getting beyond language.* It's akin to the old adage that one has to use fire to fight fire. Buddhists use language to extinguish language. Or we might say that they use language in such a way that finally the meaning of the language is there but the language has disappeared.

This is very clear in the way the Rinzai school of Zen uses *koans.* These are questions or impossible thought experiments that lead to dead ends: What is the sound of one hand clapping? What did you look like before your parents conceived you? Under the guidance of a teacher, *koans* are persistently practiced until, as it were, the student crashes into the dead end of words and thoughts so hard and with such force that he or she breaks through; the wall gives way. Or to shift the metaphor, *koans* have been described as little dynamite sticks that we implant into our discursive, empirical way of thinking that blasts it away into another level of awareness or perception.

A similar way of using words or images in order to break beyond words and images is found in the visualization practices of the form of Tibetan Buddhism that I follow. In our meditations we are instructed to visualize in front of us, in concrete particular details, a benefactor—someone who, throughout our lives or in just one particular moment, has really loved us, reached out to us, affirmed us, and so recognized our goodness and potential. Such a benefactor can be a particular person in our lives (for me, the Italian woman across the street who loved to cook wonderful pasta meals for me and my brother), or it can be a spiritual benefactor like Gautama or Jesus or Tara or Mary. The point is to feel this particular expression of love so deeply and vibrantly that we come to the point of realizing that what we feel transcends this particular expression of it.

At that point we are instructed to let go of the visualized image. The visualization becomes so intense, so real that, as it were, it burns off. It so pervades and embraces us that there is a fusion between the representation and ourselves. We become the Buddha. We become the Christ. So we visualize in order to get, not beyond, but *within* the visualization to the point where the visualization drops away. And we become it. With Saint Paul we might find ourselves exclaiming, "It is no longer I who live, but it is Christ who lives in me" (Gal 2:20).

An abiding difference? Word centered vs. silence centered? But in the end, is there an abiding difference, even a contradiction, between Buddhism and Christianity? After all, Christianity, along with Judaism and Islam, is a religion of the Book. Words play an essential, abiding role in these religions. Christians even go so far as to announce that God is Word *(Logos),* and then to proclaim that this God/Word has been enfleshed in the form of Jesus of Nazareth. Like Jews and Muslims, Christians have come to believe that the words their early communities used and eventually wrote down to communicate their early experiences of God's Word are sacred texts. The enfleshed, incarnate Word of God in Jesus and these written words bear a meaning that has to be treasured, preserved, and yes, shared with others.

In the Buddhist-Christian dialogue that we are carrying on in this book, Buddhists, I think, might understand and accept these Christian convictions about their sacred words—but with one big proviso:

> You Christians can and should continue to hold your words as necessary—as long as you also recognize that they are *as dangerous* as they are *necessary.* You can hold your words to be precious—as long as you don't *cling to them,* or *absolutize them.* As soon as you absolutize your words—including Jesus as God's Word—as soon as you make these words the *only,* or the *exclusive,* or the *final* words about God, or as soon as you forget that "the Father is greater than I," you have dangerously turned your words into idols.

So yes, for Buddhists, Christians may have good reason to hold on to their words, especially the Word of God made flesh in Jesus. But unless all these words, including the Word of God in Jesus, are held in the container of silence, they are not serving their purpose.

A Christian Response: Roger

It seems to me, Paul, that this subject matter of the connectedness with ultimate reality in spiritual practice as you lay it out once again brings to the surface some differences between a Christian and Buddhist imagination. But if they are acknowledged, they still leave room for a conversation in which the two parties can say yes to each other. To do this I set up a distinction that allows me to sort out the differences and analogies.

Two distinctions. Two distinctions lie behind this response. The first lies between epistemology and metaphysics. Epistemology reflects on what we know and how we know it. It is a complex, critical philosophical discipline about kinds of knowledge, methods of knowing, and estimates of what we really know. I use the term *metaphysics* very broadly at this point to indicate an understanding of the way things are beneath their appearances to our knowing awareness. This is also a critical and sometimes speculative way of thinking that tries to cut through *mere appearance* to *reality.* I use these terms simply to indicate two different but overlapping spheres of reference.

The other distinction notices the difference between spirituality and spiritual practice. In Chapter 1, I spoke of spirituality as distinct from spiritual practices. Spirituality refers to the way the whole of one's life defines one's relation to ultimate reality or God. A spiritual practice such as meditation is one component of this, but not the whole of it.

Apophaticism. The Buddhist emphasis on silence draws attention to the realism of Christian apophaticism: We do not know what God is (Aquinas). The Christian tradition of spiritual practices such as meditation or centering prayer resonates with Buddhist silence. It reflects a theological tradition that emphasizes the transcendence of God by a dialectical three-dimensional process: One affirms something of God, radically denies its correspondence to God's transcendent reality, and only then admits that it orients one toward God "as a finger pointing to the moon." The negative dialectic, that is, the point and counterpoint, functions more or less sharply with different sensibilities, but the mystics are generally humble in their assertions.

Spiritual practice and everyday life in the world. Spiritual practice, however, should not exhaust the entire range of spirituality lest people fail to recognize the spiritual value of ordinary life. When the range of the spiritual is viewed as comprehensive, a new polarity appears that is different from "words/silence," namely, "silence/action." This tension operates largely in the metaphysical sphere, not without epistemological relevance, but always accompanied by this question: What unites us with ultimate reality, our words, our silence, or our concrete worldly behavior? This is a question of emphasis and not exclusion. In the gospel tradition of "you will know them by their fruits" (Mt 7:16), people's self-disposition and existence are constituted by the sum total of their intentional behavior. Ignatius Loyola noted that love displays itself in deeds rather than words; I would add silence. We will be more solidly united with transcendent Emptiness and Interbeing by what we do than by periods of silence that are isolated from the moral commitments and decisions that make up our active life in the world.

A Christian Perspective: Roger

How are we to understand the relation of silence and speaking in Christian spirituality? Why does attention to God elicit these two very different reactions? In this first response to the question I illuminate a Christian perspective rather than enter into a comparison between Christianity and Buddhism. But along the way I highlight aspects that are considerably different than Buddhist spirituality and others that appear congruent with it. I want to maintain the narrow focus on being silent and being vocal and not to stray into the tension between contemplation and action, which in turn can be associated with a passive and an active dimension of a relationship with God. I want to concentrate on the tension within Christian spirituality between an apophaticism that is lost for words before transcendent Mystery and a cataphaticism that, convinced that faith entails real knowledge of God, speaks fluently of and to God. How should we understand the relation between what appears to be a necessary silence before the abyss of being and prayers of praise and petition to a personal God?

A general description of Christian spirituality. The first chapter spoke of the conception of spirituality that underlies the

Christian side of this dialogue. Some of its qualities should be recalled at this point. Spirituality refers to the way people lead their lives in relation to ultimate reality. This makes Christian spirituality the way people who encounter God in and through Jesus of Nazareth live out that relationship. Christian spirituality transpires as a conscious engagement with a personal God represented by the mediation of Jesus. The Christian is a follower of Jesus in living out a relationship with God. Being in relationship with God who is *personal* envelops the whole of a person's life.

The personal character of ultimate reality has to mark a major difference between Christian and Buddhist spirituality. A person has intelligence and a will; a person acts with intention and purpose. Being in relation to God as personal includes taking into account aspects of God that correlate with intention and will. In other words, being related to God is complex and cannot be reduced to a form of absorption into God. Since God is personal, being in relation to God is interpersonal; it involves not just what God can do for me but also what God expects of me. From one perspective the relationship to a personal ultimate reality will strongly differentiate Christianity from Buddhism. Yet from another perspective God is not *a* person, a big individual standing outside and alongside the universe. *God* also refers to the absolutely mysterious yet immanent ground of being that an apophatic spirituality recognizes *cannot be encompassed in language*. Thus, while the significance of ultimate reality being a personal God has to be underlined because it will mark a major difference relative to Buddhism, it may not be as radical a difference as it may at first seem.

The deep structure of encountering God. The route to some understanding of the relation between silence and speaking about God must pass through a description of what an encounter with God entails. All conceptions of ultimate reality, by definition, are mediated through some agent or symbol that opens up an experience of transcendence and lends qualities to what is experienced. All human experiences engage the concrete world in a particular time and place, and people formulate their conceptions through that present moment of experience. The full import of what is encountered bears a connection with the mediation and the context of the encounter. What is experienced is transcendent, but how it is experienced is always limited by the particular medium and its situation. This applies directly to the encounter of God in Jesus of Nazareth. The mediation of God through Jesus creates a tensive polarity between the transcendence of God and the immanence of God that underlies all Christian spirituality.

Working within this framework one can notice two sequences of elements in an encounter with God in Jesus that point simultaneously to a recognition of God's absolute transcendence and an experience of God's immanence. Beginning with God's transcendence, the following sequence points in the direction of God's absolute mystery: Jesus represents God; a person encounters or experiences God's presence in Jesus; the God so encountered is absolutely transcendent and experienced in awe; no words can circumscribe the transcendence of God. Each of these four points is important.

First, Jesus is the medium of a Christian's experience of God. A person may well have some notion of God before meeting Jesus. But Christian faith allows Jesus to determine the character of one's idea of God. Second, correlative to Jesus representing God, the Christian experiences God in Jesus's ministry and person, often through the mediation of the Gospels and then the church, whose role is to preserve Jesus's memory and ministry. This exemplifies the process by which the content assigned to God also comes from other mediating sources. But, third, what should be emphasized here is the tension between two dimensions of the experience: Jesus, the *finite* human person, directs the imagination to the *transcendent* reality of God. Jesus himself is presented in the Gospels as opening up a sense of awe at something sacred that empowers him and affects other people. This remains constant in the tradition. Fourth, this dimension of what is encountered in Jesus means that no words can keep up with the transcendent character of who is revealed. The transcendence of God means precisely that all words fall short of the God who is encountered in Jesus. Jesus introduces people into absolute Mystery.

By contrast, the following sequence illustrates God's *immanence* and *presence:* Jesus represents God; a person encounters or experiences God's presence in Jesus; God so encountered is made present and experienced as a power that affects human subjectivity and a light that illumines a new dimension of all reality; this generates effusive speech that describes reality as newly perceived by the light of God's presence. Each of these four points is important.

The first two points correspond with what was said above. But the third point introduces a different dimension of the encounter with God in Jesus. Jesus precisely draws attention to the *immanence* of God within his ministry. The awesome and sacred power that operates through him is concretely experienced; it is present and effective. Divine presence refers to the actual presence of God that transforms consciousness of the world and reality itself. As a result, fourth, tongues are loosened and people cannot stop talking about all the things that are now understood in a new transcendent light.

These two experiences do not relate to each other in a mutually exclusive either/or; both are present in an encounter of ultimate reality. Their co-penetration opens up the possibility of describing the relationship between silence and words in spirituality.

The relation of silence and words. Both silence and words give expression to spiritual encounter; they are not antithetically related to each other but reciprocally interact to form an integral experience. On the one hand, words proceed from silence. Silence here refers to the inner depths of the human subject. An encounter with transcendence cannot be confused with an empirical recognition, with perception stimulated by the external surface of reality. It occurs in a quiet space in human subjectivity. Words come from the surface, but recognition of transcendence comes from a region deep down within.[5] On the other hand, words bring silent encounter to the surface of objectivity, form, and meaning. Silent encounter must refer to something. Intentional silence refers to something beyond the self, and it correlates with some transcendent reality.

Whereas the human subject recognizes transcendence in silence, the content of transcendence is identified (but not circumscribed) by words. Silent encounter is the dimension in

---

[5] This description helps to explain the function of a religious symbol or sacrament. It does not communicate literal information or empirical effect, but it mediates an inner encounter that carries transcendent meaning.

experience that makes words surpass themselves in meaning. Words point transcendent encounter toward an object. Silence without words has no object. Without symbolic and mystagogical words, silent encounter would be an empty encounter with or of oneself. Words give shape to an otherwise diffuse, vague, and effectively blind consciousness and direct it toward its object. Of itself, silent encounter has no referent beyond the self. Language partners with experience to mediate awareness of the other. The experience of transcendence or ultimacy, therefore, has to be deciphered. Even the term *God* is a product of interpretation for oneself and for others, because it can mean practically anything in the imaginations of different people. The mediation that points to transcendence and the words it suggests provide the clues for that interpretation.

Therefore, Christian spirituality always involves a tension in its relationship with God. On the one hand, words never replace or supersede preverbal and silent presence of the human self to itself and to God within the self. An ounce of reflection makes it clear that the authentic words of spirituality have to be elicited from an awed reverence for God's absolute mystery and recognition that no human words can adequately comprehend God. Silence defines the embracing context for hesitant but meaningful speech about God. On the other hand, silence gives way to traditional forms of spiritual language. Silence is always called out of itself by words that interpret what is encountered in the depth of one's being. These words give form and reference to the full panoply of the world now illuminated by a new light of transcendence.

The relation with God in words. Jesus received from his tradition a faith in a personal God. He lived for the rule of this God. Faith in ultimate reality mediated through Jesus relates his followers to God as personal. Christian spirituality guides a person to the transcendent God not as a person but nonetheless as personal.

When Christian faith and spirituality take the form of speech, the language goes beyond describing God in various metaphors and symbols. Because the Christian enters a relationship to a God who is personal, the relationship easily slides into the form of direct address and a conversation. Meditation on the transcendent reality of God becomes speech that takes the form of prayer directed toward God and an attention to God that looks for a response. Reaching back into the Jewish tradition, this prayerful address to God has traditionally taken two forms, among others: praise and petition. *Benedictus benedicat*—May the blessed One bless us.

God as source of being elicits praise and thanksgiving. The creation theology elaborated in the previous chapter posits God as creator of heaven and earth. This means that along with all reality each person's own personal and reflective being has its source in the direct creative action of God. This recognition transforms self-love into a sense of gratitude toward God for the gift of one's own being. Recognition of absolute dependence on God should become a fundamental moral disposition of gratitude to God for God's continual presence and affirming acceptance. As a Christian I ask whether gratitude for being requires a gift giver. For me this is a real question. Can one have a sense of gratitude, in this case for one's being, without evoking a sense of an intentional benefactor to whom one is beholden?

Out of one's dependence in being and in an encounter with God as the continual source of one's being, human need tends to reach out to God in petition for what the fulfillment of life requires. Of course, God does not relate to creation as a finite actor, and God does not respond to human beings as an agent within the system of nature's workings. Nevertheless, the spontaneous way of expressing an absolute dependence on the personal power of being easily takes the form of a transparent request for the sustenance of one's own being.

To sum up this reflection, Christian spirituality lived before the ultimate reality of God contains polarities and tensions. Even though God is personal, the recognition of God's transcendence cautions against naive conceptions of interaction with God. The idea of God as a person interacting with another individual person does not adequately describe the relationship of God with human beings. God is transcendent and cannot be subsumed into an anthropomorphically conceived interpersonal relationship. Even in our most intimate encounters with God as personal, there is room for apophatic reserve and even silence. In this silence before the face of absolute mystery Buddhists and Christians can meet.

A Buddhist Response: Paul

I'm happy, but not surprised, to hear you state that the Christian notion of a personal God marks a "major difference relative to Buddhism" but perhaps not a "radical" difference. You recognize quite pointedly that Christians can—or should—share Buddhist reservations about imaging ultimate reality as a person: "The idea of God as a person interacting with another individual does not adequately describe the relationship of God with human beings." So the question that you explore is how Christians "interact" in their spiritual practice with "the transcendent God not as a person but nonetheless as personal."

I appreciate your advice, but I think that Buddhism can help you make it even more theologically coherent and personally satisfying for many contemporary Christians. I suspect that you may have not gone far enough in drawing out the implications of a "not-person God" for Christian spirituality.

In the way you affirm prayer as a "direct address and a conversation" in which Christians make requests of, give praise and gratitude to, and try to discern the expectations of God, such Christians are still relating to God *as a person*. You remind us that "God does not respond to human beings as an agent," but it sure looks and feels that way. And that's the problem that I, and I think a good number of Christians I know, have with asking God for favors or figuring out God's will.

In my Buddhist-Christian practice I don't pray to, or give praise to, the interconnecting Mystery I call God. I just sit in the presence of Mystery in *openness,* in *trust,* and often in *gratitude.* I don't ask for anything. I just sit in trusting openness to what one Tibetan teacher calls "the blessings that are always pouring forth."[6] And I trust that this Mystery, this all embracing-Spaciousness, holds me in what my teachers term "unconfined compassion" or "love essence."[7] And there comes a point in every meditation where I am instructed to let all these

---

[6] Nyoshul Khenpo, cited by my teacher John Makransky in *Awakening through Love: Unveiling Your Deepest Goodness* (Somerville, MA: Wisdom Publications, 2007), 15.

[7] Tsoknyi Rinpoche, *Open Heart, Open Mind: Awakening the Power of Essence Love* (New York: Harmony Books, 2012), 60–64.

words and images fall away—moments when there is, as you put it, not only "room for apophatic reserve and even silence," but there is a need, a necessity for silence. It is similar to what Paul Tillich describes as prayer or meditation in which we simply accept acceptance, even though we cannot say—indeed, it may be necessary *not* to say—what it is that is accepting us.[8]

I'm not saying that this is the way one must pray. But I am saying that is a way in which one can pray. And for many Christians who cannot help but feel uneasy in asking favors of God or in giving God worship and praise, this is a more comfortable and a more profitable way of relating to the mystery we call God. Maybe this is the only way they can pray.

Yet, if they are Christians who gather to sing and remember and celebrate Eucharist, words will be unavoidable. As I tried to explain in my statement, there are forms of Buddhism that recognize the necessity of words. These words—whether in visualizations or in chanting—are to be used with gusto. But all these words are not to be clung to; at some point they need to be set aside and recognized for what they are, that is, pointing fingers and not the moon. As you said, Roger, only when words come out of and lead back to silence are they doing their job in spiritual practice.

It Seems to Us

This chapter and the next draw us into classic polarities characteristic of a conscious relationship with ultimate reality. In the next chapter we look at the contrast between an internal appropriation of faith and active response. Here we have talked about the impulse to silence in the face of transcendence and the reflex to decipher or articulate and express what has been encountered in words or some other external form. We have compounded the abstract tension by comparing how it appears in, broadly speaking, Buddhist and Christian experience.

This conversation has to be situated in the larger context of spirituality that encompasses the whole of one's life. We are

---

[8] Paul Tillich, "You Are Accepted," in *The Shaking of the Foundations* (New York: Charles Scribner's Sons, 1948), chap. 19.

talking about how one remains in touch with what is supremely important in life. There are innumerable ways of imagining and actualizing "contact" with what ultimately grounds reality and thus one's own being. One cannot maintain such a spirituality without cultivating it. One must deploy some form of practice that formally embodies the deep meaning-giving quality of one's being and acting. Here we want to sum up how we see the complementary character of silence and speaking in spirituality.

Our conversation has arrived at a simple summary. First, we try to decide what we mean by *silence* and *words* and show how they entail each other. Then we note how following Buddha seems to favor silence and following Jesus seems to favor words. But the two can be blended in a variety of practices. Then we reach some tentative conclusions in what each faith can teach the other.

The meaning of silence and words. We feel that we have to get to a denser meaning of these iconic symbols than a contrast between no talk and garrulousness. When these terms are transferred into the sphere of spirituality they take on deeper meaning. Silence is not just non-speech or a negation of mental activity. It points to a being present to reality within the self at a level that is prior to, or at least more penetrating than, objectifying language. It is not passivity but an activity. Silence is not inert. Silence represents a kind of "dwelling in" that transpires within consciousness in a lucidity or immediacy that results from clearing away extraneous mental activity that entertains "objects." Silence can be imagined as a being present to or a being within that which, within the self, is so much larger than the self that it holds the self in being.

Words in the context of spiritual consciousness go far beyond the ordinary speech used to communicate information. Spiritual words originate in spiritual experience and refer back to it. Spiritual words can only communicate spiritual matters when they appear within a spiritual context defined by interiority, importance, depth, ultimacy, and transcendence. Sometimes spiritual words appear as something stimulated by an inner encounter or as response to a silent spiritual experience. But sometimes spiritual words may introduce a person into a sphere of reverent silence, to a place where words fail. Words seem much more active than silence: they are used to interrogate, name, interpret, and analyze. We mistakenly tend to think of silence as passive compared to the activity of formulating words to give expression to internal experiences. But sometimes words are spontaneously given to us from within. Our words are always inadequate carriers of a silent inner encounter.

Non-dual interdependence of silence and word. We have been thinking tensively and contrastively about a spiritual life with two foci or centering points that define an ellipse with a variety of uneven shapes. An imperfect oval can be fatter at either end; spiritual practice and spiritual life may lean toward silence or expression with words. We are so convinced that silence and linguistic form have to be held together that we want to go beyond linking them by alternating practices. Contemplative silence and a more active linguistic interpretation seem like alternative responses. They stimulate each other in an alternating rhythm: now silent reverence, now verbal prayer or interpretation of what is encountered in silence; now passive letting be and now active assertion and communication with others. Each element has a value, and they enhance each other by interacting. But we think that there may be a more penetrating and non-dual formula for combining these sometimes very different dimensions of a single spiritual life. Thus we propose a maxim that shows how words need silence and silence needs words: *Words without silent encounter are empty; silent encounter without words has no object and fails the community.*

This maxim may not be obvious on the reading, but a little reflection brings out the interrelatedness and mutual dependency of these dimensions of an integral spirituality. It is evident that prayer that is recited in a mechanically rote way, doctrines that express theorems that are not understood let alone subjectively appropriated, inattentive ritual observance, and so on have no more value than any other secular participatory event. They do not in themselves unite persons with ultimacy. They are empty of strictly spiritual value. And, reciprocally, silent encounter requires a more or less explicit framework of reflective intelligibility for it to yield its fruit. What is one doing in the very practice of meditation? People who meditate know very well what they are doing. And looking forward, the deepest encounter of mindfulness that does not flow out into some bodily or external expression, far from uniting people with ultimate reality and a living community, may alienate them from what should actually bind people together.

The point here is to distinguish in order to unite in a complementary and inseparable way, to show the mutual inclusion of these seemingly opposite tendencies. Silence and words are not alternating responses; rather, they are distinguishable dimensions of a single non-dual encounter with absolute transcendence. Either one may become a path of focused attention, but the other can never be left behind or completely transcended.

Buddhism favors silence; Christianity, words. These generalizations are frequently useless and misleading in their oversimplification and implied opposition. We imply no exclusion or negation here but only set out a framework for conversation. A place to situate Buddhist silence is in the practice of meditation. Many techniques, such as concentration on rhythmic breathing, aim at drawing conscious awareness away from many things into the focal point of the being of my being. Inside a person the gerund *being* indicates an actualized silent self-presence within the greater power of being itself, Interbeing. Distractions, the many words of human life, are put aside for the moment. Consciousness penetrates to the point where it becomes aware of my being as the power of being itself within me and around me. Meditation involves technique, but it is meant to lead consciousness to the stillness of being present within what Rudolf Otto, the phenomenologist of religious experience, called the mystery of being in its awesome attractiveness *(tremendum et fascinans)*.[9]

The history of Christian mysticism attests that Buddhists are not the only ones who meditate. But if meditation is formally Christian, the ultimate reality that is found within is recognized as personal. The personal character of this ground of being spontaneously invites verbal communication. Hence the long tradition of Jewish and Christian prayer. Prayer is not necessarily verbal, but encounter with a personal God decidedly tends in that direction. Whether God is imagined as out there, within, or all encompassing, the awesomely attractive One invites communication and dialogue.

---

[9] Rudolf Otto analyzes the dimensions of "mystery" experienced as "awesome power" and "attractive love" in *The Idea of the Holy* (New York: Oxford University Press, 1958), 13–40.

The nonexclusive character of these two families of spirituality can be illustrated in various examples of how they can be combined. Christians who enter into contemplations on the ministry of Jesus of Nazareth can fit them into the framework of various methods of Buddhist meditation. The icon of Jesus's ministry as it is presented in a given story in the Gospels can function like a *koan* in Buddhist meditation to fix the imagination so that it may penetrate to the divine manifestation in Jesus. Another example is found in centering prayer, a Christian method for finding God within the deepest self, which incorporates techniques that are analogous to formal Buddhist practices.

Learning from each other. These traditions of apophaticism and cataphaticism, which run deep in Christian spirituality, are not absent from Buddhism. So what these broad schools of spirituality might teach each other comes down to matters of emphasis. What can Christianity contribute to Buddhist spirituality and vice versa?

Christian spirituality of vocal prayer, instruction, commandment, and shared ritual practices show that deep internal contact with God cannot be a basis of community without these external bonds. The intimate contact with ultimate reality that resonates so deeply in a person's experience has a tendency to share itself with others, and that reveals a need to be supported by others. And this can only happen on the basis of various kinds of words that express silent encounter and rituals that enable a uniting shared experience. Without various media of communication there can be no Sangha or community.

The intense practice of Buddhist meditation that aims toward inner enlightenment typifies Buddhist practice. It reminds Christians that, in the internal-external tension of integral human experience, the forms of religion have life-giving power only when they are rooted in internal spiritual encounter. Christian spirituality constantly has to fight against the flattening out of spiritual life into a series of external practices mechanically performed. Silent encounter is the ultimate source of Christian life.

10.

To Attain Peace, Work for Justice

The theme of transforming the world brings out clearly the shared predilection for an activist spirituality that motivates these conversations. Where do Buddhists and Christians find the resources for spiritual depth that incorporates prophecy and action? We discuss how the traditions look to Buddha and Jesus to combine mysticism and prophetic criticism.

A Christian Perspective: Roger

Only in varying degrees do practicing Christians in developed Western societies recognize an intrinsic connection between their spirituality and social justice. It is important to take account of the extent, depth, and rationale of this individualist bias. Technologically advanced Western culture is largely urban and impersonal compared with the rural village. The overcrowded anonymity of the city dulls a sense of human solidarity. The pluralistic city has separated spirituality from moral conformity, and people tend to deride shallow moralizing. Peaceful religious pluralism in society must pay the price of accepting that the spiritual defines an internal sphere of being in relation to God. Nothing is more private than that inner place that defines our being; no external pressure or political coercion can reach it. This results in an internalization of social and cultural individualism into the very structure of spirituality. This structure has, in turn, released spirituality from religion. If someone from any religion wants to maintain that social problems have a bearing on our spirituality, that person will have to make the case in a way that changes the counterintuitive into common sense. What can an isolated individual do about social injustice? The pervasiveness of this individualist culture means that concern and action for social justice largely remain external and optional adjuncts to spirituality, no matter how cogent the insistence against such a view.

Much of this description of an individualist culture reflects those members of society who are financially comfortable. The poor tend to better appreciate social solidarity. This reflection addresses bourgeois culture on behalf of many groups subjected to prejudice. How does one show that situations of social injustice engage everyone, that the condition of others exerts moral, spiritual, and religious pressure on every individual? The following reflection begins with a set of presuppositions to which we assume most would agree. It then presents two basic points that add up to a straightforward response to the question. It ends by situating social concern within Christian spirituality.

Some suppositions about the human condition. The tendency to accept the world as one finds it, as an immovable status quo, sets up resistance to social change. Yet, with reflection, all will agree that objective social structures that are unjust, because they discriminate against particular groups, exist. Most will also concede that social structures depend on human support and can be changed. In fact, they are always being adjusted. But they can also be radically altered by intentional action as, for example, when lawmakers address them.

Most will also agree that human beings perform a moral act when they take a position on social issues. This can be shown by examples. The Holocaust and the anti-Semitism that supported it are commonly considered morally depraved. The structural social relations that supported Jim Crow laws elicit moral outrage. The practice of lynching is now considered repugnant. One cannot attend to such social structures and policies without a moral reaction. These examples show that seemingly objective social situations of injustice are not purely objective; they depend on human wills. But this also makes an individual's deliberate response to them a moral act. Not to respond is also a moral act. To the extent that people are socially aware, therefore, they are intrinsically and morally implicated in society, not by individual responsibility for the conditions in place, but by the duty of personal social participation. Even if we prescind from the moral correctness of a given policy or position and from the ability of any individual to act, still actual social solidarity makes radical individualism a spurious moral position.

A social conception of human existence in which one cannot adequately understand the human person as an individual apart from society provides a foundational premise to a spiritual concern for social justice. It also gives rise to the question of how this socially morality-laden condition affects a spiritual relation to God. What follows responds on the basis of two principles from Christian spirituality: the first asserts that every individual is socially constituted and exists in a double relationship to other people and to God; the second holds that in Christian spirituality love of neighbor *is* love of God.

The double relationship. These convictions lay the groundwork for appreciating the spiritual value of being in society and engaged in issues of social justice. Individualism fails to appreciate the social constitution of the individual human person. The basis of Christian spirituality in the face of social injustice lies in the fact that individuals are constituted by their relationships with other human beings and the world at every point of their existence. Human beings are "open subjects" wholly defined from within and from without by interactive relational forces. A grasp of how thoroughly each individual is socially constructed enables an appreciation of social responsibility.

The social sciences, together with the investigations of evolutionary biology, have taught us how the individual is socially constituted. We are born dependent, with a bio-identity that is given to us by our parents and ancestors. We learn from others over a relatively long period of time our speech, our social behavior patterns, and our values. As open subjects, constituted in conscious freedom to respond to the world, we acquire much of our identity by interaction with the world and other human beings. Historical and social consciousness has gradually affected the way we understand our personal selves.

This relational way of thinking has affected metaphysical and religious hopes. One cannot think of the destiny of the individual outside the circle of the species. A human being is a member of the human community. Therefore, a purely individual flourishing of personal being (salvation) is not possible without solidarity with all other human beings: individual fulfillment cannot be imagined without a connection with the history of all those who have suffered and died innocently. No isolated individual salvation is possible at the expense of others. The very hope for salvation for the individual requires an active concern for the well-being of other human beings, and the well-being of the many cannot be conceived without considering the actual conditions of particular groups.

In the Christian worldview the individual lives in a double relationship: to God and to the world of other persons and our common habitat. What one is as an individual has been socially constructed, so that one stands before God as a person in relation to the world and to other human beings. These forces and people help define who one is. Thus, how one stands before God is partly but intrinsically constituted by relationships to others. And from the perspective of God, we have to project that God relates to each individual as a God who is the creator and guarantor of the value of other human beings in the same manner that God relates to us. God's presence to each person thus releases a moral imperative to relate to those others as friends of God. God's relation to each person makes that person responsible to God for other persons.

To sum up this reflection in simple terms, all individuals are constituted by their social relationships and responsibilities. They carry their relationships with them as they stand before God. And God relates to each person as the God who loves "others" as well as each one.

Love of neighbor, personally and socially, is love of God. This is the second major principle that shows how concern for social justice forms an essential dimension of Christian spirituality. We can begin to understand this mutual entailment of love of God and love of neighbor with Jesus's acceptance of a common teaching of his day, namely, that love of God and love of neighbor together sum up the entire Jewish law (Mt 22:36–40). Considered objectively, love of God recapitulates the initial commandments of the Decalogue; love of neighbor gathers into one positive relationship all the forbidden ways of breaking this relationship as described by the other commandments. The two different loves are in parallel; God is not the neighbor, nor is the neighbor God.

But another way of looking at these two commandments appears from the perspective of the individual standing in an existential relationship before God. This is not an isolated individual, but the person seen in the previous section, constituted by bonds with other human beings and in a relationship with God along with others. The existential relationship collapses the two commandments into one complex relationship with God in solidarity with others. The quality of the relationship with God is measured by the quality of one's relationship with others. Jesus expanded the range of that relationship beyond kinship and other group boundaries. He taught that all, even the enemy, are our neighbors, so that tribally limited ethics should be transcended. He also taught that we should be neighbors actively and seek out those who need assistance (Lk 10:25–37).

This teaching reached a crescendo in the Johannine representation of Jesus's teaching where, in effect, it is said that love of neighbor is or constitutes love of God. The rationale for this is explained as follows: "Those who say, 'I love God,' and hate their brothers or sisters, are liars; for those who do not love a brother or sister whom they have seen, cannot love God whom they have not seen"(1 Jn 4:20). In the parable of the Last Judgment, Jesus said that caring for the poor, the hungry, the thirsty, and the needy was exactly the same as caring for him (Mt 25:31–46). In sum, the relationship of each person with God involves the whole of a person's life, especially his or her relationship to God's other friends. One's actual relationship with God's friends defines one's relationship with God. By an internal mutual implication, each one implying the other, love of neighbor *is* love of God and authentic love of God demands love of neighbor.

Response to social injustice measures the integrity of Christian spirituality. This assertion gains little traction in an individualist culture. Most people are so preoccupied with either themselves or their individual relationship with God that their peripheral vision is obscured. Social suffering is ignored either in itself or in its bearing on one's personal life. The following points cut through individualism to a spirituality of solidarity.

To begin, a pragmatic reflection says that without social justice there will be social unrest; as long as society has social injustice built into the public patterns of life, there can be no social peace. The lesson can be read off the surface of day-to-day history.

A society that is contrasted with one riddled with systemic inequalities need not be a "perfect" community in which all are happy in their social roles. It is more realistic simply to think of various measures of solidarity and concern for the common good. One can observe in some cultures that extended family membership places a social responsibility on all relatives. Personal self-identification does not cancel family membership; rather, the family unit supports individual identity by a social responsibility that reaches each member. With this model one can begin to imagine what a corporate concern for the common good might entail across expanded boundaries. In its vision of humanity Christianity projects the unity of the human family under God. It envisages respect for all and a concern for the common good that suffer when any group is marginalized or oppressed.

The first step of a Christian spirituality in the direction of internalizing such a vision requires breaking down any perception of an opposition between the two dimensions of one spiritual life, the one vertical in its relationship to God and the other horizontal in its relationship to other human beings, society, and the world. The tendency to contrast and oppose these two relationships distorts the single complex existence of an individual human being. Each person is simultaneously and inseparably related to God through other human beings and to society and others under the impulse of the rule of God.

To be a human being is to exist in social solidarity. Solidarity entails a person's formation by the community and responsibility to it. This reciprocity of human energy sustains individual human life. Logically speaking, one cannot think of oneself or of one's destiny outside of this framework. Without a concern for social justice individuals lack the grounds for hope for their own salvation. Individual salvation is not imaginable outside human community. In the end, the authenticity of Christian hope is measured by its appreciation of the value of others. Christian spirituality is by nature—that is, intrinsically—socially engaged.

Christian spirituality that is inattentive to this is in that measure inauthentic.

A Buddhist Response: Paul

In our reflections on the topic of this chapter, Roger, you and I take distinctly different but complementary approaches. You ask *why* spirituality must include a concern for social justice, while my question is *how* can it best do so.

The philosophical foundation to the way you answer your question is clear: It is our nature as *social beings* that grounds our concern for social justice. As a Buddhist I smiled happily at your very Buddhist description of our social nature: "Human beings are 'open subjects' wholly defined from within and from without by interactive relational forces." Roger, that's a Christian rendition of the Buddha's *anatta* or not-self teaching!

But I have found that Buddha's understanding of human nature is even more social than current Christian notions. Putting it perhaps a little too neatly, Western Christianity defines the human being as an individual who has to have social relations. Buddhism views the human being as a network of relationships that bring about an ever-changing individual. For Christianity, the individual is prior. For Buddhism, relationships are prior.

There are perhaps bigger—and also more helpful—differences that I, as a follower of Buddha, note in the way you seem to move from the notion that all humans are social beings to the conclusion that, therefore, all humans have to be concerned about social justice. You imply that when we regard a person who is suffering at the hands of others, our first and natural response as social beings will be "That's wrong" or "That's unjust."

Buddhists, I suggest, would hold that there is a prior natural response before "That's wrong." It would be something like: "How can I help? How can I alleviate your suffering?" In other words, Buddhists would say that the "natural" primary reaction to the state of suffering in a fellow sentient being is compassion—a call to extend compassion rather than a call to create justice. The need for justice follows, or arises out of, the feeling of compassion. Justice, for Buddhists, would be a way of implementing compassion. We'll explore what that means in the next chapter.

Finally, you offer a theological foundation for the essential link between spirituality and social engagement. This is the clear teaching of Jesus, expanded by John, about the *identity* between love of neighbor and love of God. This is about as clear and strong a non-dualistic teaching as you can find in the Bible: To love one's fellow human *is* to love God. Buddhists go all the way and affirm that there is no actual difference between loving neighbor and loving God, that love of neighbor and love of God are just one differently identified activity. That is because, as Buddhism teaches, the reality of God/Interbeing and the reality of finite beings are *one differently identified reality*; the difference between God (Emptiness) and the world (form) is relatively real but not ultimately true. God and neighbor are *one non-dual reality*. So when we love our neighbor, we are really and truly loving God.

A Buddhist Perspective: Paul

Buddhists and Christians would give quite different (though not contradictory) answers to a question that generally overwhelms all of us: What do we humans have to do in order to have a more peaceful world?

The Christian response is well known, often appearing on Christian bumper stickers: *If you want peace, work for justice.* This crisp sentence is, we can say, the rallying cry of Christian liberation theologians and social-environmental activists. We have a job to do—as the Jews put it, the job of fixing the world. And the centerpiece of that job is justice.

This response, Christians claim, is based on sound social and political analysis; the root cause of social strife and violence is economic. Violence among groups is generally motivated by either greed or need. It is used either to impose the exploitation of some over others or to resist the exploitation of some over others. Violence is a weapon in the hands of either the exploiters in their greed to have ever more or the exploited in their need to defend or regain themselves. Which means that the root cause of conflict and violence is injustice.

If this analysis is basically correct, the remedy is clear: There can be no real, lasting peace without justice.

Buddhists would not deny this. But they would ask how to get rid of injustice. And their basic answer is that something has to change *in* us before we can change anything *outside* of ourselves. If our resolve and our efforts to remove injustice are not originating from a deeper source within ourselves than just the desire to "do justice," we are not going to be able to do the job. There has to be a transformation *within* us before we can effect a transformation *around* us.

So there's a Buddhist bumper sticker—formulated and made famous by Thich Nhat Hanh—that answers our big question: *To make peace you first have to be peace.* He is suggesting to Christians that if justice is a prerequisite for peace, there's a prerequisite for justice. To bring about the justice that is necessary for peace, we are going to have to have that peace already in our heart.

The priority of contemplation. But just what does Thich Nhat Hanh mean by being peace? Really, it's another, perhaps more practical way of describing enlightenment—or what happens to you when you begin the process of waking up. He is saying that a precondition for the very possibility of bringing about justice in your society is that you have begun the process of waking up to the reality of Interbeing. To be able to work for justice you need to be in touch with what in previous pages we have described as the groundless Ground of your Interbeing, the stable but ever-changing energy that constitutes and is the reality of everything.

Unless we have, at least to some incipient degree, begun to wake up and feel this reality, this groundless Ground, this inter-connecting Spirit, our efforts toward justice will fail, or at least they will not have the fruits that they could have or that we hoped they would have.

This means that if—as one hears throughout Christian tra-dition—both action and contemplation are necessary for any spirituality and for all efforts to try to "fix the world," then Buddhists will want to give *a certain priority* to contemplation. While you can't have one without the other, while both action and contemplation make up a moving circle in which each leads to the other, still, for Buddhists, contemplation serves as the en-trance point to the circle or provides the main energy that keeps the circle turning.

So even if Christians point out that we experience God through our actions for justice—or as the Jesuits put it, we can experience contemplation *in* action—the Buddhists will insist that such experience of God/Interbeing in social action cannot simply take the place of experiencing God/Interbeing in contemplation. The experiences of God that we have "in the streets" or "on our meditation cushions" are indeed experiences of the same God. But they are two different kinds of experience that cannot be melded into each other. The ability to meet God or realize Enlightenment on the streets does not dispense one from also trying to meet God on our cushions.

We're back to the need for silence that we spoke about in the previous chapter. Just as words, as necessary as they are, have to come forth from silence, so do our actions, as necessary as they are, have to come forth from contemplation.

Avoiding burnout and self-righteousness. What we have been talking about so far is, for both Christians and Buddhists, vitally important. But it is also a bit abstract. We can ask more practically: *Why* must we *be* peace if we are going to be able to *make* peace? *Why* must we begin the process of waking up if we are going to have any success in bringing about justice? My Buddhist teacher Lama John Makransky offers two reasons that resonate with my own experience and, I suspect, with the experience of many people engaged in the struggle for social and environmental justice: to avoid burnout and to avoid self-righteousness.

1. To avoid burn out. If we understand the job of working for justice as a task that goes beyond charity (though requiring charity), if we are committed to fixing the world and not just tinkering with it, if we not only want to give the starving man some fish to eat but we also want to teach him how to fish (which will probably also mean dealing with the people who are not allowing him to fish)—if this is how we understand the job of justice, then we are in for a long, difficult, and some would even say impossible haul.

Working for justice is not easy. We have to deal with all the social, political, legal, and economic structures that, to use our image, make it difficult or even impossible for people to fish, even when they already know how. We have to struggle against "city hall" and all the entrenched and powerful people who control it. To fix—not just tinker with—the world, to provide real cures and not just necessary Band-Aids, we have to follow the example not only of Mother Teresa but also of Martin Luther King, Jr. We not only have to love individuals, but we also have to change structures.

And this is why many people who have signed up for the job of justice so often find that they have to change jobs. They burn out. They break down. They run out of energy. They want to continue, but they simply can't.

It seems that we don't "have what it takes" to hang in there on the job of justice. To carry on, we need an energy or resource that goes beyond our own resources. We need an infusion of something we don't presently have—or we don't think we have.

This is the energy, Buddhists would say, that comes from waking up. Enlightenment, as we have described it, is awakening to a Bigger Picture that we are part of. Our self, our identity, is no longer our own. We are working with or as part of something much larger and more powerful than ourselves. It's the truth-power of the Dharma, the energy of what Buddha discovered. To begin to be enlightened is to begin to be Dharma-driven.

Buddhists have a name for individuals who are Dharma-driven. They're called bodhisattvas, people who have so connected with and been embraced by Wisdom that Compassion naturally and necessarily flows forth from their very being. And it is compassion that can drive them to work for justice. Compassion for the starving fisherman naturally or logically impels them to teach him how to fish better or to provide him with a boat.

To be Dharma-driven means that we work for justice not primarily because we believe that justice is possible (though that may be our belief) but because we have no choice. When we gain Wisdom (Wisdom, remember, describes what we realize when we wake up to Interbeing), we automatically and naturally also realize that working for justice out of compassion is as necessary as taking the next breath. To be alive is to breathe. To be enlightened is to work for justice out of compassion. One does not burn out from breathing.

To wake up to our Buddha nature, or our Interbeing, is to feel a call to act for justice that is, as it were, self-sustaining. It does not depend on achieving results or reaching—or even moving toward—our goal. Our actions for justice are ends in themselves. They are valuable in themselves, whether we reach our goal or not. The goal we want to arrive at is already, somehow, present in each step we try to take toward it.

2. To avoid self-righteousness. From a Buddhist perspective, working for justice can become obstructed not only when we run out of energy but also when we have too much of it.

What I mean by this is something that I have experienced in myself and in my fellow social activists, that is, that we agents of social justice are often so sure about what needs to be done, about which policies are causing the exploitation, about who the "bad guys" are. In our commitment to "speaking truth to power," we are sure that we have the truth and those in power don't. This is all part of the social analysis that is integral to the method of Christian liberation theology. It has to be done. But often it is done too quickly, too much according to script, too assuredly.

Buddhists would call such too hasty, too certain analysis "clinging to one's ego-thoughts." This is the ever-lurking danger, well identified by Buddhism, of how clinging to our ego leads us to cling to and so to absolutize our own ideas and programs. I suspect that most people involved in social activism know what I'm talking about. We become so certain of our own analysis and our own programs that we end up not listening to others and missing better opportunities, better programs. And so it can and does happen that the "liberators" end up making the situation just as bad as, or even worse than it was under the oppressors. Buddhists warn us that as long as we are still clinging to our ego-identity and our own ideas, there's a little (or big) oppressor hiding in every good-willed liberator.

Again, we're back to the need to *be* peace before, or while, we try to *make* peace. The peace and the wisdom that come from waking up alert us to the ways our thinking and feeling so often obscure what is really going on. By sitting in meditation we become more aware of the danger of clinging to our own ideas and plans. If we have to "speak truth to power," we also know that we have to be as humble about what we say as we are strong in saying it. Only if we do not cling to our truth can we—and others—experience its power.

This is why in the Zen Peacemaker Order, founded by Roshi Bernie Glassman, the first principle in all efforts to make peace and restore justice is "not knowing and renouncing all fixed ideas."[1] Its followers begin every new project with "not knowing" and with the effort to silence the truth that they think they have to speak to power. In silence, they listen; they try to be aware; they allow others to express their ideas; they seek to understand what is going on in the particular context in which they are seeking to fix the world. Then, and only then, do they formulate their ideas and lay their plans—ideas and plans that they hold to but that they do not cling to.

So, in the Buddhist-Christian conversation about how to fix the world, Buddhists are suggesting to Christians that the clarion call of Christian activists has to work both ways: *If you want peace, seek justice* has to be balanced by *If you want justice, seek peace.*

A Christian Response: Roger

The human person possesses a center of consciousness that is responsible. Persons exist in a distinctive individual relationship with God and are dependent upon and responsible to communities that also subsist in relation with a loving God. This sets up various tensions between fixating on self, expressing gratitude to God for one's being, and spending oneself to support the lives of others in community. My first reaction was against the individualism that has a stranglehold on developed American culture. If commitment to social justice overwhelms people, I would emphasize protecting individuals from self-destruction. I think these different emphases can be seen in our opening statements for this chapter.

Given the uniqueness of every individual and social situation, who can define a "normative" relationship between personal and social transformation? On the one hand, no commitment that buries self-identity or undermines personal freedom can ever

---

[1] Christopher S. Queen, "Glassman Roshi and the Peacemaker Order: Three Encounters," in *Engaged Buddhism in the West*, ed. Christopher S. Queen (Boston: Wisdom Publications, 2000), 98–104.

be justified. On the other hand, no proper care of oneself can prescind from the relationships to others that sustain a person. Paul, I find nothing in your following of Buddha with which a Christian would disagree in principle. But where do your Buddhist teachings push forward Christian spirituality in the developed Western world, particularly in the United States? I find two themes that are relevant in American culture.

The deeper meaning of the world. The frenetic activism of American urban culture tends to reduce the meaning of daily living to what can be skimmed off the surface. As communication becomes faster, as the memberships that people enter into increase, as the relationships that sustain us multiply and extend over greater distances, the quality of meaning becomes thinner, shallower, and more tenuous. Life seems to shrivel into stimulus and response. The philosophical meaning of pragmatism can be quite profound. But when it describes a system of meaning, it slides toward a crass form of utilitarianism. We do what works. Goals become immediate or nonexistent or nothing more than means of self-satisfaction. It is too moralistic simply to complain that life revolves around money and is driven by greed. But, the question remains: Where in public life are questions of deeper meaning entertained?

The answer to cultural superficiality cannot lie in religious supernaturalism that adds a layer of "non-world" on top of this world. Various traditions in Buddhism and Christianity respond by drawing out deeper meaning that is intrinsic to the natural world and human creativity. Grace is within reality. This breaks through a tired dialectical relationship of transcendence expressed as judgment of the world and restores a positive God-world relation of empowerment for human fulfillment.

The broader responsibility of the individual. To a person concerned with the common good and the unequal distribution of the goods of the world, individualism carries a negative value. Can the dimensions of individuality be expanded to include a fuller positive responsibility? Does individualism always have to connote selfish, greedy, arrogant hostility to public weal and community interests? Why cannot the individual be challenged by Buddhism and Christianity to call for self-reliance *against* patterns of discrimination and social oppression, and *for* initiative, breaking barriers, exploration of new paths, and leadership in service of community and society? Society cannot change without leaders.

It Seems to Us

In this chapter we have finally reassembled the pieces of the mosaic identified in previous chapters and have built a picture of a spirituality that is both *mystical* and *prophetic*. But in our conversations about this chapter we have recognized, first of all, that in doing this—that is, in understanding the messages of Gautama and Jesus as calling for *both* individual and social transformation, for *both* contemplation and action—we are swimming against the current of our contemporary Western culture.

The unspoken values and attitudes in our American way of life are thoroughly *individualistic* and subtly *secular*. If our motto is *e pluribus unum* (out of the many, one), we seem to prefer the rights of the individual many over the duties required by the social one. Property is almost always private, rarely communal. So American society is usually a gathering of individuals—who, when they do gather, are expected to leave their religion at home.

Such are the expectations, and the suppositions, of a *secular* society. Religion may be good and valuable, but as the philosopher Alfred North Whitehead described it, "Religion is what the individual does with his own solitariness" (though religious privatization was not Whitehead's intent).[2] Religion is what we do when we step away from the world—into the quiet of the forest or of our church building. It is a private matter, not to be mixed with politics. Alarms, both internal and public, are sounded whenever someone dares to bring religious arguments into the public form. For American society, and even more so for European, there are "no trespassing" signs between religion and politics. For most Americans, to be religious may tolerably entail being a mystic but *not* a prophet.

Both of us recognize that to claim, as we do, that for Jesus and Buddha spirituality calls for a prophetic engagement with the world, we must be aware of and try to speak to a culture

---

[2] Alfred North Whitehead, *Religion in the Making* (New York: Fordham University Press, 1966), 16–17.

that has an individualistic understanding of human beings and a privatistic understanding of religion. Happily, we also discovered that Buddhists and Christians can help each other do that.

Buddhists can help Christians speak to the individualism of contemporary culture. We identified two differently labeled packages in which this help is offered: The first is pragmatic and the second is theological.

1. Pragmatic. At first we were going to label this package ontological because Buddhists can help Western Christians face what they really are: *annatas*, or non-individuals. But we also realized that Buddhism can be an effective appeal to basic American pragmatism. It offers the sobering claim, which Buddhists say can be verified by trying it out, that the best way to take care of ourselves is to take care of others. Or, the best way to be selfish is to connect with and love others. Buddhists hold up the paradoxical but invigorating truth that we can't take care of ourselves all by ourselves; we can't truly love ourselves if we love only ourselves. Why? Because we are not "I's." We are, in our deepest nature, "we."

But the helping hand that Buddhism offers to Christians extends not only to America's individualistic culture but also to its economic underpinnings. According to the theory of capitalism (at least in its present-day neoliberal and Tea Party versions), if each of us seeks our own well-being (without government interference), we will end up promoting, by a kind of magic, the well-being of everyone. Buddha, together with Jesus, turns such capitalist theory on its head: We can best promote our own well-being *only* if we are also looking after the well-being of others (and here the government might help). No magic. Just common sense.

2. Theological. As we've already recognized in this chapter, Buddhists can help Christians accept and practice the anti-individualistic message of Jesus that we can't love God unless we love our neighbor. Buddhists hold that to be true not just because our neighbor is God's friend but because our neighbor is the very presence of God. God's very self is living, acting, and beckoning in and as our neighbor. In a favorite symbol of Jesus and John, God is the vine. We together with our neighbors are God's branches (Jn 15:4–5). Such is the Buddhist and Christian non-duality between God/Emptiness and humanity/form.

In our final conversations about this chapter we also discovered a further way in which Buddhists can help Christians address the secular atheists of our culture. Tibetan Buddhist practice puts it this way: "Compassion is the source and essence of enlightenment and the heart of enlightened activity."[3] That means that if we practice compassion, we are already essentially enlightened, whether we realize it or not. This echoes Jesus's stunning announcement that if we feed the hungry and clothe the naked, we are doing that for him, whether we know it or not. For both Jesus and Buddha, loving our neighbor and promoting his or her well-being right now, in this world, is more important than believing in God or Interbeing as the ground of such action. For both of them, actions speak louder than—and are more important than—words. Many a secular atheist might agree with that.

Christians can help Buddhists respond to the secular privatization of religion and spirituality. Buddhism, as sometimes taught and practiced in North America and Europe, has been accused of falling prey to the secular privatization of spirituality. For many, Buddhist meditation is mainly a method of mindfulness-based stress reduction. It seems to forget Gautama's admonition in the Eightfold Path that if our "livelihood" or "way of life" is causing suffering for others (directly or indirectly), we cannot achieve Enlightenment and *should* be stressed—or at least concerned. Christians, we suggest, might help Buddhists be mindful of Gautama's insistence that the stress reduction that comes with Wisdom is ineffective and false if it is not accompanied by an active compassion that seeks the well-being of others.

Christians remind Buddhists that compassion must be *active* and *socially and politically engaged.* Jesus taught by example. To practice love for his Jewish brother and sisters, he, like all Jewish prophets, had to demand justice and so confront the Roman and local powers that were causing so much suffering. This is at the heart of Jesus's message as translated for Buddhists: If we are going to realize effectively the intent of the First Noble Truth—to deal with the suffering of the world—then we will have to confront the causes of that suffering not only in the

---

[3] This statement, usually credited to Sogyal Rinpoche, appears in many Buddhist sources online.

human mind and heart but also in the political and economic structures of society.

And this means that the mindfulness that will truly reduce stress and suffering—not only our own but also that of others who perhaps live on the "other side of the tracks"—will have to be a mindfulness directed not only to our own thoughts and feelings but also to the way society is organized. We need *social mindfulness* that will help us wake up to the way economic policies and voting laws can be deceiving us and keeping us from seeing things the way they really are. It is not enough, therefore, to confront greed-producing ignorance in our own heart; we must also mindfully confront the greed-producing ignorance of unjust and violent economic and military systems.

All of this means that for both Jesus and Gautama, privatized spirituality and religion are contradictions in terms.

It seems to us, then, that as in Chapters 5 and 6 we recognized a non-duality and co-inherence between God/Interbeing and the world, so now we affirm a non-duality between the *mystical* (contemplation) and the *prophetic* (action) in both Christian and Buddhist spirituality. The ideal of such co-inhering between prophetic action and mystical contemplation was described by Meister Eckhart in his widely known sermon on Martha and Mary (Lk 10: 38–42). With an insightful mystical twist, Eckhart reverses the usual meaning of this story and holds up Martha as the ultimate ideal for a disciple of Jesus. Martha, who is "busy about many things," urges her prayerful sister Mary to leave her place at Jesus's feet to help in the kitchen. Mary, Eckhart tells us, is "stuck in this pleasant feeling" of contemplation, while Martha is able to "accomplish external works [action] with the perfection that love demands [contemplation]." Indeed, "Martha was so grounded in being that her activity did not hinder her."[4] This is the ideal: to experience the love of God and the power of Interbeing as we care for others, and to hear the call of others while we, on our knees or on our cushions, abide in the silence of Presence.

But while contemplation and action, or God and our neighbor, co-inhere, and we will feel the presence of one in the other, they

---

[4] Meister Eckhart, "Sermon 86," *Meister Eckhart: Teacher and Preacher*, ed. Bernard McGinn (New York: Paulist Press, 1986), 343.

cannot be reduced to each other; one cannot take the place of the other. Like Jesus, who retreated into the quiet of the hillside, and Buddha, who called his monks to retreat during the rainy season, we need designated time for each so that our prayer or meditation can call forth our action, and our action can send us back to silence.

11.

To Attain Justice, Work for Peace

*In this chapter we agree with Hans Küng that peace and recon-
ciliation among nations call for the same among religions. Companions of Jesus insist that there can be no lasting reconciliation
without justice. Companions of Buddha add that there can be no
lasting justice without compassion. On this agenda, Christians
and Buddhists can collaborate.*

A Buddhist Perspective: Paul

In this chapter I unpack the sentence that brought my "Buddhist
Perspective" of the previous chapter to an end: "If you want
justice, seek peace."

To do that I basically draw out conclusions from the discussion in Chapter 10. If Buddhists hold to a certain priority of
being peace over *making peace*, or of *contemplation* over *action*,
then, it seems to me, they are also giving a similar priority to
compassion over *concern for justice*. In fact, Buddhists don't really have a clear concept of justice. We don't hear much talk of
justice in the teachings of Gautama. But we do hear a lot about
compassion. So it appears that what Christians seek to attain by
their emphasis on justice, Buddhists try to achieve through their
insistence on compassion.

The priority of compassion over justice. This is where Christians, especially those engaged in liberation theology, might find
themselves squirming. Compassion or charity, they point out,

does not necessarily ensure justice. In fact, it can often be a distraction from justice: the satisfying feeling from giving a starving person something to eat today may lead us to forget that he will be hungry again tomorrow. Charity or compassion moves us to address the sufferings of others; justice tells us that to do that, we have to address the social or economic causes of that suffering. Justice, therefore, always demands *something more* than charity. The "something more" has to do with structural change—new laws, new economic policies, such as the Civil Rights Act, such as anti-trust legislation.

Many of my Buddhist friends tell me that they have much to learn from these Christian admonitions about justice. But they still insist that if all such actions for justice are not arising out of a genuine feeling of deep compassion for all sentient beings, such actions will probably not bear lasting fruit. We're back to the topic of the last chapter: for real societal change to take place, for a revolution to last, the demands of justice are necessary. But they are not enough. Yes, laws that embody the requirements of justice have to be passed, and they have to be enforced, even imposed. But unless the force of law is accompanied by or eventually leads to the power of compassion, it will not work. Law can envision what a just society looks like, but law by itself, without spirit, can't get there. The change of law must eventually lead to a change of heart. And as I have learned from my Tibetan Buddhist teachers, the most powerful means of changing hearts is compassion.

Violence becomes a vicious circle. Having announced the priority of compassion, Buddhists then point out its general incompatibility with violence. How can you feel compassion and connectedness with people and at the same time inflict suffering upon them? Yes, you may have to restrain or make uncomfortable demands on those you love. But to impose suffering that diminishes them—the ultimate example being death—seems, and feels, impossible. As a Christian preacher once put it in reference to the Gospel: "If Jesus calls us to love our enemies, he probably meant not to kill them." To love and to kill would seem to be mutually exclusive.

So Buddhists draw what they believe is a coherent conclusion: The compassion that produces justice, or the justice that requires compassion, cannot be attained through violence. For them, violence always turns out to be a vicious circle. First, violence obliterates one's opponents and cuts off any chance of changing them; the putative "source of evil" is not only removed or stopped, but it is thrown away, obliterated. And this starts a vicious circle, because there will always be the karmic result of some friend or relative of the obliterated enemy who wants to avenge the violence. Those who take up the sword may not *always* perish by the sword, but they *always* produce more swords.

This is all common sense. But Buddhist teachings show the depth of such common sense by making clear both the danger and the stupidity of violence—and therefore the necessity of nonviolence. It all has to do with the Mahayana understanding of ultimate reality as the Emptiness—or Interbeing—that includes and expresses itself in every single one of us. If all of us—friends and enemies, comrades and opponents—are included in this interconnectedness, then ontologically (or deep down) we share the same identity, even though our ephemeral, always-in-flux forms are different. We live and move and have our being in one another.

So deliberately to harm or do violence to someone else is an ontological surd, irrational, for we are doing it, really, to ourselves. Violence, as it were, always ricochets off our enemy and back onto ourselves. We can't hurt someone else without hurting ourselves, which means that violence is really a form of masochism in which we ignorantly and dangerously find satisfaction in inflicting pain upon ourselves. Even more drastically, for Buddhists, violence can be looked upon as a form of suicide. In killing another, we are killing ourselves—or, killing something that constitutes our own well-being. We are cutting off relationship. And relationships, like the air we breathe, are necessary for staying alive and well.

So, *ontologically* (according to the way things work), violence *doesn't* work. It's counterproductive. According to Buddhist teachings, this is also true *psychologically* (according to the way things feel). We're talking about the link that Buddhists identify between violence and hatred. Hatred, as mentioned earlier, is one of the three poisons (along with delusion and greed) that are the primary generators of human suffering. The problem is that violence usually is the expression of, or it becomes the stimulus for, hatred. And once we feel hatred for others—or when others think or feel that we hate them—then we have cut off our relationship with them, and that means any hope of repairing our relationship. Once the smell of hatred fills the atmosphere, things can only get worse. In fact, some Buddhists hold that in particular circumstances where violence seems to be the last resort to stop suffering, one can carry out a violent act of harming or killing someone if (and only if) one can pull it off without hatred (but one would still have to take on the bad karma of having killed someone).

But this is a controversial issue—mainly because the link between violence and hatred is so tight. Even if we might be able to carry out an act of violence without hatred in our heart, that isn't the way it will look to the person on the receiving end of our violence. For him or her, it will look like, and certainly feel like, hatred. And if someone feels hated by another, the usual response is to strike back with hatred and violence—if not now, later; if not personally, then by a relative or another connection. The shout of violence almost inevitably produces the bigger echo of hatred.

The possibility of falling in love with our enemies. Shouts of violence, we have to remind ourselves, cannot arise from hearts of compassion. If we truly love and have compassion for our enemies and those we have to oppose, it will be impossible to hate them, and therefore impossible, for the most part, to be violent toward them. So the question presses: Can we love our enemies? Jesus presumed that we can when he *commanded* his followers to love their enemies (Lk 6:27). Buddha not only presumes this; he also shows how and why it is possible. Though he never put it this way (as far as I know), to begin the process of enlightenment is to begin the process of falling in love with everyone, including our enemies.

An enlightened being is someone who not only *knows* but *feels* that Interbeing is real—to the extent that the "I-Thou" relationship extolled by Western philosophers (such as Martin Buber) is transformed into a "We relationship" in which I and Thou blend into each other. Awakening enables us to *feel* that there's no difference between loving self and loving others.

But the experience of enlightenment does even more. It also alerts us to the way our thoughts and feelings have been deceiving us or preventing us from seeing all beings as grounded in, or expressions of, the Space of Interbeing. This Space, this inter-connecting Spirit, reveals to us the basic goodness and the vast potential of everyone—of absolutely everyone, no matter how deluded or greedy or hateful we *think* or *feel* that person it. Our thoughts and feelings that define others as our *enemies,* as evil people, are deceptive. Although they indicate what these *enemies* are doing to us, they also prevent us from seeing the Buddha-nature or the basic goodness and potential of our enemies. So, no matter what they are doing, we need to be able to recognize this goodness; we need to be able to feel compassion for them. Our caring for them must be stronger and more persistent than anything they do, or can do, to us. That sounds impossible. But Buddha assures us it *is* possible. We not only *must,* but we *can* love our enemies.

An option for the oppressed cannot be an option against the oppressors. This brings us to perhaps the most discomforting and bewildering challenge that Buddhists offer Christians in their shared commitment to peace and justice. It is gently but starkly stated by Thich Nhat Hanh in his little book *Living Buddha, Living Christ* when he informs Christians that for a Buddhist, God doesn't have favorites. Therefore, the preferential option for the poor that is so central to liberation theology can be dangerous.

Nhat Hanh is challenging Christians to recognize and over-come the duality between oppressed and oppressor. Both—in what each is doing and in what each is experiencing—are ex-pressions of and are held in and by Interbeing. Their actions are clearly different. But their identities are the same. That means *our* identities are linked to both oppressed and oppressors. Therefore, we do not respond to the oppressed out of compassion and to the oppressor out of justice. No, we respond to *both* out of com-passion: compassion for both the oppressed and the oppressor.

But compassion for the oppressor will be expressed differ-ently than compassion for the oppressed. It's the same compas-sion, but, as it were, in different packages. As my teacher John Makransky puts it, the compassion shown to the oppressor will be *fierce.* It will be compassion that confronts, that challenges, that calls for change. It will name the poisons that cause so much suffering: greed, hatred, ignorance. He even calls it a "wrathful compassion."

But the primary motivation for such confrontation will not be the necessity for justice but the necessity for compassion. It will be driven by a compassion for the oppressors and by the desire for their well-being, by the desire to free them from the illusions that drive them to greed and to the exploitation of others. Yes, we want to liberate the oppressed. But *just as much*, we want to liberate the oppressors. Buddhists are telling liberation Christians that compassion has no preferences. We love the oppressor as much as we love the oppressed. Our calls for justice intend the well-being of the oppressor just as much as the well-being of the oppressed.

When the oppressors see this, when they realize that they are indeed being confronted but that the confrontation arises out of compassion, respect, cherishing, when they hear from their confronter not only that they are wrong, but also, and primarily, that they are loved—then, perhaps only then, we have the possibility of changing the structures of injustice, for then there will be the possibility of a change of heart in the oppressors.

A non-preferential option for compassion that extends equally and clearly to both oppressed and oppressors will be the foundation on which justice can be built, on which structures can be changed.

A Christian Response: Roger

I notice, Paul, that you and I have responded to different aspects of human reconciliation. You formulate clearly how a Buddhist social ethical principle of nonviolence and love of enemy can promote human reconciliation. I will address how religions can live peaceably with one another.

Buddhist ontology provides the grounds for nonviolence, love of enemies, and a social option for the poor that respects the personhood of the enemy and oppressor. This is enormously important lest a cycle of violence be mounted in the name of justice and peace. The language of liberation is often aggressive; an option *for* victims often is an option *against* the intentions of those inflicting suffering. Christian creation theology offers analogous principles grounding mutual respect all around. To experience the solidarity of humans and assume corporate responsibility for our life together require acts of compassion that resist injustice while loving the enemy on a deeper level. It is also important to consider who is making the option. Ordinarily, one can presuppose a spontaneous option for the poor on the part of the poor. But as a reflective moral act, the option for the poor demands something on the part of those with power.

In the end, I think, the contrast between compassion (a human response) and justice (an objective state of affairs) may be a mistaken dualism. On the one hand, to be concerned about injustice is or entails being compassionate. And to be compassionate for all requires that we be concerned for justice. On the other hand, from the side of social relations, injustice solicits human compassion and concern for a justice that includes the well-being of all.

Interfaith dialogue creates analogous problems. We can presuppose complete mutual respect for the other religion in a social encounter. We can profess that no religion is superior to another. We can maintain a social convention of freedom of religious practice in a situation defined by separation of church and state. Yet if one religion begins to attract the members of another, there will be friction. Apart from dual belonging, which is not presently a common social phenomenon, one religion always presents itself as a concrete alternative to the others. The Western solution to this issue has been the privatization of religious belonging. But making religious commitment a private affair lowers the possibility that humane religious values will have a public impact on the discussion of the common good.

There has to be some balance between principle and historical realism in matters of social justice and interfaith coexistence and dialogue. The absolute principles of nonviolence relative to enemies and aggressors, because of our oneness in Interbeing, almost inevitably require concrete maxims or middle axioms of social ethics to negotiate actual situations.

The role of the religions in geopolitics and world peace, which can only become more and more important, can be supported by basic understanding of the relationships of religions to one another, by principles of non-superiority or religious egalitarianism, and by mutual appreciation won by dialogue. But usually religions as organized bodies behave socially, like other institutions, out of self-interest. Thus interreligious tolerance, mutual acceptance, cooperation, and friendly interfaith dialogue will always be tested by secular social conflicts. What on the level of personal spirituality may seem achievable will always require skillful means and able leadership in social relationships.

A Christian Perspective: Roger

The demand for reconciliation and peace has never been more crucial. We live in a world of violence, exacerbated by over-crowding, interdependencies, new cross-cultural invasions, and fearsome weapons to express frustrations and group hatreds. The situation has created new moral imperatives for the religions to reach accommodations with other religions that seem to exceed what their traditions allow. As a result, this reflection not only represents Christianity to Buddhists, it also interprets Christianity in ways that may seem adventuresome to Christians. But such is the depth and pervasiveness of the problem of a world that will not survive without some measure of reconciliation. And the religions play an important role in that project.

This reflection straightforwardly appeals to the Christian doctrines of God as creator, of the Spirit of God at work in the world, and of Jesus Christ to understand how Christianity can function as a force of human bonding in our common history. How can Christianity be a reconciling agency in an increasingly polarized and violent world?

The doctrine of one God contains a moral imperative for human reconciliation. The Christian conception that all reality has its origin and source in one God, creator of all things, provides a metaphysical framework for understanding oneself and the world. God is one, and God has created a single human race marked by nonessential differences. The scientific story of the emergence of the universe, the earth, life, and the human species complements the religious conception of creation and gives it concrete reference and unimaginable size. But this aesthetic and intellectual framework also contains ethical implications. The different kinds of beings are held together in a common source and ground of being. Across the development of unspeakably many species, most of which have ceased to exist, a power of being unites all things into one interrelated sphere of life on the planet. This interrelatedness transcends the competitive processes of survival. Interaction presupposes it. With the emergence of human reflection, finite beings become conscious and moral, and this involves a demand for human deliberation in the exercise of freedom. If my being has value, so does the being of others. Human beings share a common value because they are all supported by the same personal source and ground of being.

The Christian idea of the unity of the human race, not simply in bio-evolutionary terms but as creatures of a single God, means that beneath actual history a shared condition of dependence on God unites human beings. Human self-consciousness entails an awareness of the value of each individual human being, a self-importance that is bestowed on each by God. Unlike the often violent competition among other species, human beings have reached the possibility of affirming the inviolable value of other human beings. Human beings are related to each other within a common interdependent structure of mutual support. A shared condition of being urges complementary rather than competitive relationships among humans, interchanges that enhance rather than undermine or destroy life together. In other words, the positive state of being human establishes an intrinsic demand for reconciliation among human beings and of humans with the world. When this implicit desire becomes consciously appropriated it takes the form of a fundamental moral attitude, and this moral attitude corresponds with a transcendental categorical imperative of mutual respect that forms an integral part of the human condition.

A fundamental moral attitude is an interior disposition of persons or groups that orients them toward reality. It is fundamental because, as a persistent or permanent quality of subjectivity, it orients people and serves as a moral compass. It stands behind, facilitates, and becomes operative in habits that channel it in more specific directions. Fundamental moral attitudes engender vague volitional aims that double back and define practical goals for actions. They become actualized in the commitments that govern concrete decisions and actions.

The challenge to Christianity. Human beings should relate to one another in positive ways that support their mutual coexistence. But they do not. And the whole conception of humans being united as a family seems so abstract and distant from what has always been the case that, in realistic terms, it can only be regarded as fanciful and naive. This raises the question of the place of these metaphysical schemes and how they function in personal life and in the larger sphere of human history. The point here is not to resolve the question of peace among peoples. But we can discuss the obstacles to peace and the role of the religions to engage them.

Hans Küng has stated the practical problem in clear axiomatic terms: "There will be no peace among the nations without peace among the religions. There will be no peace among the religions without dialogue among the religions, and there will be no serious dialogue among the religions without common ethical standards."[1] In short, reconciliation in the world cannot happen without reconciliation among the religions. But no reconciliation among religions is possible without recognition of the autonomous value of the other religions. Otherwise, as a distinct religion, one religion will always represent an alternative to the other religions and thus cause conflict. In fact many of the religions understand themselves in an absolute way that renders other religions untrue or of lesser value. The challenge to Christianity is whether it can understand itself and portray itself as a reconciling agency in history, something that demands a self-understanding that simultaneously recognizes the autonomous integrity and validity of religions other than itself.

These premises allow for a fairly exact formulation of the question posed to Christianity: How is Christianity to be understood in a way that is faithful to its origins and history and at the same time supports the autonomy, validity, and integrity of other religions.[2] Such an understanding has to be a genuine Christian self-understanding acceptable to the community; it must also allow Christianity to be a reconciling and peace-making power in history. The rest of this reflection presents an outline of such a self-understanding using the terms *God as Spirit* and Jesus as the *Word of God*.

---

[1] Hans Küng, "The World's Religions: Common Ethical Values," lecture at Santa Clara University, March 31, 2005.

[2] As Edward Schillebeeckx formulated it: "The problem is, rather, how can Christianity maintain its own identity and uniqueness and at the same time attach a positive value to the differences of religions in a non-discriminatory sense?" E. Schillebeeckx, *Church: The Human Story of God* (New York: Crossroad, 1990), 165.

God as Spirit urges the autonomous authenticity of other religions. Christians have within their story the symbols that allow them to recognize the autonomous authenticity of other religions, even though the history of Christianity testifies to confessions of absoluteness and superiority. The key to this interpretation lies in the language of God as Spirit and a theology of creation. God as Spirit is not other than God; the symbol Spirit refers to God. It calls attention to God's immanent presence in and to the world, to all creation, and potentially to human consciousness.

The most straightforward rationale for God's immanence appears in the theology of creation, and I am repeating ideas expressed earlier. God creating is not a single act that God completed in the beginning of the universe; rather, it is the continuing action of God that holds finite or created reality in being. In other words, all finite reality absolutely depends on God's actual creating power that maintains it in existence. This conception places God not up there or out there but everywhere as the suffusing and sustaining inner power of all that exists. God's creative energy operates within the evolutionary process. Transcendent God is the "within" of all finite being. The creating power of God makes all things good. Everything that exists has ontological value; finitude is not evil; the lack of perfection does not make something bad. In terms of morality and sin, the axiom that God loves the sinner but not the sin carries profound implications.

Specifically, then, Christianity finds the grounds for the integrity of other religions in the doctrine of creation. Creation out of nothing implies the universal presence and influence of God as personal and loving Spirit. The religions are the ways in which God's presence has come to public awareness. This view neither implies the perfection of any religion as a set of symbols and practices nor affirms the moral goodness of its practitioners. But it affirms the universal presence and availability of God and God's gracious power of love implicitly present to human experiences and given different names according to these experiences.

Following Jesus entails a spirituality of the rule of God that can be noncompetitive and reconciling. Recognizing that all religions exist within the sphere of the working of God's grace does not go far enough to allow Jesus to represent the power of reconciliation. This is so because whenever Jesus Christ is introduced into a dialogue with other religions, he appears as potential alternative, if not an actual rival, to the mediations of ultimate reality that are in place. This statement of the case is commonly recognized in missiology: How can Jesus not be divisive if he is proposed by Christians as *the* true revelation and mediation of God?[3]

The premise of the Christian church is precisely that its faith in God is formed by Jesus Christ. Jesus was himself a human being and as such is universally available and approachable. As a human being, Jesus bore theocentric witness to God and acted as an agent of the rule of God. The rule of God as Jesus represented it cannot be reduced to a formula because its reality consists of a social-existential dialogue and movement sustained by God's presence. One can characterize it *formally* as the way things would be and will be according to the Creator's intention. But the rule of God is always moving, and other religions offer conceptions of what Jesus called the rule of God. This sets up a tension between the particularity of Jesus and the universality of his message of the rule of God that comes to a fine point in the dialogue with other religions. For Christians, Jesus is behind the message. But the content of the witness can be presented in the more universal categories of creation, and these can be appreciated apart from revelation through Jesus or the mediation of the church. An ultimate ground of being can be expressed in the symbols of other religions.

For Christians, that which opens up the possibility that Jesus can be a reconciling and not a competitive religious mediator lies in the exegetical consensus that historically Jesus did not preach himself but the rule of God. Jesus's mission and being were oriented toward making God's values, the will and the rule of God, operative in the world, in personal lives, and in society. The most basic response of a Christian to Jesus consists of being attracted to him and appropriating his message, that is, a spirituality of following Jesus. Doctrines developed out of that spirituality and

---

[3] If Christians held that Jesus was not the only and the absolute mediator of God, but rather one among others, the theoretical problem would be resolved. Jesus would not be presented as an alternative but as a complementary mediator. But for Christians the question of how this is a legitimate interpretation of the tradition has to be engaged.

refer back to it. Jesus is reconciler on the basis of the spirituality he engenders. As Paul Tillich insisted, the self-negation of Jesus to the rule of God is what allowed him to be the Christ.[4]

Jesus's role of reconciler lies in his revelatory message of the rule of God as the ultimate reality that supports and guarantees the value of all human existence. Appreciation of that message allows dialogue about the meaning of teachings or doctrines on all sides. On a new basis of mutual respect, doctrines can be discussed around a table of exchange that involves genuine listening and learning, and that does not threaten the deep status of one's own or the others' religions. This deeper dialogue intensifies the unity of human existence before what is commonly recognized as absolute Mystery.

A Buddhist Response: Paul

As a companion of Buddha, I certainly resonate with your call for *reconciliation* as the "transcendental categorical imperative" for all nations and for all religions. I also believe that your Christian dialogue with Buddhism can help you strengthen and clarify that call.

You rightly point out that in order to achieve reconciliation of our differing views and differing needs, we human beings must "transcend the competitive processes of survival." The interconnectedness of cooperation must have a priority over the bottom line of competition. To ground and inspire such cooperative connections you appeal to the "common value" that each individual has as a creature of the same "personal source and ground of being." Each created individual has inherent value.

As a Buddhist, I want to clarify and expand. Again, appealing to the basic *anatta* (not-self) teaching of Buddha, I find the real value of each of us not in our *individuality* but in our *relatedness* to one another and to the larger, interconnected whole. Our real

---

[4] "He proves and confirms his character as the Christ in the sacrifice of himself as Jesus to himself as the Christ." Paul Tillich, *Systematic Theology*, vol. 2, *Existence and the Christ* (Chicago: University of Chicago Press, 1957), 123. There is more to be said here about the divinity of Jesus, a doctrine which I hold. But it need not be held in an exclusive way.

happiness results not from preserving ourselves but from con-necting ourselves in mutual giving and receiving. This is part of the Buddhist teaching on *impermanence*. Our individuality is not permanent; our value—and our happiness—is not in maintain-ing and augmenting what we are but in offering what we are to the flourishing of the community. The value of each and every one of us is, ultimately, not to cling to our selves but to give of ourselves. As Jesus said, we can find ourselves, paradoxically, only if we lose ourselves.

We're back to the primacy of compassion over justice. The ability and the necessity of "transcending the competitive pro-cesses of survival" are grounded primarily in the compassion that we can feel for each other, not in the justice that affirms and requires the value of each individual. Of course, compassion will call for justice. I'm talking here about what seems to have more effective motivating power to overcome the competitive processes of survival. And I think compassion can provide the energy to get this difficult job done more effectively than justice alone.

How can the religions—specifically Christianity and Bud-dhism—effectively promote such reconciliation? There is an in-herent contradiction in religious teachings between *reconciliation* and *supersession*—for instance, between Christianity's announce-ment that God loves everyone but that Christ and Christianity are meant to replace or supersede all other religions. (Buddhism has its own forms of supersessionist teachings.)

You're right, Roger, that such a supersessionist attitude was not part of Jesus's message about the universal rule of God. But, as you know, while Jesus in the Synoptic Gospels preached the primacy of the rule of God, the early church in the rest of the New Testament preached the primacy of Jesus. Christians have to deal with a lot of "one and only" language that runs through the Christian scriptures.

Buddhists might offer some help in how to do that. Buddhist sacred texts also abound in ringing praises of the excellence and power of the Buddha. But they also have more explicit warnings than do Christians about the need to be careful of all language. Buddhists are instructed not to *cling to* their language, not to absolutize it. No language is free of the need to be qualified and reinterpreted. Christians need to keep that in mind in all the wonderful things they say about Jesus.

It Seems to Us

In reflecting together on our exchanges in this chapter, we found ourselves in agreement that a primary expectation that most people—whether they are believers or atheists—have of the religions is that they be peacemakers. One of the most urgent tasks facing all religions today is to show that they are a greater source of peace and reconciliation than they are of conflict and violence. Undeniably, throughout history and still in our present world, filled as it is with the terrorism of warfare and injustice, religions have inspired and justified violence and hatred. Unless they make clear that they can function much more effectively as instruments of peace and reconciliation (Saint Francis Assisi), they will—and perhaps should—lose their validity in the eyes of many.

It seems to us that our conversations in this chapter have shown how Buddhists and Christians can help each other both in promoting reconciliation among nations and in promoting reconciliation *among religions*.

Reconciliation among nations. As companions of Jesus and Buddha, trying to listen to each other, we recognize that the urgent task of achieving lasting peace and reconciliation *among nations* requires a constant and creative combination of concern for justice and a commitment to compassion. Roger the Christian has reminded Paul the Buddhist that in order effectively to practice compassion, *justice* is necessary. And Paul reminds Roger that it is impossible to achieve lasting justice without *compassion*. To once again apply a theme that resonates throughout our conversation, there is a non-dual relationship between a concern for justice and compassion. One calls forth the other. Neither can be reduced to the other. As we have reminded each other in this chapter, compassion without justice can be naive, and justice without compassion will break down.

But in balancing this non-duality, we acknowledged that perhaps Christians have a bit more to learn from Buddhists than vice versa. What we're getting at can be expressed by an image we used back in Chapter 6: Just as there is an "asymmetrical reciprocity" between God and the world, so there is an asymmetrical reciprocity between compassion and a concern for justice. In other words, compassion bears a certain practical priority in the non-dual balancing with justice. In saying that

God and the world "need" each other, we recognized that the world's need for God is greater than God's need for the world. So too in the necessary mutuality between compassion and concern for justice, compassion plays the role of a precondition for the realization of justice.

By recognizing this prior or preconditioning role of compassion in the work of justice, we are recognizing a teaching that is at the heart of both Christianity and Buddhism: We realize and achieve who or what we are through loving our brothers and sisters, through living as bodhisattvas. For Christians, the first commandment that Jesus gave his disciples was to love one another, not to strive for justice (although, to repeat, love will demand justice) (Jn 15:12). For Buddhists, the first and necessary result of enlightenment is compassion. We human beings realize who we are and what makes for our happiness primarily and initially by *giving ourselves,* not by demanding our rights (although we will have to demand our rights when they are violated). In traditional Christian language, we can be ourselves only by emptying ourselves in love *(kenosis).* Our *hypostasis* (underlying state or foundation) requires *kenosis* (giving ourselves). That, Saint Paul tells us, is what Jesus taught and embodied (Phil 2:6).

The practical priority we are assigning to compassion summarizes what we talked about in this chapter: Unless the tree of justice grows in the soil of compassion, its roots will not go deep enough to bear lasting fruit. That in no way minimizes our demands for justice. But a demand for justice that arises from and is inspired by compassion is very different from a demand that comes out of hatred or anger. Angry demands usually elicit anger and defensiveness. Compassionate demands have the possibility of opening and changing hearts. Both Jesus and Buddha taught this. "For hatred can never put an end to hatred; love alone can. This is an unalterable law" (Dhammapada 1:1). "But I say to you that listen, Love your enemies, do good to those who hate you, bless those who curse you, pray for those who abuse you" (Lk 6:27–28). The only hope we have of turning enemies into friends who will work for justice with us is to love them. It would seem, therefore, that if love does not precede a concern for justice, justice does not hold out much hope.

The necessity of compassion lays the foundation for the necessity of non-hatred. We agreed that while there might be grounds for controversy about whether Jesus and Buddha insisted on non-violence, there can be no doubt that they preached non-hatred. To love our enemies means not to hate them. And non-hatred will generally, if not always, call for nonviolence.

Reconciliation among religions. If Christians and Buddhists can help each other in the task of promoting peace among nations, how might they do likewise in promoting peace among religions? If there is any validity to Han Küng's dictum that there will be no peace among nations without peace among religions, we have to address the questions of hostility and division among families of faith. Our friendly conversation as companions of Buddha and Jesus convinces us that we have to speak about the reconciliation of Buddhists and Christians and find the skillful means of showing why we do not compete with each other.

It seems clear enough that a number of interpretations of Jesus and Christianity and of Buddha and Buddhism diminish their potentiality for being a reconciling force in history. We are thinking here of convictions that are exclusive, that see faith traditions in a competitive relationship, that generate a self-understanding of superiority over other faith traditions, and that relate to other faiths with a desire for conversion of the other and thus ultimate usurpation. We need interpretations of Jesus and of Gautama that allow them to appear as reconciling agents among the religions. But how is that possible? It is not easy, but we agreed that three considerations, even though they are not developed at length, indicate a direction. We focus on Christianity in the hope that on this issue, Christians may offer a helpful example for Buddhists.

The first consideration stresses the need to distinguish between efforts to interpret Jesus of Nazareth and Gautama and efforts to interpret later conceptions of them. There is a natural tendency within traditions for interpretation to build on interpretation, and this gradually leads further away from the one being interpreted. For example, by the end of the first century some Christians were interpreting Jesus, the Jewish prophet and teacher, in a way that made him appear hostile or alienating to Jews. The classic way of continually reforming and purifying our understanding of Jesus is to go back to the source. Biblical criticism gives us the ability *in some measure* to distinguish Jesus of Nazareth from later interpretations of him even in the New

Testament. Interpretation of Jesus must keep the original ministry and followers of Jesus in view as much as this is possible.

A second consideration for interpreting Jesus stresses how he reveals a God of all people. This does not mean that our present understanding of God is uniquely revealed and can therefore be imposed on all others. Rather, entering into Jesus's portrayal of the God of all means that the Spirit of the God he preached is actually present and at work in all creation, all people, and all religions, broadly conceived. Therefore, with the language of the rule of God, Jesus refers to what can be and in some ways is experienced by all. When Buddhists point to emptiness, they do not mean "their" emptiness but rather what subsists in all and can be found within each one as his or her Buddha-nature. The God of Jesus's rule of God bears functional analogies to emptiness, and Jesus's teaching should be understood as having analogues in the experiences of other faiths.

A third consideration comes from earlier chapters: Jesus not only reveals ultimate reality but also authentic human existence or nature in the face of transcendence. Jesus does not represent Christians but all human beings. Jesus reveals all people as God's people, all people as loved by God, and all people as chosen and full of grace. When Jesus is recognized as representative of all, it is right to think of him as awakened or enlightened. Therefore Jesus, like Moses, Buddha, and Muhammad, does not stand above or between people but among us all.[5] He points to a God who as Spirit is at work in all faiths. Interpreting Jesus as a revealer of authentic human existence as a whole enables the Christian to find God at work in manifestations of authentic human living among other faiths. Analogously, Buddhists and others may find their revealed conceptions of ultimate reality operating within Christianity.

These considerations begin to open a way of understanding how Jesus and other religious mediators can be seen as reconcilers between religions and not sources of division. Jesus, a revealer of the God of all and a representative of authentic human existence,

---

[5] Christian theology has more to say here, much more, but nothing that contradicts these affirmations of Jesus being a human being. People who understand incarnation recognize that this is the point of the doctrine.

cannot be treated as a possession of one faith over against others but should be considered as one who shows how God is at work in the world and within all spiritual traditions. Buddhists who consider Jesus as enlightened and Christians who follow Buddha have received this insight. An appreciation of Jesus as reconciler forces one to reconsider the character of religious boundaries and to question the meaningfulness of religious "enemies" or "competitors" in the light of the rule of God revealed in Jesus. If God is parent of all, and all people are our neighbors, and we should treat them with loving respect, it is not possible to hold up Jesus as a ground for religious division. Inversely, every interpretation of Jesus as a deep dividing factor of people into friends and enemies is a false interpretation.

These reflections on Jesus, and analogous reflections on Buddha, lead us to be very cautious in speaking about a Christian mission except in terms of dialogue with brothers and sisters. We want to communicate, but never without listening and learning. Are we entering a new "axial age," not of loosening borders, but of conversation and cooperation among the religions in the common cause of mutual acceptance and reconciliation?

12.

Is Religious Double Belonging Possible? Dangerous? Necessary?

We end with an exchange on a controversial topic. In fact, many writers, representing many more people, profess being at home in more than one religion. We talk about what this means and how it is possible. Finally, we reflect on what it entails for the relationship between spirituality and religion.

A Christian Perspective: Roger

My reflections for this chapter lack the existential perspective of one who experiences dual religious belonging from inside. An adequate understanding of the phenomenon requires that kind of witness. But something can be said for an analysis in more objective terms. The progression of these reflections begins with the idea of religious belonging; this seems like a logical lead into dual belonging. I move toward dual belonging by noting how Christian belonging always involves interpretation, ever new interpretations in new times and cultures. As a bridge to dual belonging I consider being religious, being spiritual, and being curious. These define a path that leads many to discover that they are dual belongers.

The meaning of religious belonging today. What is entailed in religious belonging in the highly literate, critical, and secular culture of the Western developed world? So pervasive is the secularity of especially our urban societies that by a certain age most persons who are religious are so by choice and on their own terms rather than by default. Many distinguish between being spiritual and being religious. I understand spirituality as the whole tenor of the way persons direct their lives in face of some transcendent reality and value. Being religious adds to that a community and tradition. This does not mean that every religious person must participate in synagogue, mosque, or church, but without such participation a particular religious tradition will eventually cease to exist. Belonging to a religious tradition entails a community even when the community is kept at arm's length. Participation in a religion today often involves criticism of various aspects of the common, public face of the community. Yet beneath all the details of being church, most Christians are aware that what summons them transcends church and remains absolute Mystery. It is precisely this unknown mystery that elicits a basic loyalty to a community and tradition, and this loyalty helps define the self at its deepest level in relation to mystery.

Two analogies may help us understand aspects of the deep priority that belonging to a religious community can attain in a person's life. One is kinship. Although kinship is understood differently across cultures, in places where family ties are important one can often see kinship bonds transcending almost every form of alienation. The bond of kinship requires acceptance of someone who belongs to you despite chasms in social standing, sharp political differences, economic class, and even religious contradiction. The relative, no matter what, is simply part of one's family. Kinship bonds have roots that are prior to all learned behavior, and they withstand other sources of separation. Common religious belonging usually runs thinner than blood in social relations, but the more society becomes plural in its religious commitments, the more people experience the need for a common spirituality as an inner bond that holds them together and gives each one an identity. Like the bond of kinship, common spiritual belonging provides mooring for a person's being; it grounds the context of meaning in which everyday existence goes forward. The analogy of kinship shows how deeply religious belonging merges with ontological self-definition that goes well beyond sharing a set of beliefs.

Language provides another analogy to appreciate the depth of religious belonging. Language is more than an arbitrary external tool that enables us to speak. It helps to define the way a community thinks, values, and responds to the world. Language both emerges out of human freedom and bends back to shape it. Language codifies the basic meanings and values of a culture and enables people to learn and to interpret reality. Language provides the shared symbol system that, once a person has internalized it, allows a person to communicate with others and participate in society. This symbiosis shows how religious speech and practice reflect an internal sphere of human freedom within and beneath the religious externals. Religious belonging has roots that sink deeply into a person's self-appropriation. The beliefs and values that are provided and nurtured in a religious community function like a language that is used to define the self and formulate one's identity. Religious belonging shapes the consciousness of a person's being.

In sum, religious belonging has the potential for comprehensively shaping a person's identity. This puts considerable pressure on the idea of dual belonging.

Every Christian is in some measure eclectic. This consideration is another preliminary step moving in the direction of outright dual belonging. An eclectic Christian is one who is open to, learns from, or participates in the religious practices of one or more religions other than Christianity. I'm not saying that all Christians are eclectic to the same degree, but I want to indicate that we all are to some degree.

The point of noticing that all Christians are eclectic is to counter a false impression that most Christians understand the meaning of the doctrines and practices of their faith in exactly the same way. This is not the case. Individuals appropriate the religious values and meanings of the common faith on their own terms, according to their life context and their abilities. To know is to interpret, and no two persons appropriate reality in exactly the same way. Generally speaking, doctrines and religious practices are received at a naive level of common sense, and members of the community interpret their meaning as best they can, ranging from imaginative scenarios to critical revisions. As for the communities to which each person belongs, they are all different, slightly in the same society at the same time, more so as contexts change over time, and greatly in different cultures at different times across the world. The religious practices and public statements of belief and value are always shifting as they respond to new situations and emergent crises.

Eclecticism may seem like overstatement to describe the ordinary life of the churches. But it forces notice of the great variety of persons that make up the church and how they are alive and interacting with the world around them. Many people are constantly adjusting their deep convictions and commitments to the world as they know it through their commerce with it. Deep religious belonging endures because it allows for new learning and growth in personal formation, not because it inhibits personal appropriation.

On being religious, spiritual, and curious. To be religious means to participate in a community that nurtures one's spirituality within a specific faith tradition. To be spiritual means to be attentive to the transcendent reality that provides the center of gravity for all one's actions. To be eclectic means that one's spiritual life continues to grow in the dialogue with the world of which human existence is a part. Life in the present-day world includes the presence of, knowledge about, and social interchange with people of other religious traditions. To be curious is to be open to and religiously interested in the spirituality and religious traditions that nurture other people.

Because the ultimate is absolute Mystery, in today's world the closeness of people of other religions makes it difficult to suppress curiosity about their religions and spiritualities. A fascination with other religions may manifest itself in various ways. In some cases it is a desire to learn the basic logic of other religious traditions. In others, fascination runs toward spirituality. Many different conceptions of spiritual ideals and established sets or techniques of spiritual practice have become available in Western societies that were relatively unknown fifty years ago. Granted, in some cases we may be witnessing something that is no more than *mere* curiosity. Accounting for the motives driving the new interest remains difficult. But one has to think that some degree of hunger for spiritual nourishment is also at work.

Active fascination with other religious and spiritual practices inevitably leads in different ways to self-discovery. In some cases a people may discover a new sense of the logic of their traditional spirituality in the contrast with another worldview or set of practices. For example, in contrast to an ultimate reality that is characterized as not personal, one more deeply appreciates what a personal relationship with a personal God entails. Such a relationship can no longer be taken for granted but resonates with new depth. In other cases people may enhance their traditional spirituality with new learning. Seeing things in a new and different light adds dimensions and implications to what one already possesses. The experience of the other deepens and expands self-possession. For example, the concept of no-self *(anatta)* may stimulate a new appreciation of the total dependence of the creature on the creator. This translates into a self-appreciation in relation to a personal God that can have transforming effects in one's life. In still other instances persons may discover their inner selves in a wholly new way in the encounter with a new set of beliefs and practices. One has to assume that all religions have dimensions that resonate with some deep structures of human existence as such.

Dual belonging happens when persons are drawn to live within the practices and beliefs of more than one religion. This statement describes the possibility of dual religious belonging as something deep and complex transpiring first of all on the level of spirituality. Four considerations help to show how it is possible.

One can begin by simply calling to mind the deep character of religious belonging. Participation in a religion rests on an attachment more profound than belonging to a club. It is rooted in a spirituality as this was defined earlier: a consistent way of life in relation to transcendent reality. Such a commitment to life defines one's being by the relationship with ultimacy that presses in and sustains the self. This spirituality has a rationale in beliefs and an overt manifestation in religious practices shared by the community. They make sense for the community because of the prior inner shared faith of each one. Religion is the external superstructure of beliefs, practices, and functional community that houses a spiritual way of life.

A second factor revolves around the polarity between activity and passivity. The depth of religious identity implies that a sense of being attracted to and, more strongly, of belonging to another religion are as much things that happen to a person as they are a deliberate choice. Like conversion, belonging to another religion is complex. It mixes an active and a passive voice. We speak of people who converted, but the same people may insist that something happened to them; they may even have been taken by surprise. Like faith itself, attraction to a new spirituality comes as gift from transcendence and elicits gratitude. The process of curiosity, appreciating, trying on, and appropriating new dimensions of a spirituality that fits will often have a character of gift rather than achievement.

Third, when dual belonging is approached through spirituality, as distinct from adherence to religious systems, it becomes much more plausible as an authentic place to be. Spirituality is an existential reality; it is life lived, the logic of human action in relation to an ultimate, transcendent reality. On the surface personal human existence is always encountering new reality, being affected, accommodating, and changing. Each person is in some measure a hybrid, a life absorbing some bit of new reality into itself with every fresh encounter. More deeply, the existential depth of each subject's self-possession in relationship with transcendence allows for different symbols, beliefs, and practices to all have some influence on the religious belonger that one actually is. In the face of transcendence a dual spiritual belonger can handle pluralism.

From a Christian perspective, finally, the possibility of an authentic dual belonging lies in some form of the creation theology outlined in the last chapter. Creation theology justifies the transcendence of ultimate reality and its immanent presence, both of which are needed to ground dual belonging. Because spirituality unfolds in relation to an ultimacy that is beyond all finite reality, no set of symbols can represent it in an encompassing or exhaustive manner. But its immanent presence, when it affects human consciousness, does allow human beings to respond to it in a conscious way. In objective terms dual belonging may not fit in any exact place between traditions. It does not entail a third religion that is located between two others. It exists today within the subjectivity of those who profess it. It is possible because all persons in their uniqueness bear distinctive relationships with ultimate reality.

A Buddhist Response: Paul

Your input, Roger, helped me to sort out what I think are the *preconditions* that have to be present before anyone, especially a Christian, is going to feel the desire or the courage to explore the possibilities of double belonging. If any of these predispositions is missing, a religious person will probably choose to stay put in his or her own backyard.

Without becoming overly analytic (a not uncommon problem for us theologians), let me list, with your help, four preconditions for the possibility of double belonging.

Theological preconditions. Unless persons make or feel—consciously or subconsciously—the *distinction between spirituality and religion*, they will feel no incentive to explore how they might expand their spirituality beyond their religion. You say it so crisply: "Religion is the external superstructure of beliefs, practices, and functional community that houses a spiritual way of life." A "house" should not become a "prison." Visiting, even renting, someone else's house can become an opportunity to expand one's spiritual way of life.

Christian preconditions. Taking seriously Jesus's reminder that "the Father is greater than I" (Jn 14:28), Christians must recognize two realities: the God they have experienced through Jesus is greater than Jesus; and this God waits to meet them also in other religious houses. Without this recognition, Jesus imprisons them.

Personal-experiential preconditions. What I'm suggesting here is that one's own religion must "work" before one will feel attracted by other religions. In one's own religious practice one, as it were, "gets a whiff of the sacred." And this whiff prepares one—really, requires one—to pursue the scent of the sacred wherever it might be found. This is why Thomas Merton is such a telling example of double belonging. It was only after he spent years of breathing in the Christ-Mystery in the Abbey of Gethsemani that he felt the need to start "sniffing around," as it were, in other traditions. And what he discovered in others deepened his knowledge of Christ.

Psychological preconditions. Here is where Buddhism can help clarify and prepare the way for double belonging—mainly in its teaching that we are *anattas* (not-selves). Listen to a contemporary Buddhist's description: "*Anatta* doesn't mean that you don't have a self, but that it isn't separate and isolated. Nor is it solid and immutable as we like to think. Nor is it always right. Nor the center of the known universe."[1] But that is a description of the self of a double belonger—one who realizes that to be who I am, I must be in life-changing and faith-changing relations with others.

And this brings me to a final, and rather unsettling, sharpening of your statement. You say that it is curiosity that impels many Christians to explore double belonging. That is certainly the case for many Christians. But for many others, it is not just curiosity. It is starvation—or malnutrition. Their standard diet of doctrinal instruction and spiritual-sacramental practice is not meeting the nutritional needs of many American and European Christians. They don't want to leave their church communities, but they need help. And they seem to be finding that help through the teachings and practices of other religions. Without some form of double belonging, they could not be Christian.

A Buddhist Perspective: Paul

In this final chapter we take up what this book is all about, or more cautiously, what this book can lead to: double (or multiple) religious belonging.

Double practice/double nourishment. Double or multiple belonging points to the growing number of people in Western cultures who find that they are spiritually nurtured by more than one religious tradition. The nourishing comes from engaging the practices and exploring the teachings of another religious community. For many of these people, this is not an intentional project, a pre-planned undertaking. They didn't decide that they were going to be, or try to be, double belongers. Rather, it often just happens, sneaking up on a person, as it were. That's pretty much how it happened for me.

The growing phenomenon of double religious belonging confirms the prophecy made by Notre Dame University theologian

---

[1] Kimberly Snow, "The Peril and Promise of Selflessness: A Psychologist Explores the Path into Depression or *Anatta*," in *Mind and Life* (Spring 2014): 15.

John Dunne over forty years ago. In *The Way of All the Earth: Experiments in Truth and Religion* he predicted that "the spiritual adventure of our time" will not be to pursue only one religious path but to "pass over by sympathetic understanding from one's own religion to other religions and come back again with new insight into one's own."[2]

Double belonging is what happens when this dialogical process of "passing over and passing back" starts to work; when it begins to take on a life of its own; and when it assumes a sustaining, guiding, and even necessary role in one's life.

More precisely, double belonging begins to take shape when in the passing back to one's own religion one discovers that one is not leaving the other religion behind. In passing over to and back from Buddhism, a Christian brings something of Buddhism back into his or her Christianity. It's not just that Buddhism throws new light on what one already has in one's "Christian house"; besides doing that, Buddhism also adds to what is now to be found in the Christian house. Buddha becomes an occupant of the Christian house. The house is no longer just a Christian house.

So, in the process or experience of double belonging, a Christian remains a Christian but becomes a different kind of Christian—a Christian who now sees differently and acts differently, whose religious experience, we might say, is expanded. What one feels when one hears the word *God* is somehow different, deeper, fuller. What one learns from another religion begins to define one's own religious identity. The dialogue becomes life-sustaining.

Distinct and equal. It should be clear that double belonging is not what scholars call *syncretism*—when two religions are so mixed together in a kind of New Age blender that it is impossible to tell one from the other. They form a tasty spiritual cocktail whose ingredients merge into something new. In double belonging, on the contrary, the two religious teachings or practices, or the two narratives or stories, remain distinct. Both Buddha and Jesus speak in their own voices and deliver different messages. And yet, for the double belonger they feed into and off of each other. One enhances, clarifies, and even needs the other. One without the other is somehow incomplete.

---

[2] John S. Dunne, *The Way of All the Earth: Experiments in Truth and Religion* (New York: Macmillan, 1972), ix.

Marriage might serve as a helpful, though limping, analogy for double belonging. Two different people, who clearly and necessarily remain distinct, now find fulfillment in and through each other. While distinct, they can no longer be separate. In their differences they need each other. Their differences call out to each other. They can't imagine being who they are without each other.

But in this marriage of religious identities, does one partner, or one religion, have priority over the other? In most contemporary marriages couples do not make an agreement that one of them is the "boss," or that in situations of conflicting viewpoints, one of them will always have the final, decisive word.

And yet, especially in the early stages of double belonging, something like that does seem to be the way things work. Generally, one steps onto the path of double belonging with a given, a primary spiritual identity formed in the cultural, psychological conditioning of the religion one was born into. This is the religion where one, for the most part, feels at home. It is this religious story and practice that is clarified and strengthen by the practice of another tradition. In such situations one would call oneself a Buddhist Christian. *Christian* is the substantive, the original and primary identity; *Buddhist* is the adjective, the important "add-on."

That's how I described myself when I first woke up to the reality that I had become a double belonger. But as I deepened my dual practice, as I faced questions from friends about what was really going on, I came to a point where I realized I couldn't make such neat, prioritizing distinctions. Like other double belongers with whom I compared religious notes, I discovered that I had arrived at a blended religious life in which both my Christian and Buddhist practices play essential roles—in a way that makes it impossible to say that one is dominant over or more important than the other.

In my double religious identity my relationship with Buddha and Jesus became increasingly less a question of dominance. Neither was the "decider." Neither had the last word. On some issues I find myself preferring the path that Jesus followed; on others, Buddha's message and practice are preferable. But in giving one the right of way over the other, I don't feel I'm leaving the other behind. Though one sometimes precedes the other, we keep moving in the same direction.

So now it is difficult to say either that I'm a Buddhist Christian or a Christian Buddhist. Rather, I'm a Buddhist and a Christian. It's impossible to say which comes first, which is more important, or which has the last word. Given the humility that seems to have marked both of their lives, I suspect Buddha and Jesus would be comfortable with that.

Double belonging can become a necessity. For some religious seekers, especially in our contemporary context in the West, double religious belonging is not just something that can enrich their spiritual lives. It is, rather, something that *saves* their spiritual lives. In order to carry on their spiritual journey, they have no choice but to explore multiple religious belonging. This, I think, is what John Dunne started to realize some forty years ago. As some contemporary scholars put it, more and more people are coming to the surprising realization that if they want to be religious, they have to be religious interreligiously.[3]

Such a need arises, I think, out of two different but complementary sources. One, we might say, is the natural result of any authentic spiritual experience. When a religious practice works, it puts us in touch with a Reality that, when we know it, we know we do not really know it. To know it is to know that we can never fully know it, and that therefore there will always be more to know. Different spiritual paths put us in touch with Mystery. There's always more to Mystery than any one path can find. So if one's particular religion is working, one will realize what Edward Schillebeeckx phrased so neatly: "There is more religious truth in all the religions together than in one particular religion."[4] Double belongers draw the evident conclusion: to start exploring other religions.

Or, usually more painfully but pressingly, the need to draw on other religious teachings and practices can arise from difficulties within one's home religion. These can be theological differences that arise when traditional formulations or explanations about the nature of God or the meaning of salvation or the end of the world just don't make sense. Such struggles can also be more

---

[3] Peter C. Phan, *Being Religious Interreligiously: Asian Perspectives on Interfaith Dialogue* (Maryknoll, NY: Orbis Books, 2004).

[4] Edward Schillebeeckx, *Church: The Human Story of God* (New York: Crossroad, 1990), 166.

spiritual or more practical; that is, the practices or the forms of prayer or ritual that one grew up with are no longer doing their job—they no longer touch and tingle within one's feelings. They need to be repolished, readjusted, refreshed.

For either, or both, of these reasons, many people feel the need to *add to* and/or to *clarify* their given religious practices and creeds. They need help. And so they begin the path of double belonging. Exploring the teachings or creeds of another tradition throws light—often transforming light—on their own. Different meditational or ritual practices enliven or replace those that have grown stale or stolid.

Double belonging: An example of the "mutual fecundation" of religions. Now, a brief theological aside. What I have just described about why double belonging is a necessity for some spiritual seekers is an illustration of what Raimon Panikkar called the necessary "mutual fecundation of religions."[5] Religions evolve in many ways; one of them is through what they learn from or adapt to in other religions. This has been the case throughout the history of religions, but it's much more evident and urgent in our globalized world. There are real differences among the religious families of the world. Some families have traits and gifts that others do not have. And *that's why they need one another.*

In each tradition certain themes are stressed; certain types of spiritual practices are preferred. There are those traditions that emphasize the mystical, while others speak more of the prophetic. Some stress the singularity of the Ultimate (monotheism), others acknowledge the diversity within Ultimacy (polytheism). Some focus on the transcendence, others on the immanence of the Ultimate. Some are theistic, others non-theistic. To the historian such differences seem to be contradictory. For mystical multiple belongers like Panikkar, they are complementary.

Double belongers are discovering that the differences among the religions are generally (not always!) much more "fecundating" and enriching than opposing and excluding. For a growing number of people, without such fecundation, without multiple religious practice, it would be hard, maybe impossible, to be religious.

---

[5] Raimon Panikkar, *Intrareligious Dialogue* (New York: Paulist Press, 1978), 61.

The dangers of double belonging. Yes, there are dangers in this venture of religious double belonging. The Dalai Lama alerts us to such dangers when he warns of the incongruity and even violence of "putting a yak's head on a sheep's body."[6] There are beliefs within the world of religions that may simply be incompatible, or their meaning may be so embedded in a particular culture or history that they are meaningless in other contexts. To try to coordinate such teachings or practices runs the risk of deforming at least one of them. In trying to adopt something new, it is possible to end up watering down or maiming one's own practices.

There are other dangers. One is captured in the image of people flitting around a "divine deli" selecting delectable tidbits now from the Hindu section, then from Islam, and how about a little Christianity? One ends up with a collection of sweets without much substance. One enjoys the tastes but misses real nourishment and so ends up with a spiritual diet limited to what one likes and missing what one needs. In double or multiple practice, there's the danger that people can become so scattered in their practice that they do not expend the required energy and dedication to any one of them. Or they can focus on practices and beliefs that feel good but that don't challenge and correct.

To recognize such dangers is to be reminded that any spiritual search or practice calls for serious engagement. To explore another religion, one cannot just taste. One has to learn how to cook and prepare, as it were. Serious study and serious practice—often under a teacher—is essential to double belonging. Otherwise, one is only a multi-religious dilettante, or voyeur.

Realistically recognizing the dangers, double belongers still claim that the possibilities of spiritual enrichment far outweigh the dangers of distortion or dilution. In the end, the bottom-line criterion for assessing whether double belonging is authentic is simple: Does it yield the spiritual fruits of peace and compassion? Does it deepen one's personal peace and centeredness? Does it connect one with others in compassion and commitment? If it does, one can consider himself or herself part of what John Dunne called the new "spiritual adventure of our time."

---

[6] Dalai Lama, *The Good Heart: A Buddhist Perspective on the Teachings of Jesus* (Boston: Wisdom Publications, 1998), 105.

A Christian Response: Roger

I recall an incident at a theological conference at which a theologian described a long experience with two religious practices that culminated in his becoming a dual belonger. In response to this experiential testimony another theologian declared that this was impossible. One could not coherently internalize two antithetical religious traditions. Behind this judgment, beyond the ideological arrogance that denied a living fact, rests a premise shared by many, that is, that openness to diverse religious systems entails relativism that effectively undermines the truth of Christian revelation. If in fact dual belongers exist, I want to confirm the possibility with three cumulative reasons.

Human apprehension of ultimate reality is limited. I presuppose that ultimate reality is absolutely transcendent and not a finite thing of this world. Knowledge of it is explained in various ways, but none is a function of taking a look. Because ultimacy is an object of faith and not worldly knowledge, no apprehension adequately encompasses it. All awareness of it is limited and partial. But a limited concept can be true if it corresponds with its referent. A particular conception can live with assertions about different aspects of an immeasurable transcendence. Even affirmations of opposing qualities may truthfully characterize ultimate reality in what Nicholas of Cusa called a *coincidentia oppositorum* (coincidence of opposites) within God. God is both just and merciful.

Religious truth entails engaged existential encounter. The idea of God is such that recognition of its meaning entails an existential relationship with the one who entertains it. Whether we speak of ultimate reality, or Emptiness, or God, the meaning encompasses all human beings. This explains why religious truth entails an existential encounter whether one affirms or denies its content. The epistemology of transcendence is unique because its object is not a sensible or finite object among others. Spiritual encounter thus refers to a process of being drawn into a sphere that utterly transcends finite representations. *Encounter* means a personal engagement that cannot be reduced to the limits of reason but involves intuition and feeling, that is, emotional and voluntary dimensions that form part of a holistic response.

All spiritually relevant religious truth develops. Because the object of religious faith is transcendent, its representation is always limited, and the content overflows rational acuity; all spiritually relevant religious truth changes. Impasse, coming up against resistance, the feeling that "this does not fit," provides the catalyst for developing truth. Its relevance requires adjustment to new cultural experiences, responsiveness to new questions, and openness to new dimensions of truth in new situations. Spiritual relevance involves being in conversation with life in the present-day world. Since religious pluralism is a constitutive element of our world, all spiritual and religious truth has to respond to it by engaging it.

These three characteristics of spiritual and religious truth make it flexible, and that flexibility entails the danger that what is revealed in any given religion could be lost or distorted by historical development. But we should not confuse care to preserve the meaning of religious truth with stasis. The greatest threat to religious truth is failure to engage human life.

It Seems to Us

In our conversations about this final chapter we first reminded ourselves that we live in a new and distinctive religious situation. The urban centers of the Western world have been transformed. Migrating people bring their religions with them. All the major religions are everywhere. This change has been accompanied by a shift in corporate consciousness. People of different religions who previously did not speak with one another now do. Friendship, colleagueship, neighborhood, children's schools, marriages, and a thousand other shared things override religious differences and bring people together. Actual interchange is creating a pluralistic religious consciousness. Religious diversity describes the given situation; no one thinks about massive religious unity. Religious pluralism is the natural condition of human history, as Rita Gross puts it in her recent book *Religious Diversity—What's the Problem?*[7]

---

[7] Rita M. Gross, *Religious Diversity—What's the Problem? Buddhist Advice for Flourishing with Religious Diversity* (Eugene, OR: Cascades Books, 2014).

Spiritual reflection today has to unfold within a context of religious pluralism and interchange. Extensive religious sharing shows that what we desire is cross-communication. When this happens, religious pluralism begins to appear as more a gift than a problem. People hope that inevitable clashes between religions and cultures will give way to toleration and then to new opportunities for enrichment and collaboration. We want to reflect together on these possibilities.

Clear and porous borders. Borders are interesting. They enclose and define space; they mark where different territories meet; they keep out and are crossed; they divide; and they provide the spot where peoples are connected. We cannot live without all sorts of borders. We have to respect them.

The border supplies a fruitful metaphor for how people of different cultures relate to one another. We conclude this chapter on double belonging by suggesting how various degrees of eclecticism in spirituality might strengthen the faith of every religious community and how this may be conceived as border crossing. We then talk about interreligious belonging.

Border crossing. Let's begin with passing over and coming back.

1. Strong borders. The new situation of religious pluralism and the constant bombardment of the new and the strange require strong religious borders. In contrast to the unity within differences, relativism abandons every boundary that claims to be normative because it seems to diminish the other. But self-definition is not a claim to superiority, only to identity. And a pluralistic situation demands self-definition. Borders provide clarity about identity. Borders locate persons and allow them to know where they are in relation to the other. One cannot fully participate in a pluralistic enterprise without an identity. Loss of identity undermines coherent agency and consistent interchange. Pluralism, which by definition entails interchange with others who also have an identity, requires clear borders.

Many religious leaders do not promote conversion of others to their own religion.[8] Religious belonging is or should be too

---

[8] The Dalai Lama clearly indicates that the point of entering into dialogue is not to seek conversion of the other. See *The Good Heart*, 97–98.

deep to enable an easy permanent border crossing or migration. To go deeply into transcendent reality, one has to take care of a lot of business on the surface level of community and society. Religious identity is like home as distinct from a dwelling place; home always provides the familiar space and tools needed to burrow down into the foundations of reality. No matter how cosmopolitan one becomes, identity always has a home to return to. All of this adds up to high respect for religious borders. In a situation of extraordinary religious fragmentation, they provide a stable relationship with ultimate reality and only very serious reasons should be allowed to move a person to leave home.

2. Flexible borders. Borders are strongest when they are flexible. We do not want to weaken borders, but we need to make them flexible. They must be there so that people can meet at them, cross them, visit on the other side, and come back all the richer, because they transport something across them. If borders are not flexible, they define a reservation; identity does not expand but becomes stunted; persons become rigid and lose touch with what is going on in the spiritual world.

We have defined eclectic spirituality as one that is open to and learns from or authentically participates in other religious traditions. This open conception allows for a wide variety of learning and practice that may be appropriated into a Christian faith. What remains central and constant are the essentials of following Jesus so that the substance of one's commitment is Christian. The history of the development of the Christian church is strewn with eclectic historical borrowing from other faiths beginning in its early Jewish history and continuing all through Christian expansion.

One of the most prevalent and obvious forms of this eclecticism in Christian spirituality uses Buddhist forms of meditation. Hybrid forms of Christian prayer and Buddhist meditation such as centering prayer are commonplace in Western Christian spirituality. But the formula opens out into many different degrees of learning from Buddhist practice. The benefits of eclectic spirituality are as many and as specific as the people who participate in other religious practices. Generally speaking, these include a breakdown of barriers between people and of fear of others and their religious traditions, and this leads to the growth of a spontaneous and differentiated "we consciousness."

Double belonging. Today, with the phenomenon of double belonging, that "we consciousness" seems to be taking on new contours—richer but also more ambiguous depths. Here, Paul, self-identified as a Buddhist and a Christian, is speaking from his own experience of double belonging. For him, and it seems for other double belongers,[9] the borders between two traditions—in this case, Buddhism and Christianity—certainly remain. But for the double belonger, within his or her own practice, these borders become more flexible and porous than clear and strong. This is not easy to explain.

What we have so far described as eclectic spirituality pretty well fits what has been called, especially since Vatican II, inter-religious dialogue. In dialogue one has a primary, enduring identity or home. This home is perhaps marvelously enriched, even transformed, through dialogue with another religious tradition. But it remains the primary identity, the one home. There is much border crossing in this dialogical exchange, but the borders remain clear. One knows well whether one is standing on one side of the border or the other.

In the experience of double belonging, this is not always the case. The borders seem to blend. One becomes fully at home on both sides of the border, although the two sides remain clearly marked. Gospel and Dharma are two different teachings. There is a real difference between receiving the Eucharist and sitting on one's cushion. But it seems that these clear differences are more external than they are internal—that is, they mark two evidently different practices passed down through the centuries; but in the internal practice of the double belonger, they influence and blend with each other. How one experiences one's unity with Christ in the Eucharist this morning at mass is influenced—clarified or deepened—by the meditation that one practiced on one's cushion last night. And the way one feels one's Buddha-nature in meditation is affected by the way one experienced one's "being in Christ" at mass. Differences between Buddhist and Christian practice and teachings certainly remain. But in distinctive ways they become united in the practitioner.

---

[9] Described in Rose Drew, *Buddhist and Christian? An Exploration of Dual Belonging* (New York: Routledge, 2011).

To try to understand and explain what is going on here, Paul has used the analogy of the hypostatic union of two natures in one person as those categories were adopted by theology following the Council of Chalcedon to explain the divinity-humanity of Jesus.[10] In the double belonger two different religious practices, Buddhist and Christian, remain truly different ("not confused, not changed" as Chalcedon put it), but they become one in the person of the double-belonging practitioner.

So it is not that double belongers have two religious homes in which they feel equally at home. Rather, they have only one home, but it has both Christian and Buddhist furniture and decorations. And both motifs blend into a beautiful, living environment.

So how does one talk about borders, and border crossing, for double belongers? We are not entirely clear on how to answer that question. Religious double belonging is, as they say, a cultural interreligious work in progress. While in some multireligious Asian countries multiple religious identities are not an uncommon cultural phenomenon, in the West, consciously to embrace two different spiritual practices is still a new and unmarked path. It has to be further followed and pondered in order to know where it is leading.

We recognize that it is a path that is not for everyone. Yet, while this is true, while the *border blending of double belonging* may not be for everyone, the *border crossing of interreligious dialogue* is a possibility, and perhaps a requirement, that is offered to all. If for most Christians the borders that mark their religious home remain clear, they also have to be porous. Our Christian churches, like our world, need to dialogue and cooperate with one another and with other religions. As fellow Christians, both of us affirm the assurance of the Asian Catholic bishops that dialogue is the new way of being church.

Whether and how that new way of dialogue might lead to greater double belonging is one of the open questions and adventures of this dialogical church.

---

[10] Paul F. Knitter, *Without Buddha I Could Not Be a Christian*, 2nd ed. (Oxford: Oneworld, 2013), 220–21.

Glossary

Bhikku: A Buddhist term for monk. The feminine form is *bhik-kuni.*

Bodhisattva: One who has attained enlightenment and who resolves to share that experience with others. A bodhisattva has attained the wisdom that is synonymous with compassion. Having seen reality, a bodhisattva wishes to bring others to the same enlightenment.

Buddha: The title that was given to the historical Gautama to signify that he has awakened and reached enlightenment. As Jesus was called the Christ, Gautama was called the Buddha.

Creation: In an active sense, creation refers to the action of God exclusively because it means making reality out of nothing; in contrast to forming something out of preexisting materials, nothing precedes creation. Creation should not be imagined as a past event but understood as the deep structure of finite reality. In a passive sense, as an effect, creation refers to objective reality that has been created and is being held in existence by the power of God.

Dependent Origination: The fundamental Buddhist teaching that all things arise and have their being in dependence on other things. Reality consists of "no-things"; no-thing is a substance, existing unto itself.

Dharma: In Buddhism, Dharma has multiple meanings. Principally, it refers both to the cosmic order that sustains reality and to the teachings of Buddha. Such teachings are understood not simply as lessons but as the energy of truth. Thus, in the Triple Refuge, Buddhists take refuge in Buddha, the Dharma, and the Sangha.

Dukkha: The suffering that, according to the First Noble Truth, characterizes all existence. It is related to another fundamental teaching of Buddhism that all reality is impermanent. *Dukkha* results when we try to cling to things that are "unclingable" because they are changing.

Eightfold Path: Constitutes Buddha's Fourth Noble Truth and outlines the practical steps by which one can, as it were, put Buddha's teaching to the test. The eight steps divide into three movements: (1) trust Buddha's teachings (right view and right intention); (2) avoid unnecessary harm of others (right speech, right action, and right profession/job; and (3) practice some form of meditation (right efforts, right mindfulness, right concentration).

Eschatology: Based on the Greek word eschatos, meaning "last." Eschatology is theological reflection on the last things: the end of time and the final destiny of human existence. Since the end-time is not available to human perception, much of eschatology is imaginative projection into the future of the convictions of present-day faith. It responds to the question of what God has prepared for finite reality, especially human beings, but inclusive of other forms of being.

Emptiness: A translation of the Sanskrit *Sunyata*, which points to the insubstantiality or the non-individuality of everything. Everything is therefore an "inter-thing." To realize and to "be" emptiness is to attain, or begin to attain, the wisdom of enlightenment.

Four Noble Truths: The content of Buddha's first sermon and the heart of his message: (1) life unavoidably contains suffering; (2) suffering is caused by greed and clinging; (3) to stop suffering, stop greed and clinging; and (4) to stop greed and clinging, try Buddha's Eightfold Path.

Gautama: The family name of Buddha, usually used to refer to the historical figure, Siddhartha Gautama, who became the Buddha, that is, he who has awakened.

Grace: At its source grace refers to God's love (kindness, mercy, forgiveness, active care) for creation and most particularly for each human being. Grace in its origins is interpreted in innumerable ways by theology depending on how it is experienced. Grace is purely gratuitous in its character of being gift. Objectively, or in its effects, many different things are named grace insofar as they flow from or express God's love. Theology provides a multitude of root metaphors explaining how grace works in the world and human life.

Hermeneutics: The principles and theory of interpreting (1) the Bible; (2) more broadly, texts; and (3) existence itself. In its widest sense it merges with a philosophical theory of understanding and knowledge.

Historical consciousness: In broad terms, the critical awareness of being in time and the change that this entails. More pointedly it refers to recognition of the degree to which all ideas and values are conditioned by the historical and social context in which they exist. Historical consciousness stands in contrast to a standardized universal understanding of anything subsisting above or within but unaffected by context.

Interbeing: A translation used by contemporary Buddhists like Thich Nhat Hanh for Emptiness or dependent origination, pointing to the Groundless Ground of Being.

Jesus of Nazareth: This proper name refers to the historical person as he appeared in history to his contemporaries.

Jesus Christ: In the first century, *Christ*, from the Greek *Christos*, meaning "anointed," was a title signifying that Jesus was the Messiah. This became a proper name, and it refers to Jesus of Nazareth as he was in history and most pointedly as he is alive today in God's sphere and in the Christian communities.

Kenosis: A Greek word meaning "emptying." Saint Paul used it in the hymn in Philippians 2:5-11 that says Jesus "emptied" himself to become a slave. Kenosis has come to represent the self-emptying of the divine Son in fully becoming a human being, as in the phrase "kenotic Christology."

Mahayana: A reform movement within Buddhism that began as early as 100 BCE. It stressed the availability of enlightenment for laypeople and held up the bodhisattva as the idea for all Buddhists.

Orthopraxis: Literally, "right action." It is often balanced with *orthodoxy* or "right beliefs." Orthopraxis prepares us to perceive, and then to corroborate, orthodoxy.

Really Real: The phrase used by the authors as a general or neutral indicator of the Ultimate, a pointer to what Christians intend with the word *God* and to what Buddhists might mean by *Emptiness* or *nirvana*.

Redemption: A theory of salvation. Its premise is that the human race has fallen from grace and is marked by sin. The basic metaphor is that Jesus of Nazareth, by means of his death and resurrection, has restored human existence to a new positive and saved relationship with God. There are variations among different theologies of redemption.

Salvation: Based on the Latin word *salus* meaning "health" or "wholeness," this broad term expresses the experience of believers in Jesus Christ. It refers to the restoration that was and is accomplished by God through the mediation of Jesus of Nazareth. The New Testament uses many different metaphors and theologies to describe or to understand how God brought about human fulfillment through Jesus. *Liberation* is often considered a modern equivalent.

Samsara: The general term used by Buddhists to indicate the human condition caught in change, frustration, suffering, and the constant rounds of rebirth. *Samsara* is contrasted with nirvana, which is the liberation from *samsara*. Mahayana Buddhists hold up the ideal of realizing that nirvana is to be found within *samsara*.

Sangha: Buddhist term for the community of followers of Buddha and practitioners of the Dharma. It is part of the Triple Refuge that all Buddhists take.

Siddhartha: The personal name of the historical Gautama (Gautama is the family name). Siddhartha means "he who achieves his goal."

Soteriology: The study of the salvation Jesus mediated. It responds to such questions as what salvation is, why we need it, and how Jesus effected it. These questions have generated different conceptions of how Jesus saves. For example, there are theories or conceptions of divinization, redemption, sacrifice, atonement, satisfaction, substitution, and revelatory example.

Spirituality: Sometimes related to the human spirit and sometimes, as in Christianity, to the Spirit of God. On a concrete or existential level spirituality refers to the depth dimension of how persons view themselves connected with reality. It is understood differently as a sphere of distinctive transcendent experiences, or as a set of specific practices, or as a whole way of life that connects one to what is supremely and ultimately important. Spirituality as a discipline is the study of various forms of spirituality.

Sunyata: A Sanskrit word usually translated "Emptiness," "Voidness," or "Vast Spaciousness." It indicates the interrelatedness of everything, to the extent that *everything* is *no-thing*, that is, devoid of substantial, individual existence. We are not "beings" but "beings-with."

Synoptic Gospels: The Gospels of Mark, Matthew, and Luke. They share many stories that can be laid side by side and viewed together (synoptikos). Compared with the Gospel of John, these three appear to be less stylized and closer to history, even though each has its own distinctive theological theme.

Teleology: Based on the Greek word telos, meaning "end" or "goal," this term refers to an inner structural orientation toward a specific way of acting and a goal. Organic things, like seeds, have an inner program of development that illustrates one form of teleology.

Trinity: A Christian doctrine promulgated in the year 380 CE. Trinity refers to the three "Persons" of the one God: Father, Son, and Spirit. *Person* here does not have the same meaning as the term *person* with reference to a human individual. What theologians call Persons are drawn from the distinct places where God can be experienced: in creation, in Jesus, and as spiritual empowerment in and of the community. These experiences of God acting are called the economic Trinity. The so-called immanent Trinity refers to the inner constitution of God: three Persons forming one single nature and life of God.

Triple Refuge: Part of becoming a Buddhist consists in taking the Triple Refuge to Buddha, to the Dharma, and to the Sangha. It is also called the Three Jewels.

Upaya: A Sanskrit word for a method of Buddhist teaching. The word means "skillful or expedient means." This method recognizes that one must adapt one's teaching to the person's needs, limitations, context. Thus, one might use a procedure that is not entirely accurate or true in order to bring the student to a deeper realization of Buddha's teachings.

Vajrayana: One of the major traditions of Buddhism, sometimes included in Mahayana Buddhism and sometimes understood as a movement beyond it. Literally, it is the Diamond Way associated with Tantric Buddhism and often refers to the Buddhism that took form in Tibet.

Index

Adam and Eve, 124, 129, 131, 133

anatta
  describing, 221–22
  non-individuality, 26, 190
  not-self, 123, 125, 140, 181, 207, 219

anthropocentrism, 114

apophaticism, 161, 162, 163, 167, 169, 173

Aquinas, Thomas, 83, 93, 94, 109, 156, 161

Aristotle, 83, 151

Assisi, Francis of, 209

asymmetrical reciprocity, 90, 103, 148, 209

Athanasius, 138

atheism, 77–78, 93, 191

Augustine, 7, 110, 120, 132, 143, 156

avidya, 133. *See also* ignorance

bhikku, 40, 235

Bigger Picture
  caring for others as natural, 3
  death and, 139
  enlightenment as awakening to, 185
  Interbeing, 123

  mindfulness, getting in touch with, 126
  non-dual unity, 4–5
  realization of, leading to meaning and energy, 1–2
  security within, 127
  ultimate reality, waking up to, 5–6

Bodhi tree, 41, 67, 78, 135

bodhisattvas
  Christian spirituality, parallel to, 7
  compassion of, 108, 185, 210
  defining, 235
  in Mahayana Buddhism, 82, 238
  samsara, return to, 108
  service to others as bodhisattva ideal, 151
  suffering, lessening of as goal, 107

Buber, Martin, 198

Buddha
  awakening of, 155
  as benefactor, 159
  on death, 139
  defining, 235
  Eightfold-Path, 3–4
  enlightenment and, 29, 52, 53–54, 135–36